# The Changing Face of Management in China

China is one of the fastest developing emerging economies in the world today. The country has a huge influence on a global level, both politically and economically. Despite this, very few books cover both the full range of management functions and the key issues facing managers in this unique business environment.

*The Changing Face of Management in China* explores the key challenges facing businesses and managers in China, across management functions as well as across a range of sectors and organization types. Written by prominent scholars with direct experience in this market, this book adds to the existing body of knowledge by examining a range of areas of Chinese management in the context of local political, economic and social traditions, and the global economy.

Part of the successful *Working in Asia* series, this book includes case studies that allow the voices of local managers to be heard, as well as extensive bibliographies pointing students and researchers to the most up-to-date sources of information in this important area.

**Chris Rowley**, PhD, is Professor of HRM and Director of the Centre for Research in Asian Management at City University, UK, and advisor to the HEAD Foundation, Singapore, on research and publications. He is editor of the leading journal *Asia Pacific Business Review* and has published widely in the area of Asian business and management with more than 350 articles, books, chapters, pieces and other knowledge transfer output.

**Fang Lee Cooke**, PhD, is Professor of HRM and Chinese Studies and Deputy Head (Research and Innovation) of the School of Management, RMIT University, Australia. Her research interests include HRM, employment regulations, knowledge management and innovation, outsourcing, Chinese outward FDI, Chinese Diaspora, and comparative studies of HRM practices in China and India. She is the author of *HRM, Work and Employment*, published by Routledge in 2005.

# Working in Asia

General Editors:
**Tim G. Andrews**
University of Strathclyde
**Keith Jackson**
School of Oriental and African Studies, University of London
and **Chris Rowley**
City University, UK; HEAD Foundation, Singapore

This series focuses on contemporary management issues in the Asia-Pacific region. It draws on the latest research to highlight critical factors impacting on the conduct of business in this diverse and dynamic business environment.

Our primary intention is to provide management students and practitioners with fresh dimensions to their reading of standard texts. With each book in the *Working in Asia* series, we offer a combined insider's and outsider's perspective on how managers and their organizations in the Asia-Pacific region are adapting to contemporary currents of both macro- and micro-level change.

The core of data for the texts in this series has been generated by recent interviews and discussions with established senior executives as well as newly fledged entrepreneurs; with practising as well as aspiring middle managers; and women as well as men. Our mission has been to give voice to how change is being perceived and experienced by a broad and relevant range of people who live and work in the region. We report on how they and their organizations are managing change as the globalization of their markets, together with their business technologies and traditions, unfolds.

Drawing together the combined insights of Asian and Western scholars, and practitioners of management, we present a uniquely revealing portrait of the future of working and doing business in Asia.

*Titles in the series include:*

**The Changing Face of Multinationals in Southeast Asia**
*Tim G. Andrews, Nartnalin Chompusri and Bryan J. Baldwin*

**The Changing Face of Japanese Management**
*Keith Jackson and Miyuki Tomioka*

**The Changing Face of Chinese Management**
*Jie Tang and Anthony Ward*

**The Changing Face of Management in South East Asia**
*Chris Rowley*

**The Changing Face of Women Managers in Asia**
*Chris Rowley and Vimolwan Yukongdi*

**The Changing Face of Korean Management**
*Chris Rowley and Yongsun Paik*

**The Changing Face of People Management in India**
*Pawan Budhwar and Jyotsna Bhatnagar*

**The Changing Face of Management in Thailand**
*Tim G. Andrews and Sununta Siengthai*

**The Changing Face of Vietnamese Management**
*Chris Rowley and Quang Truong*

**The Changing Face of Management in China**
*Chris Rowley and Fang Lee Cooke*

# The Changing Face of Management in China

Edited by
Chris Rowley and Fang Lee Cooke

Routledge
Taylor & Francis Group
LONDON AND NEW YORK

First published 2010
by Routledge
2 Park Square, Milton Park, Abingdon, Oxon OX14 4RN

Simultaneously published in the USA and Canada
by Routledge
270 Madison Avenue, New York, NY 10016

*Routledge is an imprint of the Taylor & Francis Group, an Informa business*

Typeset in Times New Roman
by Keystroke, Tettenhall, Wolverhampton
Printed and bound in Great Britain by
CPI Antony Rowe Ltd, Chippenham

*British Library Cataloguing in Publication Data*
A catalogue record for this book is available from the British Library

*Library of Congress Cataloguing-in-Publication Data*
The changing face of management in China / edited by Chris Rowley and
Fang Lee Cooke.
p. cm.
Includes bibliographical references and index.
1. Industrial management–China. 2. Personnel management–China.
3. Business enterprises–China. I. Rowley, Chris, 1959– II. Cooke, Fang Lee.
HD70.C5C3927 2010
658.00951–dc22
2009038589

ISBN10: 0–415–46333–5 (hbk)
ISBN10: 0–415–46332–7 (pbk)
ISBN10: 0–203–85514–0 (ebk)

ISBN13: 978–0–415–46333–1 (hbk)
ISBN13: 978–0–415–46332–4 (pbk)
ISBN13: 978–0–203–85514–0 (ebk)

For Professor Rowley's former PhD students
Li Xue Cunningham, Qi (Jean) Wei and Hun-Fun (Irene) Poon for
their great assistance and friendship on our joint
journey over the past few years.

# Contents

# Illustrations

## Figures

## Tables

# Case studies

# Contributors

**Richard Chamblin** is a professor of accounting at the Millikin University in Illinois and has had a long professional career in private accounting and consulting.

**Fang Lee Cooke**, PhD, is Professor of HRM and Chinese Studies and Deputy Head (Research and Innovation) of the School of Management, RMIT University, Australia. Previously, she was a chair professor at Manchester Business School, University of Manchester. She received her PhD from the University of Manchester. Her research interests are in the areas of HRM, employment regulations, knowledge management and innovation, outsourcing, Chinese outward FDI and Chinese Diaspora. Her current research interests also include comparative studies of HRM practices in China and India. She is the author of *HRM, Work and Employment in China* (2005) and *Competition, Strategy and Management in China* (2008).

**Dr Li Xue Cunningham** is an RCUK research fellow and Deputy Director of Centre for Research in Asian Management, Cass Business School, City University. Before she embarked on her research career, she worked as a manager in international business for several large Chinese corporations. Dr Cunningham's research interests include international and comparative human resource management, organizational behaviour, corporate management, small and medium enterprise business and development, especially in China.

**Hui Feng** is currently a PhD student in the Marketing Department of Indiana University at Bloomington.

**Kun Huang** is a senior human resource manager in a large state-owned enterprise in China. She received her PhD at Manchester Business School, University of Manchester.

**Ng Sek Hong** is Reader in the School of Business at the University of Hong Kong. He attended the London School of Economics and Political Science of the University of London for an MSc degree in industrial relations and, later, also for his PhD, specializing in the field of industrial sociology. He teaches and has published several books and a number of articles in the areas of employment and labour study, industrial relations and human resources.

**Dr Olivia Ip** is Associate Professor in the Management Department at the City University of Hong Kong. She works on human resource management and labour market studies. She has published articles on human resource management, trade unions, and manpower in Hong Kong and Mainland China.

**J. Mark Munoz** is a professor of International Business at Millikin University and is an internationally recognized author and consultant.

**Irene Hon-fun Poon**, CCP, CIPD, MBA, has been a management consultant and HR practitioner for many years in various countries. Her research interests include cross-cultural management and Asia Pacific management and business. Her recent publications are in the *Asia Pacific Business Review, 21st Century Management, Handbook of Technology Management* and *Management through Collaboration*.

**Chris Rowley**, PhD (Oxford), Professor of Human Resource Management, Cass Business School, City University, is Director of the Centre for Research on Asian Management. He is editor of *Asia Pacific Business Review*, series editor of *Studies in Asia Pacific Business* and *Asian Studies: Contemporary Issues and Trends*, and has published widely including in *California Management Review*, *Journal of World Business* and *International Journal of HRM*, with more than 350 articles, books, chapters, pieces and other knowledge transfer output.

**Russell Smyth** is Professor and Head of the Department of Economics, Monash University, Melbourne. He has honours degrees in Economics and Law from Monash University and a PhD in Economics from the University of London. His research interests include enterprise restructuring, labour market reform, migration and social protection in China. He has published widely on these areas. In 2008 he was a recipient of the Economic Society of Australia Honorary Fellow Award for services to the economics profession in Australia.

**Yonggui Wang** is currently co-editor of the *Journal of Chinese Entrepreneurship*, a professor and an academic leader in the Department of Marketing, Business School, University of International Business and Economics (UIBE), Beijing, with more than ten publications in international journals such as *Journal of Engineering and Technology Management, International Journal of Managing Service Quality, Competitiveness Review, Information System Frontiers*. Before joining UIBE, he had worked for Nanjing University as a professor of Marketing and Associate Director in the Department of Marketing. His new monograph 'Marketing Competences and Strategic Flexibility in China' (coauthored with Dr Richard Lihua) was published by Palgrave Macmillan in 2007.

**Jean Qi Wei**, CIPD, MBA, PhD, has been a HR practitioner for many years. Her research interests include reward management, performance management, and comparative studies in IHRM. Her recent publications are in *Asia Pacific Business Review, Journal of Global Business Advancement* and *HRM: The Key Concepts*.

**Qingguo Zhai** is Professor, School of Business and Economics, Liaoning Shihua University. He has a PhD in Engineering from Shenyang University and is currently completing a second PhD in Management in the Department of Management, Monash University, Melbourne. His research interests focus on enterprise restructuring, job satisfaction and subjective wellbeing in China. These are topics on which he has published in English and Chinese.

**Xiu Ying Zheng-Pratt**, CPA, MBA, is currently a corporate consolidations financial analyst at Caterpillar Inc. Thus far in her career with Caterpillar she has held various positions in both the managerial cost accounting and the corporate financial accounting fields of accountancy.

# Abbreviations

| | |
|---|---|
| ACFTU | All-China Federation of Trade Unions |
| CCP | Chinese Communist Party |
| CEO | Chief executive officer |
| CFO | Chief finance officer |
| CNPC | China National Petroleum Corporation |
| COE | Collectively owned enterprise |
| EDS | Equity-for-debt-swap |
| ERP | Enterprise resources planning |
| FDI | Foreign direct investment |
| FMV | Fair market value |
| FPC | Fushun Petrochemical Company |
| GAAP | Generally accepted accounting principle |
| GACC | General Administration of China Customs |
| GDP | Gross domestic product |
| HRM | Human resource management |
| HPMS | High-performance management system |
| IAS | International Accounting Standards |
| ICT | Information communication technology |
| IFRS | International Financial Reporting Standards |
| ILO | International Labour Organization |
| IPR | Intellectual property right |
| IT | Information technology |
| JV | Joint venture |
| KM | Knowledge management |
| KPI | Key performance indicator |
| M&A | Merger and acquisition |
| MIAD | Management of International Accounting Disparities |
| MNC | Multinational corporation |
| NIE | Newly industrialized economy |
| OEM | Original equipment manufacturer |

| | |
|---|---|
| PA | Performance appraisal |
| PM | Performance management |
| PMS | Performance management system |
| POE | Privately owned enterprise |
| PRC | People's Republic of China |
| PRP | Performance-related pay |
| R&D | Research and development |
| RM | Risk management |
| SAR | Special Administrative Region |
| SASAC | State Assets Supervision and Administration Commission |
| SME | Small and medium-sized enterprise |
| SOE | State-owned enterprise |
| TVE | Township and village enterprise |
| WTO | World Trade Organization |

# 1 Setting the scene for the changing face of management in China

*Fang Lee Cooke and Chris Rowley*

## Introduction

A number of scholarly works have now emerged that capture the dynamic changes that have taken place in Chinese business and management in recent years. For example, Smyth *et al.* (2005) charts the institutional challenges facing China in a globalized economy. It covers corporate governance and financial reforms, human resources (HR) and labour market reform, social welfare reforms and the growth of the private sector in the context of China's accession to the World Trade Organization (WTO). Hassard *et al.*'s (2007) book documents in depth the transformation of the state-owned enterprises (SOEs) over more than a decade. More recently, Warner (2009) provides a reassessment of HR management (HRM) with 'Chinese characteristics'. It explores some of the less studied but increasingly relevant aspects of HRM in China, particularly organizational relationships/behaviours and psychological outcomes of the employees.

However, few books are available that cover a range of management functions (e.g. accounting, marketing and HRM) and issues (e.g. knowledge management (KM) and performance management (PM)) across a number of sectors and organizational forms (e.g. multinational corporations (MNCs) and small firms). Yet, these are the very areas where important changes are taking place, resulting in new challenges being encountered by managers in China. The aim of this book is therefore to examine a range of areas and issues in Chinese management in the light of the national political, economic and social traditions and the global economy.

While providing a broad context for each function or issue featured in this volume, each chapter also focuses on a couple of key aspects within each discipline/issue to capture the latest developments in China and to reflect what is happening as international trends. Written by authors from different continents based on their recent research findings, this book adds to the existing body of knowledge by analysing key strategic choices and constraints as well as management challenges facing Chinese managers in a context of marketization and internationalization.

More broadly, this book continues in the vein of recent texts in the innovative *Working in Asia* Routledge series in terms of developing in some fresh ways the original purpose and conceptualization of the series. The intention of this unusual series is to provide accessible, easy-to-read and -use books written by experts, many local, and critically which give 'voice' to individuals, especially local managers within organizations. This 'voice' can come via illustrative case studies and vignettes, used to examine and exemplify the changing practices, issues and the 'face' of management in Asia. These aims and format of the series in turn require a commensurate downplaying of more research monograph-type content and structure. With the ongoing widespread interest in Asia, the time is ripe for books using such a focus and format.

This book on China follows the generic rubric of the series and focuses on the broad area of management in the country set within its background, context and contemporary changes. The aims of the book are to examine a range of key management and business practices, strategies, areas and issues in the framework of the local political, economic and social traditions and the global economy and challenges, and to give 'voice' to local managers and practitioners and illustrative organizational case studies and vignettes (two of each for the substantive chapters, except Chapter 5, with its single-organization focus; see Table 1.4, pp. 24–5). Also, the book not only covers a wide range of management areas but does so in a common three-part framework (key issues and new developments; organization and manager cases; challenges), to allow greater consistency across chapters and quicker and easier inter- and intra-cross-chapter comparisons, depending on the reader's particular interests and focus. In addition, it allows cross-book comparisons within work in this series, such as on Korea (Rowley and Paik, 2008) and Vietnam (Rowley and Truong, 2010).

The book is useful and important for several reasons. Often, much that is written in the field comes from non-Chinese authors and sources and uses Western perspectives, models and theories, while concentrating on only a single or a few practices, issues or areas. Moreover, much of what we know about Chinese management is more commonly drawn from studies conducted with quantitative methods or at the macro level, although some qualitative studies at organizational level do exist. Less is known of the perspectives of Chinese managers on specific issues at work. This book fills that gap. Furthermore, the book's stance is different – the aim is to allow the 'voice' of local managers, practitioners and organizations to come through more.

This book is also important because the topics and area have relevance to many different types and levels of qualifications and subjects, researchers and readers. These include business and management, such as international business, cross-cultural management and functional areas covering HRM, marketing and accounting, and such issues as type of ownership and size. As such, the book's broad coverage and content will also be of use to fields such as Asian studies and sociology, as well as issue-related areas, among many others. Additionally, the diverse range of organizational and manager cases can be used in a variety of ways, including teaching and education and other illustrative purposes.

Therefore, many levels and types of educational and training programmes would benefit from this text. The book has both country-specific and international appeal, especially in other parts of Asia, Australia, North America and among English-speaking and Western-educated managers from Asia and those with an interest in this fascinating country. Another market includes practising managers, both expatriates and locals, of organizations with a Chinese aspect, and those who may be thinking of setting up activities in China. Furthermore, the chapter bibliographies are important as many students and teachers in the area often find it difficult to locate up-to-date sources of information for topics and issues covered in this book that are written in an easily accessible manner.

## Analytical framework

Businesses operate within a societal context shaped by a broad range of institutional and cultural factors at various levels. At the international level, a country's business environment is influenced by policies, regulations and other pressures and incentives from international organizations. It is also influenced by the way multinational firms operate, both globally and in the host country. For example, an increasing number of Chinese firms and industries are now subject to a rising level of competitive pressure as a result of China's accession to the WTO in 2001 and the subsequent gradual removal of barriers to multinational firms operating in China. At the national level, the role of the government, the legal system, the economic and finance system, the technological innovation system, the education and training system, and the stock of human capital in the labour market are all important institutional factors that determine the business environment.

The role of the government includes: 'the extent to which markets are administratively regulated, the degree of centralization in government economic policy, and the extent of government ownership in business' (Child, 2001: 696). The technology and innovation environment includes: government spending on research and development, government and industry focus on technological effort, new discoveries and developments, speed of technology transfer, and rates of obsolescence (Johnson and Scholes, 2002). The education and training system is important as it determines the pool of human capital of the country, including knowledge, skills and managerial competence essential to its competitiveness. It is also a determinant of the workforce's earning power and the nation's living standard and consumption power. At the industry level, many of the factors identified at the international and national levels manifest themselves but exhibit characteristics that are specific to particular industries (Cooke, 2008).

In the context of managing business operations in China, Li and Zhou (2005: 3) identified six major institutional environmental factors that firms must scan, monitor and design strategies to deal with. These include:

- Continued transition to a market economy;
- Opening up to world stages;
- Continued development of laws and regulations governing economic activities;

- Paramount role that various levels of government play in economic activities;
- Geographical diversity and development stage disparity; and
- Rapidly developing emerging product markets.

The factors identified above serve as a guide in the analysis of the business environment, competitive pressure and business strategy of the industrial sectors and firms throughout this book. The rapid changes in China's institutional and social environments provide a timely opportunity to explore how the business environment is evolving and how firms are adapting to these changes in order to survive and succeed. Context and challenges are therefore the common threads in each chapter of this book for us to understand the pressures and opportunities facing each industrial sector and firms selected here for study.

In the next section of this chapter, we outline the key context within which management, organizations and business operate. This is followed by a summary of key challenges that these are facing. These sections are useful as they also set the context for the substantive chapters on management functions and issues that follow. Finally, an outline of the structure of the book is provided with overviews and coverage of the contributions and cases.

# The changing context of management in China

## History

The history of China as recorded in traditional records extends as far back as the Three Sovereigns and Five Emperors, about 5000 years ago. Recorded history is supplemented by archaeological records dating back to the sixteenth century BC. China is one of the world's oldest continuous civilizations. Turtle shells with markings reminiscent of ancient Chinese writing from the Shang Dynasty have been carbon dated to around 1500 BC. Chinese civilization originated with city-states in the Yellow River (Huang He) valley. However, 221 BC is commonly accepted to be the year in which China first became unified under a large kingdom or empire by Qin Shi Huang. Successive dynasties developed bureaucratic systems that enabled the Emperor to control a large and diverse physical territory. Following the turbulent pre-Second World War era and the success of the Communists in 1949 after the civil war, the People's Republic of China was established (Wei and Rowley, 2009b).

## Geography

Stretching some 5026 kilometres across the East Asian landmass, China borders the East China Sea, Korea Bay, Yellow Sea and South China Sea, between North Korea and Vietnam in a changing configuration of broad plains, deserts and mountain ranges, including vast areas of inhospitable terrain. The eastern half, its sea coast fringed with offshore islands, is a region of fertile lowlands, foothills and mountains, deserts, steppes and subtropical areas. The western half is a region of sunken basins, rolling plateaus and towering massifs, including a portion of the highest tableland on earth. China is one of the world's largest countries in total area, almost the exact same size as the US, but smaller than both Russia and Canada (Wei and Rowley, 2009b).

## Climate

The climate of China is extremely diverse, from subtropical in the south to subarctic in the north. Monsoon winds, caused by differences in the heat-absorbing capacity of the continent and the ocean, dominate the climate. Alternating seasonal air-mass movements and accompanying winds are moist in the summer and dry in the winter. The advance and retreat of monsoons account in large degree for the timing of the rainy season and the amount of rainfall throughout the country. Tremendous differences in latitude, longitude and altitude give rise to sharp variations in precipitation and temperature. Although most of the country lies in the temperate belt, its climatic patterns are complex (Wei and Rowley, 2009b).

## Natural resources

China has substantial mineral reserves and is the world's largest producer of antimony, natural graphite, tungsten and zinc. Other major minerals are bauxite, coal, crude petroleum, diamonds, gold, iron ore, lead, magnetite, manganese, mercury, molybdenum, natural gas, phosphate rock, tin, uranium and vanadium. With its vast mountain ranges, China's hydropower potential is the largest in the world (Wei and Rowley, 2009b).

Based on 2005 estimates, 14.86 per cent (about 1.4 million sq km) of China's total land area is arable. Some 42.9 per cent of total land area is used as pasture, and 17.5 per cent is forest. However, only about 1.3 per cent (some 116,580 sq km) is planted with permanent crops and the rest with temporary crops. With comparatively little land given over to permanent crops, intensive agricultural techniques are used to reap harvests that can feed the world's largest population, with some surplus for export (Wei and Rowley, 2009b).

China's water resources include 2711.5 billion cubic metres of runoff in its rivers and 828.8 billion cubic metres pumped annually from shallow aquifers. As pumping draws water from nearby rivers, the total available resource is 2821.4 billion cubic metres. 80.9 per cent of these resources are in the Yangtze River basin (Wei and Rowley, 2009b).

## Environment

China has many environmental problems. To begin with, the country's population of 1.3 billion accounts for around a fifth of the world's population, but the nation possesses less than one-tenth of the world's arable land. Furthermore, almost the entire population lives in the well-watered eastern half of the country, where virtually all farmland has been developed. Indeed, China has very little land that has not been altered in some way by human intervention. The sheer size of the population means that forests, wetlands, grasslands and agricultural fields are stretched beyond the limits of sustainable use. Dramatic growth in the economy and the continuing need to raise living standards for some of Asia's poorest people mean that urban areas face a similar crisis: coal dust, untreated factory and vehicle emissions and wind-blown desert sand make Chinese cities some of the most polluted in the world; many of the rivers are polluted and virtually all water in urban areas is heavily contaminated. Some sixteen of the twenty most polluted cities on earth are in China (Wei and Rowley, 2009b).

Two of the serious negative consequences of rapid industrial development have been increased pollution and degradation of natural resources. Much waste is not properly treated. Water pollution is a source of health problems and air pollution causes up to 750,000 premature deaths each year. The polluted environment is largely a result of the country's rapid development and consequently a large increase in energy consumption, which is primarily provided by coal power plants (Wei and Rowley, 2009b).

## Population

The population experienced a rapid growth between the 1950s and early 1980s until the government realized the problems that this dramatic growth imposed on the country. Since the late 1970s, especially since its introduction of the reform and opening-up programme, China has formulated a basic state policy to promote family planning in an all-round way so as to reduce population growth and improve its quality in terms of health and education. The government encourages late marriage and late childbearing and advocates the principles of 'one couple, one child' and of 'having a second child with proper spacing in accordance with the regulations'. The government pays great attention to the issue of population and development and has placed it high on the agenda of the overall plan of its national economic and social development. It consistently emphasizes that population growth should be compatible with socio-economic development and should be concerted with resource utilization and environmental protection (Wei and Rowley, 2009b).

After nearly thirty years of effort, China has successfully developed an integrated approach to the population issue with its own national characteristics. The excessive population growth has been brought under control. The natural growth rate was decreased from 12 per 1000 in 1978 to 5.17 per 1000 in 2007 (*China Statistical Yearbook 2008*). Great achievements have been made in various social undertakings, such as education and public health. By the end of 2000, nine-year compulsory education had been made almost universal, and illiteracy among young and middle-aged people eliminated (see p. 11 for more on education). The maternal mortality rate declined from 94.7 per 100,000 in 1990 to 56.2 per 100,000 in 1998. The average life expectancy increased to 71.4 years in 2000 (Wei and Rowley, 2009b).

## Economy

Since the late 1970s the Chinese leadership has been moving from a sluggish, Soviet-style, centrally planned economy to a more market-oriented economy through the 'Four Modernizations' (of agriculture, industry, science and technology) and 'Open Door' policies, albeit still within a rigid political framework of Communist Party control. To this end, the authorities switched to a system of household responsibility in agriculture in place of the old collectivization, increased the authority of local officials and plant managers in industry, permitted a wide variety of small-scale enterprise in services and light manufacturing and opened the economy to increased foreign trade and investment (Wei and Rowley, 2009b).

In late 1993 additional long-term reforms aimed at giving still more play to market-oriented institutions and at strengthening the centre's control over the financial system were approved. SOEs would continue to dominate many key industries in what was now termed 'a socialist market economy'. Since the reforms, China has transformed its economic system from a highly centralized, planned economy to a market economy. Though people hold different views on whether China has set up a complete market economic system, the transformation has certainly been profound. Moreover, it has been necessary to speed up the reform process, especially since China's entry into the WTO (Wei and Rowley, 2009b).

## Evolving business environment

Management and businesses in China have witnessed significant changes in the last three decades. This is consequential of the broader economic reform that is market-oriented and increasingly global-focused. The 'Open Door' policy adopted by the Chinese government in 1978 and the abundance of cheap labour have attracted a large amount of foreign direct investment (FDI), making China one of the largest recipient countries of FDI (see Table 1.1). This investment initially came mainly from Chinese diaspora entrepreneurs but has been dominated in recent years by MNCs from developed economies. The investment has spread across a wide range of sectors, with manufacturing, retail and financial industry among the key recipient sectors (see *China Statistical Yearbook 2008*).

Fuelled by FDI, China's GDP had increased from 364.52 billion yuan in 1978 to 24952.99 billion yuan in 2007; GDP per capita increased from 381 yuan to 18,934 yuan in the same period (*China Statistical Yearbook 2008*). Industrialization and urbanization have led to a continuous decline in the primary sector's contribution to GDP (i.e. agriculture, forestry and fishery) and a rise of the tertiary sector (i.e. commercial and service). In 1978, some 28.1 per cent of the GDP came from the primary sector; this had fallen to 11.3 per cent by 2007. By contrast, 23.7 per cent of the GDP was contributed by the tertiary sector in 1978; this had risen to 40.1 per cent by 2007. Export made up over one-third of China's GDP

**Table 1.1** Utilization of foreign capital, 1979–2007 (end-of-year figures) (Value figures in 100 million US$)

| Year | Total | | Foreign loans | | FDIs | | Other foreign investments |
|---|---|---|---|---|---|---|---|
| | No. of projects | Value | No. of projects | Value | No. of projects | Value | |
| **Total amount of contracted foreign capital** | | | | | | | |
| 1979–1984 | 3,365 | 287.69 | 117 | 169.78 | 3,248 | 103.93 | 13.98 |
| 1985 | 3,145 | 98.67 | 72 | 35.34 | 3,073 | 59.31 | 4.02 |
| 1989 | 5,909 | 114.79 | 130 | 51.85 | 5,779 | 56.00 | 6.94 |
| 1990 | 7,371 | 120.86 | 98 | 50.99 | 7,273 | 56.96 | 3.91 |
| 1995 | 37,184 | 1,032.05 | 173 | 121.88 | 37,011 | 912.82 | 6.35 |
| 1996 | 24,673 | 816.10 | 117 | 79.62 | 24,556 | 732.77 | 3.71 |
| 1997 | 21,138 | 610.58 | 137 | 58.72 | 21,001 | 510.04 | 41.82 |
| 1998 | 19,850 | 632.01 | 51 | 83.85 | 19,799 | 521.02 | 27.14 |
| 1999 | 17,022 | 520.09 | 104 | 83.60 | 16,918 | 412.23 | 24.26 |
| 2000 | 22,347 | 711.30 | – | – | 22,347 | 463.80 | 87.50 |
| 2001 | 26,140 | 719.76 | – | – | 26,140 | 691.95 | 27.81 |
| 2002 | 34,171 | 847.51 | – | – | 34,171 | 827.68 | 19.82 |
| 2003 | 41,081 | 1,169.01 | – | – | 41,081 | 1,150.70 | 18.32 |
| 2004 | 43,664 | 1,565.88 | – | – | 43,664 | 1,534.79 | 31.09 |
| 2005 | 44,001 | 1,925.93 | – | – | 44,001 | 1,890.65 | 35.28 |
| 2006 | 41,473 | 1,982.16 | – | – | 41,473 | 1,937.27 | 44.89 |
| 2007 | 37,871 | – | – | – | 37,871 | – | – |
| 1979–2007 | 633,969 | 16,616.22 | 1,683 | 1,385.38 | 632,286 | 14,794.01 | 436.80 |

Source: adapted from *China Statistical Yearbook 2008*, p. 729.

(*China Statistical Yearbook 2008*). There are many examples of Western and Eastern MNCs in China (see Poon and Rowley, 2009).

The continuous high growth rate of GDP has provided employment opportunities to millions of rural migrant workers who have either lost their land for farming as a result of urbanization or have decided to migrate to cities to improve their economic conditions. It was reported that by the mid-2000s, there were over 100 million rural migrant workers working in urban areas. They made up 58 per cent of the workers in the industrial sector and 52 per cent in the service sector (State Council, 2006). As Table 1.2 shows, employment in the primary sector has been in steady decline since 1978, with workers absorbed by the manufacturing, construction, wholesale and retail sectors, and other industries. Since the wage levels are generally considerably higher in the secondary and tertiary sectors than in the primary sector (see *China Statistical Yearbook 2008*), the growth of employment opportunities in the urban areas has led to an increase in wage income and an improvement of living standards in the population in general. According to the World Bank (2006), 400 million people in China have been lifted above the poverty threshold in the last twenty years. The growth of wage income means growing purchasing power and a more vibrant domestic consumer market. This creates new opportunities for new products as well as new product markets.

Accompanying the economic reform and the growing wealth of the nation is the rising level of education in China. In particular, increases at the higher education level are marked. In 1978, 402,000 students were enrolled in universities nationwide, with 10,708 of them at the postgraduate level. In 2007, nearly 5.7 million students were enrolled, 418,612 of them at the postgraduate level. The majority of them were full-time students. Much of this growth took place in the last decade, following the state's decision to expand the higher education sector radically. In 1998, the enrolment figure was 1.08 million. In 1999, enrolments in universities had increased by 48 per cent to nearly 1.6 million students (*China Statistical Yearbook 2008*).

Another defining feature of China's economic development is the dramatic growth of the private sector (e.g. Child and Tse, 2001; Garnaut and Huang, 2001; Nolan, 2004; Parris, 1999). The growth of the private sector has been more significant since the mid-1990s as a result of the contraction of the state and semi-state sectors through the downsizing, privatization and closure of SOEs and collectively owned enterprises

**Table 1.2** Number of employed persons at the year-end by sector (in thousands)*

| Industry | 1978 | 1985 | 1990 | 1995 | 1998 | 2000 | 2002 |
|---|---|---|---|---|---|---|---|
| Farming, Forestry, Animal Husbandry & Fishery | 283,180 | 311,300 | 341,170 | 330,180 | 332,320 | 333,550 | 324,870 |
| Mining & Quarrying | 6,520 | 7,950 | 8,820 | 9,320 | 7,210 | 5,970 | 5,580 |
| Manufacturing | 53,320 | 74,120 | 86,240 | 98,030 | 83,190 | 80,430 | 83,070 |
| Electricity, Gas & Water Production & Supply | 1,070 | 1,420 | 1,920 | 2,580 | 2,830 | 2,840 | 2,900 |
| Construction | 8,540 | 20,350 | 24,240 | 33,220 | 33,270 | 35,520 | 38,930 |
| Geological Prospecting & Water Conservancy | 1,780 | 1,970 | 1,970 | 1,350 | 1,160 | 1,100 | 980 |
| Transport, Storage, Post & Telecommunication Services | 7,500 | 12,790 | 15,660 | 19,420 | 20,000 | 20,290 | 20,840 |
| Wholesale, Retail Trade & Catering Services | 11,400 | 23,060 | 28,390 | 42,920 | 46,450 | 46,860 | 49,690 |
| Finance & Insurance | 760 | 1,380 | 2,180 | 2,760 | 3,140 | 3,270 | 3,400 |
| Real Estate | 310 | 360 | 440 | 800 | 940 | 1,000 | 1,180 |
| Social Services | 1,790 | 4,010 | 5,940 | 7,030 | 8,680 | 9,210 | 10,940 |
| Healthcare, Sports & Social Welfare | 3,630 | 4,670 | 5,360 | 4,440 | 4,780 | 4,880 | 4,930 |
| Education, Culture & Art, Radio, Film & Television | 10,930 | 12,730 | 14,570 | 14,760 | 15,730 | 15,650 | 15,650 |
| Scientific Research & Polytechnic Services | 920 | 1,440 | 1,730 | 1,820 | 1,780 | 1,740 | 1,630 |
| Governmental Organizations, Party Agencies and Social Organizations | 4,670 | 7,990 | 10,790 | 10,420 | 10,970 | 11,040 | 10,750 |
| Others | 5,210 | 13,190 | 17,980 | 44,840 | 51,180 | 56,430 | 62,450 |
| **Total** | **401,520** | **498,730** | **647,490** | **680,650** | **706,370** | **760,850** | **737,400** |

Note: a complete set of figures beyond 2003 is not available from subsequent yearbooks.

* 'Employed persons' refers to the persons aged sixteen and over who are engaged in social working and receive remuneration payment or earn business income. This indicator reflects the actual utilization of total labour force during a certain period of time and is often used for research on China's economic situation and national power (original note from *China Statistical Yearbook 2005*, p. 181).

Source: adapted from *China Statistical Yearbook 2005*, p. 125.

(COEs) (e.g. Hassard *et al.*, 2007; Smyth *et al.*, 2005). In 1978, over 78 per cent of the urban workforce was employed in the state sector. This had been reduced to less than 23 per cent by 2007. In the five-year period between 1998 and 2002, when the state sector restructuring was at its peak, over 27 million workers were laid off (*China Statistical Yearbook 2003*).

Despite operating initially under the guarded freedom granted by the state and other institutional constraints that still persist, the private sector has been growing steadily since the 1980s in terms of the number of firms, size of the workforce and industrial outputs. In 1998, the sector employed a total of 17.1 million workers (both urban and rural). By the end of 2007, it employed 72.53 million (*China Statistical Yearbook 2008*; figures do not include self-employment). While private businesses have expanded into a diverse range of industrial sectors, commercial services and labour-intensive light manufacturing industries remain their main territory. The majority of the private businesses are relatively small, mainly due to the difficulty of securing bank loans for business development. They are highly profit-driven and therefore more adventurous and opportunistic (Cooke, 2008).

Institutional constraints notwithstanding, private entrepreneurship has played an important role in product innovation and product market development in areas where the state sector has been too slow and rigid to respond. While the overall level of China's innovation capacity remains relatively low, Chinese privately owned enterprises (POEs) are now the main drivers of technological innovation (Cooke, 2008). For example, over 80 per cent of the enterprises in the 53 high-tech zones in China are privately owned. POEs hold 66 per cent of the patents, 74 per cent of the technological innovations and 82 per cent of the new product developments in China (*People's Daily Overseas Edition*, 13 January 2007). Vital to these innovative activities are the increasing level of higher education and the entrepreneurship of overseas Chinese scholars and students (Khanna, 2007). There has been growth of small and medium-sized enterprises (SMEs) and different management practices within the private sector (see Li and Rowley, 2007; 2008a; 2008b). In addition, some particular HRM practices have evolved, as in the area of rewards (Wei and Rowley, 2009a; 2009c).

# Key challenges

The transformation of the economic and social landscape of China presents a number of significant, key challenges to management. The relatively heavy reliance on FDI and an export-driven manufacturing economy means that the Chinese economy can be highly vulnerable to the global politico-economic climate. For example, the global financial crisis triggered by the credit crunch in the banking and insurance sector in late 2008 has had considerable impact on Chinese enterprises that are export oriented. A large number of private factories have gone bankrupt or been closed in export manufacturing zones such as the Pearl River Delta Area of Guangdong Province. This has led to job losses for millions of migrant workers.

Creating internal demand to sustain economic growth has become a key task for the Chinese government. At the enterprise level, developing products and marketing techniques appropriate for different market segments becomes a more pertinent strategic concern than ever. One of the negative consequences of China's market economy is the widening income gaps between the poor and the rich. According to the World Bank, income of the bottom level of the population has increased by 42 per cent over the last ten years. Income of the middle level has increased by 115 per cent within the same period, while income of the top level has increased by 168 per cent (Dong, 2008). Affordability remains low at the bottom and lower levels of the population. Politico-economic turmoil and the consequent employment insecurity impact further on consumers' spending confidence and affordability, particularly at the lower level of the market segment. The Chinese culture of saving for rainy days, one that is reinforced by the absence of social security protection for the majority of the population, presents another challenge to marketing and sales.

Chinese culture affects business and management not only in the marketing area (e.g. Lasserre and Schütte, 2006), but in how business is conducted and people are managed. The importance of *guanxi* (personal relationships) has been widely noted (e.g. Luo, 2000; Warren *et al.*, 2004). Chinese people are *guanxi*-oriented and have acquired sophisticated skills to develop interpersonal relationships. *Guanxi* has to be developed to overcome institutional deficiency caused by market imperfection and regulatory failure. The emphasis on *guanxi* over and above laws and rules sometimes means that foreign businesses find it very hard to accept and adapt to the Chinese business culture. Likewise,

Chinese managers may find themselves in an awkward position when they apply their Chinese mindset to conducting business in Western countries, where the interpretation of business ethics differs. In addition, Chinese managers may find that the collectivistic and egalitarian approach to managing workplace relationships and reward distribution that they use in China is difficult to implement in countries with individualistic cultures (Cooke, 2005). Moreover, this Chinese traditional value is now also being challenged by the younger and more educated generation of the Chinese workforce.

Perhaps the most serious challenge to managing business in China is the twin problem of skill shortage and innovation capability. The rising level of human capital, measured by the increased level of educational attainment of the workforce, has not alleviated the worsening skill shortage of the country. This is occurring in a context of labour surplus (see Zhang and Liu, 2009). The education level of the workforce remains relatively low compared with that of developed countries (see Table 1.3, p. 16). A more serious problem is that the educational system in China is not conducive to innovation and creativity. The vocational education system has also been criticized for being grossly inadequate for what is needed by employers. Few businesses invest sufficiently in training and development, partly due to the poaching practice (e.g. Cooke, 2005). Even fewer firms invest in research and development (R&D) for innovation as a result of rampant violations of intellectual property rights (IPR). While transformation of China from largely a 'made in China' country to a 'created by China' country to sustain its economic and social development is a formidable challenge for the government, operating successfully under these institutional constraints is the ultimate test for business managers.

The aim of this volume is therefore to examine in detail how the context for business management may have changed in the last two to three decades, and how managers address the challenges identified here and many more that have not yet been mentioned.

## Management functions and issues – structure of the book

This volume is structured in two parts. The first part contains three chapters that cover a management functional area each, including HRM, marketing and accounting. The second part consists of five chapters. Four of these cover certain aspects of management issues, including SOE reforms, management in SMEs, performance management (PM) in

**Table 1.3** Educational attainment composition of male and female employment in China in 2007 (percentages)

| Education level | Total | Illiterate and semi-illiterate | Primary school | Junior high school | Senior high school | College | University | Post-graduate |
|---|---|---|---|---|---|---|---|---|
| National total | 100 Male: 53.6 Female: 46.4 | 6.0 | 28.3 | 46.9 | 12.2 | 4.3 | 2.1 | 0.20 |
| Male | 100 | 3.4 | 25.0 | 50.2 | 14.3 | 4.6 | 2.3 | 0.25 |
| Female | 100 | 9.0 | 32.2 | 42.9 | 9.8 | 4.0 | 1.9 | 0.14 |

Source: compiled from *China Labour Statistical Yearbook 2008*, pp. 63–5.

different types of organization, and mergers and acquisitions among domestic private and international firms in the IT and telecom industries. The fifth provides an overview of management in Hong Kong, which became a special administration zone of China in 1997 but has retained much of its unique management context and challenges. Below is a summary of the content of each chapter.

## Management of human resources

HRM in China has experienced a period of transformation in the last two decades. The traditional personnel management policies once characteristic of the dominant state-owned sector have been replaced by a diverse range of HRM practices. Organizational leaders are facing a new set of challenges in linking their HR strategy with organizational performance as a result of the diversification of ownership forms and business portfolios, heightened market competition, and the changing values and work ethics of the younger generation of the workforce, who are more exposed to the influence of Western culture and ideology.

As the pace of globalization gathers speed, internationalizing Chinese firms also face challenges in how to design HR systems that suit the Chinese environment, on the one hand, and are acceptable in the international arena, on the other. Meanwhile, the enactment of a series of new employment regulations in 2008 signals the Chinese government's determination to raise the level of protection of its workforce. Firms are no longer able to hire and fire people at will and offer exploitative terms and conditions, at least in principle. Employees are afforded greater power to seek justice through legal channels when these regulations are violated by employers. The implementation of these regulations therefore presents further challenges for employing organizations as well as HR professionals. In Chapter 2, Cooke reviews major changes that are taking place in HRM in China at both macro and micro levels and the reasons for these changes. A number of case examples are drawn from different industrial sectors and ownership forms to illustrate the changes, new HRM practices and challenges.

## Uniqueness and diversity in marketing

China is a large country with a huge population and many (fifty-six) ethnic groups. The consuming habits are quite different for consumers living in urban and rural areas, southern and northern China, eastern and western China. The fast economic development has widened the income gap between the different areas. Firms need to conduct in-depth investigations of local customers' income level, consumption habits and environment and then adjust their marketing strategies to build strong brands and win customers. Many famous brands, such as Whirlpool, Valentino and NEC, abandoned the Chinese market after several years of operation because they failed to address the uniqueness of brand building.

Incorporating research conducted both in Western countries and in China, Wang and Feng (Chapter 3) highlight the importance of brands in the Chinese market and the uniqueness of that market. They provide an overview of the historical development of marketing in China, the unique characteristics of Chinese consumers and unique compositions of the customer-based brand equity. Wang and Feng argue that brand equity in the Chinese market can be divided into four parts: perceived quality, brand awareness, brand associations and brand loyalty. They propose a brand-equity-based marketing strategy to guide practitioners in brand building in China by using the examples of two reputable companies that are famous for their successful branding strategies in China – Haier Group and McDonald's (China). Finally, Wang and Feng address challenges confronting brand building in China, such as regional differences, stricter legal and media supervision, crises of customer confidence towards brands, stronger patriotism etc.

## Issues and differences in accounting

As companies around the world expand internationally, diverse strategies have been employed to establish global presence. With the internationalization of Chinese enterprises, it becomes imperative for executives to understand the differences in the operational environments of the home and host countries. While there are several cultural, business, economic and management differences across countries, an important area of examination is accounting practice. Chapter 4 describes the current state of accounting in mainland China, identifies differences between China and countries such as the US, and discusses business implications for the internationalizing Chinese enterprises.

Chamblin, Munoz and Zheng-Pratt identify twelve significant accounting issues: revenue recognition, disclosure of related party transactions, disclosure of cash flow statements, intangible assets, borrowing costs, leases capitalization, inventories valuation, fixed assets valuation, R&D costs, accounts receivable, effects of currency conversion, and income taxation. In dealing with these issues, the authors recommend a seven-step process for the Management of International Accounting Disparities (MIAD). The MIAD Model includes such steps as: market environment assessment, accounting system evaluation, identification of key accounting differences, assessment of business impact of accounting differences, implementation of selected measures, evaluation and monitoring, and review and update. The authors further recommend specific measures for internationalizing Chinese firms.

## Reforming state-owned enterprises

China's economic reforms commenced in December 1978 when the Third Plenum of the Eleventh Central Committee issued a communiqué calling for a reduction in the degree of centralization of economic management and reform of the commune structure. The initial reforms focused on agriculture, but in the 1980s spread to the SOE sector. In the first period of SOE reform, lasting from 1984 to 1993, SOEs were made responsible for profits and losses in the market and contract arrangements were introduced that rewarded managers for meeting specified performance targets. These reforms had some success in reducing government intervention in the management of SOEs, but the rights and responsibilities of SOE managers remained ill-defined. The second period of SOE reform, which commenced in 1993 and is ongoing, has focused on establishing a modern corporate governance structure in China's large and medium-sized SOEs and enterprise groups.

Smyth and Zhai (Chapter 5) examine the outcomes of the latest stage of China's attempts to corporatize its SOE sector and consider some of the major challenges that exist for further economic restructuring of China's large SOEs three decades on from the Third Plenum of the Eleventh Central Committee. To illustrate their points, they draw on a case study of Fushun Petrochemical Company (FPC), which is a large SOE in Liaoning Province under the control of the China National Petroleum Corporation (CNPC). Drawing on interviews with managers and local government officials, the authors use the economic restructuring of FPC that commenced in 1999 to illustrate how the reforms have been implemented on the ground and some of the major difficulties that further economic restructuring poses. They also examine how managers used an emerging environmental awareness in China in the lead-up to the Beijing Olympics to promote a positive image of FPC.

## Small and medium-sized enterprise management

The importance of large firms in China's economic development has received a considerable amount of attention in the political and popular discourse, media and academia. But since the 1990s, SMEs have played an increasingly important role in this economic growth. SMEs have become important as a source of employment and as contributors to the economy and structural reform. Though SMEs contribute 60 per cent of the country's GDP and over 75 per cent of urban job opportunities, they face enormous challenges as China integrates more into the world economy. Influences such as globalization, technological innovation and demographic and social change, as well as the level of technology deployed, innovative ability, financial support and entrepreneurship, can be found in the business environment, impacting as both external and internal factors. However, little is known about the historical trajectory of SMEs in China and the challenges they are facing.

Cunningham and Rowley (Chapter 6) provide us with an overview of SMEs in China by looking at their historical development and examining their current situation in a socio-economic environment. They argue that key political and economic reforms form a backdrop to the development of SMEs in China and highlight the significant role of SMEs in the national economy. Drawing on case study examples, they illustrate that institutional and cultural factors play a critical role not only in the development of SMEs but in shaping entrepreneurship. Cunningham and Rowley identify a number of key challenges encountered by entrepreneurs in SMEs in China.

## Managing performance

Managing performance is a thorny issue for managers in most societal contexts. In China, the end of job-for-life and the growing popularity of performance-based rewards have called into question the relevance of the traditional styles of performance appraisal that were based on seniority, political orientation and moral integrity instead of competence and technical performance. In Chapter 7, Poon, Wei and Rowley outline recent developments in performance management in China, particularly in knowledge-intensive industries. They argue that economic reforms, new labour legislation, China's accession to the WTO as well as the focus on an 'informatization' strategy have brought significant changes to management practices. An important consequence of this change is the introduction of greater market mechanisms in HRM practices with commensurate change in performance management.

Poon, Wei and Rowley argue that HRM practices, including a performance management system (PMS), can be shaped by many factors, such as the Chinese institutional environment, cultural values and type of firm ownership. They compare and contrast PMS adopted in different types of firm ownership to illustrate which elements and functions of PMS have changed (*change content*). They also discuss what factors facilitate or hinder the implementation of new performance management in knowledge-intensive industries (*change context*). Four cases are provided to exemplify the characteristics of PMS and to explore issues that have emerged during the change process from individual and organizational perspectives.

## Managing mergers and acquisitions

Despite the fact that mergers and acquisitions (M&As) has been a major strategy deployed by firms to grow, access resources, strengthen their market positions and exploit new market opportunities in the Western economies, M&A activities have started to emerge in China only since the mid-1980s and have gained popularity only since the mid-1990s. However, much of the M&A activities have taken place between Chinese firms. Cross-border M&A deals remain a relatively small proportion and insufficiently understood. This is in spite of the fact that China is one of the largest FDI recipient countries in the world. What is known is that cross-border M&As in China mainly occur in the form of acquisitions and that acquisition activities in the twenty-first century are shifting away from traditional industries towards new, high-tech and high-value-added industries. With the explosive growth of mobile phone and Internet subscribers in the last decade, the Chinese information communication technology (ICT) market has been a lucrative as well as a competitive arena for many Chinese and foreign firms.

In Chapter 8, Huang and Cooke provide an overview of the brief history of mergers and acquisitions in China, with a focus on foreign investors' acquisition activities. They then detail the motives and post-acquisition integration processes of four sets of acquisitions of private Chinese firms by foreign-owned MNCs in the Internet and telecom industries. These four sets of case study examples reveal the processes of the acquisitions, the bargaining power held by the two parties and the new business dynamics that emerged during the post-acquisition integration. Huang and Cooke also identify some of the key challenges facing cross-border acquisitions in China. These include: regulative confusions, limited availability of professional services to facilitate M&As, competence deficiency of Chinese management in handling cross-border M&As, and interventions from local government.

## Management in Hong Kong

Management in Hong Kong owes its current features and pattern largely to the cultural and normative heritages extending from both Chinese and British custom and practices. In Chapter 9, Ng and Ip trace the evolution of management and management practices in Hong Kong under the context of globalization and Hong Kong's reversion to China in 1997. They identify and discuss a number of key issues which provide the historical and theoretical backdrop to the development of management practices in Hong Kong in the age of modernity/ post-modernity.

It is acknowledged that there is conspicuous propensity for Hong Kong businesses to converge with and benchmark themselves against industrially advanced economies and societies, while evolving practices to emulate them. However, the authors also argue that Hong Kong has attained its current position not only through the world's convergence movement, but due to experiences unique to its history. In this respect, Ng and Ip discuss two issues relevant to developing economies – the role of the state in fashioning the development process; and the alleged excellence of Asian values, as popularized by the thesis of the spirit of Chinese capitalism – which have purportedly contributed to the East Asian legend of hastened economic growth. Drawing on several studies conducted on businesses in Hong Kong and their management practices during the 1980s and early 1990s, Ng and Ip illustrate how the contextual variable of culture has affected managerial characteristics and performance in the territory. They point out that although globalization has affected Hong Kong visibly since the 1990s, Hong Kong has remained a hybrid melting-pot that echoes as well as defies the logic of theoretical statements advanced by convergence, culturalist, and late-development theories.

## Conclusion

It is now widely recognized that China is a fast-developing country that has a major political and economic influence on the global stage. However, the challenges that China faces in sustaining its economic and social development domestically and as a key global player are immense. This collection delineates the macro context under which organizations of diverse ownership forms operate. Many of the management issues and obstacles identified in the case studies are generic and serve as important lessons for organizations in other sectors and regions. A key component of managing organization is managing people. The centrality of HRM runs through the volume and forms a core part of the discussion in many chapters (see Poon and Rowley, 2007 for the foci and changes in research interests). The shortage of skills and talent, the problems of PM and the psychological contract of the employees informed by the Chinese cultural tradition are some of the most unique features in HRM. In other management functions, while a sound understanding of Chinese culture proves crucial for successful marketing and product branding, a mindset with Chinese culture may be detrimental in the accounting practices. This has important implications for an increasing number of Chinese firms that are seeking global expansion.

As is often the case, edited volumes are constrained by space and the availability of expertise at the time needed. As such, this volume has not been able to cover as many functional disciplines and management issues as we would have desired. Nevertheless, we feel that it is a useful addition to the growing body of literature on Chinese business and management for students, practitioners and researchers who are interested in learning more about China and the changing face of management therein.

**Table 1.4** List of case studies: types of organizations and managers

| Chapter | Organization | | Manager | |
| --- | --- | --- | --- | --- |
| | Name | Sector | Position | Organization |
| **HRM** | | | | |
| Case 2.1 | Huawei | IT | | |
| Case 2.2 | Service Co | Facilities maintenance | | |
| Case 2.3 | | | HR manager | Company A (speakers) |
| Case 2.4 | | | Director | Company B (detergent) |
| **Marketing** | | | | |
| Case 3.1 | Haier | White & brown goods | | |
| Case 3.2 | McDonald's | Food retailing | | |
| Case 3.3 | | | Marketing manager | Coca-Cola |
| Case 3.4 | | | Call centre manager | Motorola |
| **Accounting** | | | | |
| Case 4.1 | Haier | White & brown goods | | |
| Case 4.2 | Firm X | Commercial goods | | |
| Case 4.3 | | | Partner | Henderson Consulting |
| Case 4.4 | | | Accounting manager | XYZ Corp |
| **SOE** | | | | |
| Case 5.1 | Fushun Petroleum | Oil | | |
| Case 5.2 | | | Former general manager | Fushun Petroleum |
| Case 5.3 | | | Current general manager | Fushun Petroleum |

| | | | | |
|---|---|---|---|---|
| **SME** | | | | |
| Case 6.1 | Oriental | Fruit processing/sales | | |
| Case 6.2 | NPG | Automatic door production | | |
| Case 6.3 | | | Owner manager | Oriental |
| Case 6.4 | | | Owner manager | NPG |
| | | | | |
| **PM** | | | | |
| Case 7.1 | Bank of China | Finance | | |
| Case 7.2 | Bank of America | Finance | | |
| Case 7.3 | | | Deputy MD | Zhan Investments Holding Co. Ltd |
| Case 7.4 | | | Marketing manager | Estra |
| | | | | |
| **M&A** | | | | |
| Case 8.1 | Oriental Power and US Magic | Telecom equipment | | |
| Case 8.2 | Quick Rabbit and Asian Dragon | Software development | | |
| Case 8.3 | | | HR Director | Paradise and Online Star |
| Case 8.4 | | | Founder | Matador and RichTech |
| | | | | |
| **Hong Kong** | | | | |
| Case 9.1 | HKE | Power generation | | |
| Case 9.2 | Company W | Property management | | |
| Case 9.3 | | | Senior manager | HKE |
| Case 9.4 | | | HR manager | Company W |

# Bibliography

Child, J. (2001) 'China and international business', in J. Child, *Oxford Handbook of International Business*, Oxford Scholarship Online, 1, 29: 681–716.

Child, J. and Tse, D. (2001) 'China's transition and its implications for international business', *Journal of International Business Studies*, 32, 1: 5–21.

*China Labour Statistical Yearbook 2003, 2005* and *2008*, Beijing: China Statistics Press.

*China Statistical Yearbook 2003, 2005* and *2008*, Beijing: China Statistics Press.

Cooke, F. L. (2005) *HRM, Work and Employment in China*, London: Routledge.

Cooke, F. L. (2008) *Competition, Strategy and Management in China*, Basingstoke: Palgrave Macmillan.

Dong, B. H. (2008) 'From the Labour Law to the Labour Contract Law', Paper presented at the 'Breaking down Chinese Walls: The Changing Faces of Labor and Employment in China' International Conference, Cornell University, Ithaca, New York, 26–28 September.

Garnaut, R. and Huang, Y. P. (2001) *Growth without Miracles – Readings on the Chinese Economy in the Era of Reform*, Oxford: Oxford University Press.

Hassard, J., Sheehan, J., Zhou, M., Terpstra-Tong, J. and Morris, J. (2007) *China's State Enterprise Reform: From Marx to the Market*, London: Routledge.

Johnson, G. and Scholes, K. (2002) *Exploring Corporate Strategy: Text and Cases* (6th edition), Harlow: Pearson Education Ltd.

Khanna, T. (2007) *Billions of Entrepreneurs: How China and India Are Reshaping Their Futures and Yours*, Boston: Harvard Business School Press.

Lasserre, P. and Schütte, H. (2006) *Strategies for Asia Pacific: Meeting New Challenges* (3rd edition), Basingstoke: Palgrave Macmillan.

Li, M. and Zhou, H. (2005) 'Knowing the business environment: the use of non-market-based strategies in Chinese local firms', *Ivey Business Journal*, November/December: 1–5.

Li, X. and Rowley, C. (2005) 'Chinese SMEs: development and HRM', in E. Mrudula and P. Raju (eds) *China: Trading Empire of the New Century*, India: ICFAI University Press, 108–19.

Li, X. and Rowley, C. (2007) 'HRM in Chinese SMEs', *Personnel Review*, 36, 3: 415–39.

Li, X. and Rowley, C. (2008a) 'HRM in Chinese SMEs', *Asia Pacific Journal of Human Resources*, 46, 3: 353–79.

Li, X. and Rowley, C. (2008b) 'HRM in SMEs in Jiangsu, China', in R. Barrett and S. Mayerson (eds) *International Handbook of Entrepreneurship and HRM*, Cheltenham: Edward Elgar, 285–301.

Luo, Y. (2000) *Partnering with Chinese Firms: Lessons for International Managers*, Aldershot: Ashgate.

Nolan, P. (2004) *Transforming China: Globalisation, Transition and Development*, London: Anthem Press.

Parris, K. (1999) 'The rise of private business interests', in M. Goldman and R. MacFarquhar (eds) *The Paradox of China's Post-Mao Reforms*, Cambridge, MA: Harvard University Press, 262–82.

*People's Daily Overseas Edition*, 13 January 2007.

Poon, I. and Rowley, C. (2007) 'Contemporary research on management and HR in China', *Asia Pacific Business Review*, 13, 1: 133–53.

Poon, I. and Rowley, C. (2009) 'Company profiles: East Asia', in C. Wankel (ed.) *Encyclopaedia of Business in Today's World*, Los Angeles: Sage, 320–25.

Rowley, C. and Paik, Y. (2008) *The Changing Face of Korean Management*, London: Routledge.

Rowley, C. and Truong, Q. (2010) *The Changing Face of Vietnamese Management*, London: Routledge.

Smyth, R., Tam, O. K., Warner, M. and Zhu, C. (2005) *China's Business Reforms: Institutional Challenges in a Globalised Economy*, London: Routledge.

State Council, The (2006) *Report on Rural Migrant Workers in China*, Beijing: The State Council of China.

Warner, M. (ed.) (2009) *Human Resource Management 'with Chinese Characteristics'*, London: Routledge.

Warren, D., Dunfee, T. and Li, N. (2004) 'Social exchange in China: the double-edged sword of guanxi', *Journal of Business Ethics*, 55: 355–72.

Wei, Q. and Rowley, C. (2009a) 'Changing patterns of rewards in China', *Asia Pacific Business Review*, 16, 4: 489–506.

Wei, Q. and Rowley, C. (2009b) 'China', in C. Wankel (ed.) *Encyclopaedia of Business in Today's World*, Los Angeles: Sage, 268–72.

Wei, Q. and Rowley, C. (2009c) 'Pay for performance in China's non-public sector enterprises', *Asia Pacific Journal of Business Administration*, 1, 2: 119–43.

World Bank, The (2006) *World Development Indicators 2006*, Washington, DC: The World Bank.

Zhang, W. and Liu, X. H. (2009) 'Introduction: success and challenges: an overview of China's economic growth and reform since 1978', *Journal of Chinese Economic and Business Studies*, 7, 2: 127–38.

# 2 The changing face of human resource management in China

*Fang Lee Cooke*

- Introduction
- Context
- Case studies
- Key challenges
- Conclusion

## Introduction

People management in China has experienced a period of transformation in the last two decades. The traditional personnel management policies once characteristic of the dominant state-owned sector have been replaced by a diverse range of human resource management (HRM) practices. Organizational leaders are facing a new set of challenges in linking HR strategy with organizational performance as a result of the diversification of ownership forms and business portfolios, heightened market competition, and the changing values and work ethics of the younger generation of the workforce, who are more exposed to the influence of Western culture and ideology. As the pace of globalization gathers speed, internationalizing Chinese firms also face challenges in how to design HR systems that suit the Chinese environment, on the one hand, and are acceptable in the international arena, on the other. Meanwhile, the enactment of a series of new employment regulations in 2008, namely the Labour Contract Law, the Employment Promotion Law, and the Labour Dispute Mediation and Arbitration Law, signals the Chinese government's renewed and stronger determination to raise the level of protection for its workforce. Firms are no longer able to hire and fire people at will and offer exploitative terms and conditions, at least in principle. Employees are afforded greater power to seek justice through legal channels when these regulations are violated by employers. The implementation of these regulations therefore presents further challenges to employing organizations as well as to HR professionals.

This chapter first reviews major changes that have taken or are taking place in HRM in China and the reasons for these changes. It outlines changes in the HR environment at a macro level before drawing attention to some of the changes in HR practices at a micro level. It then provides a couple of case studies to illustrate which HR practices are adopted by large companies in China and what effect these practices may have on employees and organizational performance. In addition, two mini-case studies of HR managers are presented to illustrate the challenges they encounter in managing the workforce and their perception of the role of HR professionals. The chapter then highlights a number of key challenges in people management, notably the skill shortage problem and the related talent management problem. The chapter concludes that HRM in China has moved away from its traditional personnel management system to be more strategic and performance-oriented. Not only are there signs of convergence across different ownership forms in the adoption of HR practices, but there is evidence to suggest that the conventional belief that Western multinational corporations are more progressive in their HRM than Chinese firms is open to question.

## Context

As mentioned above, diversification of ownership forms has been a key feature in China's contemporary economic reform that has a profound influence on how employment is structured and people are managed in workplaces. As we can see from Table 2.1, employment in the state-owned sector, which includes government organizations, the public sector and state-owned enterprises (SOEs), has been in steady decline since the mid-1990s. This is a direct consequence of the downsizing and restructuring drive of the government (see Chapter 5, this volume, for more details). Similarly, employment in collectively owned enterprises (COEs), often owned by local district government, has also experienced steep decline. Characteristics of employment and management in SOEs and COEs possess considerable similarities, although the latter are generally less developed and offer lower levels of employment terms and conditions to their employees than SOEs (Cooke, 2005). Parallel to the shrinkage of employment in SOEs and COEs has been the emergence of a variety of ownership forms and the growth of employment in these

**Table 2.1** Employment statistics by ownership in urban and rural areas in China (in millions)*

| Ownership | 1978 | 1980 | 1985 | 1990 | 1995 | 1998 | 2000 | 2003 | 2006 |
|---|---|---|---|---|---|---|---|---|---|
| **Total** | **401.52** | **423.61** | **498.73** | **647.49** | **680.65** | **706.37** | **720.85** | **744.32** | **764.00** |
| Number of urban employed persons | 95.14 | 105.25 | 128.08 | 166.16 | 190.93 | 206.78 | 231.51 | 256.39 | 283.10 |
| State-owned units | 74.51 | 80.19 | 89.90 | 103.46 | 112.61 | 90.58 | 81.02 | 68.76 | 64.30 |
| Collectively owned units | 20.48 | 24.25 | 33.24 | 35.49 | 31.47 | 19.63 | 14.99 | 10.00 | 7.64 |
| Co-operative units | – | – | – | – | – | 1.36 | 1.55 | 1.73 | 1.78 |
| Joint ownership units | – | – | 0.38 | 0.96 | 0.53 | 0.48 | 0.42 | 0.44 | 0.45 |
| Limited liability corporations | – | – | – | – | – | 4.84 | 6.87 | 12.61 | 19.20 |
| Share-holding corporations | – | – | – | – | 3.17 | 4.10 | 4.57 | 5.92 | 7.41 |
| Private enterprises | – | – | – | 0.57 | 4.85 | 9.73 | 12.68 | 25.45 | 39.54 |
| Units with funds from Hong Kong, Macao & Taiwan | – | – | – | 0.04 | 2.72 | 2.94 | 3.10 | 4.09 | 6.11 |
| Foreign-funded units | – | – | 0.06 | 0.62 | 2.41 | 2.93 | 3.32 | 4.54 | 7.96 |
| Self-employed individuals | 0.15 | 0.81 | 4.50 | 6.14 | 15.60 | 22.59 | 21.36 | 23.77 | 30.12 |
| Number of rural employed persons | 306.38 | 318.36 | 370.65 | 472.93 | 488.54 | 492.79 | 489.34 | 487.93 | 480.93 |
| Township and village enterprises | 28.27 | 30.00 | 69.79 | 92.65 | 128.62 | 125.37 | 128.20 | 135.73 | 146.80 |
| Private enterprises | – | – | – | 1.13 | 4.71 | 7.37 | 11.39 | 17.54 | 26.32 |
| Self-employed individuals | – | – | – | 14.91 | 30.54 | 38.55 | 29.34 | 22.60 | 21.47 |

Note: * Since 1990, data on the economically active population, the total employed persons and the subtotals of employed persons in urban and rural areas have been adjusted in accordance with the data obtained from the Fifth National Population Census. As a result, the sum of the data by region, by ownership or by sector is not equal to the total (original note from *China Statistical Yearbook 2003*, p. 123).

Source: adapted from *China Statistical Yearbook 2003*, pp. 126–7; *China Statistical Yearbook 2007*, p. 127.

business entities. In particular, privately owned enterprises (POEs), in both urban and rural areas, have seen significant growth. So have foreign-funded enterprises, including those funded by Hong Kong, Macao and Taiwan.

The increasing dominance of non-state-owned/invested firms as the primary employer means that these firms have greater autonomy than their state counterparts in determining HR practices that are more closely linked to market competition and organizational performance than those in the state sector. This has resulted in the rising level of adoption of performance management, often associated with performance-related pay, and work intensification for the majority of employees in these firms.

# Performance management

It has been noted that performance management is currently being promoted as a modern, Western HRM concept in China. This is in spite of the fact that performance appraisal practices have long existed in China with strong Chinese characteristics (Cooke, 2008). During the state-planned economy period, performance appraisal for ordinary workers mainly focused on attendance monitoring and skill grading tests. The former was used as the basis for wage deduction and the latter for pay rises. For professional and managerial staff (broadly classified as state cadres), performance appraisal (PA) was used primarily as a means for selecting and developing cadres and as evidence for promotion (Zhu and Dowling, 1998). In the early years of Socialist China, ideological and technical elites were promoted. During the Cultural Revolution period (1966–76), political performance (e.g. loyalty to the Communist Party) and moral integrity were the key criteria of performance measurement instead of technical competence and output (Cooke, 2008). Since the 1990s, PA systems have been more widely and systematically adopted by organizations in both the state-owned and private sectors than in the past (Zhu and Dowling, 1998; Lindholm, 1999; Bai and Bennington, 2005).

Changes are now taking place in PA practices that depart from the traditional form. Generally speaking, performance appraisal for ordinary workers was mainly about linking their productivity and level of responsibility with their wages and bonuses in order to motivate them to work towards the organizational goals. By contrast, results of performance appraisals for professional and managerial staff are often linked to annual bonuses and promotion (Cooke, 2008). Changes in cultural outlook are also occurring in China. For example, Bai and Bennington's (2005) study revealed that the Chinese cultural values did not impede the implementation of individual performance-related reward schemes. A study of sixty-five Chinese private firms by the author during 2007 and 2008 also showed that profit-sharing and stock option schemes were the most widely used and perceived to be the most effective HR mechanism to retain key employees. These findings suggest that new materialism has overtaken traditional cultural forces that tend to promote egalitarianism and suppress materialistic desire.

However, performance management as an HR function presents a number of challenges to managers. One is how to design a performance-related reward system that is seen as fair by employees and affordable by the company. The majority of firms still do not have a well-developed and comprehensive performance management scheme in place. Another challenge is to develop line managers' interest and competence in performance management as they are the key to people management. Research evidence suggests that performance management has not been fully accepted by managers as an effective tool in managing human resources (Cooke, 2008). According to a study conducted by Zhang (2005), who surveyed managers and workers across the five subsidiaries of a large stock market-listed state-owned enterprise, junior managers appeared to be more conservative and resistant than workers in terms of implementing a new performance management scheme which aimed to relate performance more closely to financial rewards. By contrast, over half of the workers surveyed had a positive attitude towards performance-related pay, and only a small minority (10–15 per cent) felt that competition pressure and distributional variations should be minimized.

## Work–life balance

Heightened market competition and the fast growth of firms have generally resulted in work intensification for employees in the private sector. This is particularly the case for firms in such fast-growing industries as telecommunications, IT, consultancy, finance and estate management. Work intensification has led to health problems and retention issues. Some firms are now beginning to address these problems by organizing after-work social events for their employees and hiring professionals to provide counselling services. For example, according to an HR manager interviewed by the author in October 2007, McKinsey (Shanghai) is introducing a range of social activities to offset the negative effects of long working hours and to stem the turnover problems. These include wine-tasting events and several social clubs. Other employee assistance programmes (EAPs) are being introduced by MNCs and high-performing private firms to help employees cope with stress. While organizing social events for employees (and their families) has long been a workplace welfare provision in SOEs and to a lesser extent in private firms as part of the Chinese paternalistic culture, EAPs are relatively new in China and are mainly provided to professional and managerial employees. It must be noted that work intensification associated with long working hours is endemic in the manufacturing sector, particularly in sweatshop factories where workers are primarily rural migrants. They rely on long hours in order to compensate for their low wages. Managers interviewed by the author reported that employees are not very interested in participating in the social activities, preferring to work more hours to earn extra money. These examples suggest that work–life conflicts in China derive from a range of sources that may be different from those manifested in Western societies and so require different HR initiatives in the Chinese context.

## Mentoring

Mentoring is being adopted by MNCs and larger Chinese private firms as an HR method for employee development. The mentoring system is different from the traditional Chinese apprentice system, which was used particularly in state-owned enterprises during the state-planned economy era. The apprentice system focuses on the development of craft/technical skills and behavioural conduct/personality of the protégé within the moral framework defined by the Socialist state. By contrast, the mentoring system that is promoted in the Western HR literature and adopted by a small, albeit increasing, number of firms in China has a broader focus. In principle, the mentor is not only responsible for inducting the mentee into the system of the organization, but is instrumental in guiding the career development of the mentee. The emphasis is both on the professional development and personal growth of the mentee and on alignment of their needs with those of the organization. Here, the mentor plays an important role in sharing his/her knowledge about the organization with the mentee, hence reinforcing the organizational culture. As we can see from Organization case 2.1, below, the mentoring system forms an important part of the training and development system for junior employees and is an integral part of the supervisor/mentor's job in Huawei Technologies Ltd.

## Towards a strategic approach to HRM

Earlier studies of HRM in Chinese firms have found that they tended to be less strategic than their Western counterparts in their approach to HRM (e.g. Warner, 1993; Child, 1996). More recent studies, however, have observed that HRM in China is becoming more systematic and market oriented, with evidence of adaptation of Western HR techniques (e.g. Warner 1998; Ding and Akhtar, 2001; Zhu and Dowling, 2002). Battling in the war for talent (see p. 44 for skill shortage problems), Chinese firms are starting to be more strategic in linking their HR practices to organizational performance (e.g. Law *et al.*, 2003; Wei and Lau, 2005; Zhu *et al.*, 2005; Wang *et al.*, 2007). Studies by Wei and Lau (2005), Zhu *et al.* (2005) and Wang *et al.* (2007) found that the differences in key HR practices among firms of different ownership forms in China are diminishing, indicating a trend of convergence in the HR practices adopted by foreign-invested and Chinese firms. There is a continuing trend and increasing movement away from the traditional Chinese HR practices to the more Western HR practices, and the gaps in the HR competence between Chinese-owned private firms and MNCs are closing. In addition, Wang *et al.* (2007: 699) found that 'while foreign-invested companies emphasize humanistic goals the most, it was private-owned enterprises that linked these goals most tightly with the high-performance HR practices'. According to Wang *et al.* (2007: 699), '[t]he pattern of the organizational goals and HR practices linkage reflects that private-owned enterprises are more aggressively utilizing their HR functions to accomplish their organizational goals'. This is in spite of the fact that they have adopted fewer high-performance HR practices than the foreign-invested companies. In addition, there is evidence that flagship domestic private firms are adopting commitment-oriented HRM practices (e.g. Ding *et al.*, 2001; Gong *et al.*, 2006).

## Case studies

This section aims to illustrate some of the developments and challenges in HRM in four companies in China. It first provides two mini-case studies of HR practices in two large companies operating in China. One is a privately owned Chinese multinational company (Huawei Technologies Ltd) operating in the information communication technology (ICT) industry. The other is a French-owned multinational company operating in the service sector. These two cases are selected to provide examples of how firms operating in different sectors and at different ends of the labour market may face different sets of HR problems and formulate their HR policies to deal with HR challenges in different ways. While both are multinational firms, we focus only on the HR practices in their Chinese operations, which may differ significantly from their overseas operations. These two company cases are then complemented by two mini-case studies of HR managers. Each has been in their position for at least four years. Ms Zhang works for a privately owned speaker manufacturing firm, while Mr Ye works for an SOE that was once a joint venture of P&G. These two cases illustrate HRM issues in domestic manufacturing firms that have, or have had, connections with foreign businesses in one way or another. It must be noted that management practices found in these four companies are not necessarily representative of the respective industry in which they operate or the entire category of their ownership form.

## Organization case 2.1  Huawei Technologies Ltd

### Company background

Huawei Technologies Ltd (hereafter Huawei) was founded in 1988 as an IT product sales and distribution company and headquartered in Shenzhen (southeast China). In less than two decades, it has developed into a leading supplier of next-generation telecom networks and currently serves nearly three-quarters of the world's top fifty operators. It has operations and representative offices in more than 100 countries and regions round the world that serve over one billion users. Nearly three-quarters of its sales now come from the international market. Highly innovation driven, Huawei invests 10 per cent of its revenue in research and development (R&D), where 48 per cent of its 62,000 employees are deployed.

Huawei has set up at least twelve R&D centres in different regions round the world to strengthen its position in the region and customize both products and services. These include: Silicon Valley and Dallas in the USA, Bangalore in India, Stockholm in Sweden and Moscow in Russia. In addition, Huawei has set up some thirty training centres worldwide to help its customers and local people to study advanced management and technologies. Huawei is arguably the most high-profile Chinese-owned ICT firm.

continued

## HR policies

Huawei recruits its employees both at the entry level from top universities in China and at mid-point from the market, often taking employees from competitor companies. Employee referrals are used in which existing employees will be given a bonus when they have successfully introduced a job candidate to the company. The majority of Huawei's employees are employed on a fixed-term contract between one and three years. However, this type of contractual relationship is likely to change since the Labour Contract Law was enacted in January 2008.

Huawei established Huawei University in 2005 to provide tailored training courses to its employees and customers. New employees received one to six months' induction training at the university on corporate culture, product knowledge, marketing and sales techniques, product development standards, etc. Huawei University is responsible for training and developing workers, technicians, managers and future leaders of Huawei. Chinese employees are also sent abroad for assignments to gain wider experience of the product and understanding of local customers' needs and technical environment. Interviewed employees all agreed that Huawei offers excellent training and development opportunities to its staff, which is a key attraction for job candidates.

Huawei adopts a mentoring scheme in which each new recruit is assigned to an experienced employee as his/her mentor to help them adapt to Huawei's way of working and living as quickly and effectively as possible. The mentor is responsible for the new recruit's performance in the first three months and the latter's performance forms part of the mentor's performance. In addition to the mentoring system, Huawei's Chinese operations employ a team of external experts, mainly professors from renowned universities in China, to provide further coaching and advisory support to its employees on various issues related to the employees' work and life.

Huawei offers a Dual Career Development Path for its employees, which comprises a managerial path and a technical/professional path, and allows employees to choose an appropriate career goal for their personal development based on their characteristics and career interests.

Huawei adopts a competitive reward strategy through regular benchmarking with its competitors and makes adjustments to its wage levels annually based on market information and Huawei's financial performance. International HR consultancy firms such as Mercer and Hay Group are used to conduct salary data surveys regularly. An individual bonus system has been adopted in which the bonus plan of a Huawei employee is closely linked to his/her level of responsibility, performance and tasks completed in each quarter. In addition, Huawei is privately owned and about 80 per cent of its stocks are held by its Chinese employees who joined the company in its early years of development. This stock option scheme is no longer available to new employees.

Huawei is an intensely performance-driven organization and high performers are put on a fast track for career growth. Performance pressure is internalized. For example, a mentee's performance forms part of the mentor's performance, and long working hours and performance-related pay are the norms. As a long-established corporate culture, Huawei's employees have a tradition of bringing their sleeping cushion to the office and they work there nearly eighteen hours a day, catching only a brief nap underneath the desk when exhausted. The sleeping cushion is seen as a symbol of Huawei's hard-working culture. Aspirational young graduate employees feel the peer pressure to work long hours and achieve results. Huawei's corporate ideology is that those who can endure hardship and are prepared to research hard will get a good return. Each year employees go through their performance assessment, and the bottom 3–5 per cent of performers are dismissed. A similar proportion of managerial staff who are deemed poor performers are also demoted or dismissed.

There is a general proportion of performance assessment grading: Excellent (top 10 per cent), Good (40 per cent), Normal (45 per cent) and Needing Improvement (5 per cent). Those who are ranked in the last category twice successively will be dismissed. This percentage is adjustable based on the overall performance of the department. High-performing departments can have a higher proportion of people in the top categories while poor departments will have a larger proportion of staff in the lower categories. Many new employees feel 'the survival threat', as it is widely known among the workers.

Huawei provides additional welfare benefits to its employees on top of the provision of social insurance specified by local employment laws. For example, over 20,000 of Huawei's employees work in its Shenzhen headquarters. Single employees are provided accommodation, subject to availability, at a low rate in a full-facility holiday-resort-like environment on site. In addition, Huawei HQ has a wide range of employees' clubs that aim to enhance the social life of its employees and achieve work–life balance. This is typical of the Chinese paternalistic style of employee care.

Huawei's cultural values include: professionalism, good customer services, devotion, diligence, pursuit of high quality, continuous learning and innovation. Many of these are typical Chinese/Oriental social values. Corporate culture training runs through the whole training process.

## Tensions in the HR system

On the whole, Huawei's HR system is essentially a high-performance work system (HPWS) influenced by Western HR techniques, such as mentoring schemes and performance appraisal linked to reward and development. The common characteristics of employees that Huawei seeks – young, ambitious, highly educated and motivated – make it possible for Huawei to implement an HPWS. This HPWS is coupled with extensive workplace welfare provision and non-financial recognition programmes typical of Oriental societies. Recognition and award is an honour that is highly valued in the Oriental and collective culture.

Although Huawei is a highly prestigious and much sought-after employer in China and its HR strategy is one that rewards high performance with good remuneration and welfare benefits, performance pressure on individual employees is intensive. In recent

continued

years, Huawei has attracted much publicity as a result of employee suicides and health problems related to work pressure. Huawei senior management is now turning its attention to this problem and taking action to reduce the work pressure for its employees: for example, banning employees from working (voluntarily) late at night in their offices. However, according to interviewed employees, the workload and expectation are so high that they need to work (unpaid) overtime to get their work done.

Another source of tension in Huawei's HR system is its reward system. An employee stock option has been advocated by strategic HRM writers (e.g. Bhattacharya and Wright, 2005) as one of the mechanisms for firms to retain employees. However, this option, which was initially adopted to boost morale and incentivise performance in the firm's early days, had served its function in Huawei. It has become a problem in motivating longer-serving staff, whose profit sharing is far higher than their salary income, as well as new employees, who are aggrieved by not being given the options, as disclosed by interviewees (see *China View*, 2007). In November 2007, when the enactment of the new Labour Contract Law was imminent, Huawei decided to dismiss *en masse* its 7,000-plus employees who had been with the company for eight years or more. They received a generous redundancy package and were given the chance to reapply for their old jobs as new employees. This decision has invoked wide criticism from all corners, as it was seen as an overt gesture by Huawei to pre-empt the Labour Contract Law. However, Huawei explained that the decision was taken to end the 'job number culture' of the company (each employee was assigned a job number when they were recruited) in which longer-serving employees felt complacent and often demanded privileged treatment. It was believed that the termination of their seniority in the company, measured by job tenure, would bring them back down to a lower hierarchy and incentivize them to perform more effectively.

Finally, although Huawei has been employing prestigious international HR consultancy firms to help it develop state-of-the-art HR systems, managers who were interviewed felt that the company still has not got a corporate HR strategy to support its international business portfolio. Many of the HR interventions are designed and implemented at the local level. As an operational manager pointed out: 'Huawei is expanding too quickly. The headquarters cannot cope with all the queries and demands from local operations. They leave it to us to decide how to manage the operations as long as we meet the key performance indicators set by the company' (Manager 1, Huawei).

Source: Huawei company websites and interviews with twelve employees and four ex-employees of Huawei in 2007–08.

## Organization case 2.2 ServiceCo

## Company background

ServiceCo (pseudonym) is a large French-owned subsidiary based in Shanghai. It provides cleaning, catering, security and facilities maintenance services to industrial parks and commercial centres/shopping malls. The French multinational firm has been operating in China for over ten years, with subsidiaries in several cities, including Beijing and Kunshan (near Shanghai). At the time of the study, ServiceCo employed 1,500–2,000 employees in Shanghai. About 10 per cent of them are white-collar and the remaining 90 per cent are mostly semi-skilled workers on low pay. There are ten people in the HR department. The HR director, Ms Yang, is Chinese in her early thirties. She has a bachelor's degree but no HR qualification. Nor has she received any professional HR training. According to Yang, none of her HR officers has an HR qualification, although *ad hoc* training sessions targeted at specific HR aspects are provided as and when they are deemed necessary. The majority of the HR people have an administrative work background, including Yang herself.

The HR officers, who are based at the regional headquarters, have very little contact with shopfloor employees, who are spread across many sites. Instead, line managers have the major responsibility of managing people on a day-to-day basis. The line managers and HR officers have weekly team management meetings in which the latter will identify key HR problems and provide basic HR training to the former. These are often remedial actions when certain HR problems occur repeatedly. Trainings are done in house, and in Yang's words, in a somewhat 'blind leading the blind' manner. According to Yang, the company does not micro manage the shopfloor employees, but focuses on the line managers. Once the line managers are kept under control by the senior management, they will manage their subordinates well as part of their responsibility.

The HR department plays a mainly administrative role, with no strategic input in the business. There is no formal HR policy in ServiceCo. This is partly a result of the high staff turnover of HR officers. As Yang said, 'Ironically, it is the HR department that has the highest staff turnover rate among all the departments that have professional and administrative staff. HR skills are highly transferable and there is a short supply of HR professionals in the market. They can walk into a job very easily.' It is interesting to note that Yang, having joined ServiceCo only six months prior to the interview with the author, is about to leave the company. The reason for her leaving is because her new manager, an American Chinese woman, disagrees with her approach.

## HR practices

Although the French-owned operation has been established for over ten years, there is no identification from the Chinese employees that they are working for a foreign firm. Most of the staff are Chinese, with only about ten French expatriates heading up the senior management positions. All HR practices are developed locally, without any

continued

influence from the French headquarters. 'The French are even more Chinese than the Chinese. The General Manager has been here for a long time and is very familiar with the labour regulations and knows exactly how to take advantage of them' (Yang). Managers are promoted internally when vacancies arise, often through the development of new projects. There is no systematic planning for employee training other than basic induction training. According to Yang, 'In some firms, employees complain of no training. When you provide training, they complain of no effect. So you can't win.'

A major HR problem in the company is recruitment, due to the high turnover rate. There are normally 200–300 posts vacant. Overtime is used constantly to cover some of the vacancies. Having a 10–15 per cent vacancy rate is also a strategic decision because, on the one hand, it gives employees overtime opportunities to boost their wages and, on the other, it reduces employment costs for the firm. A different strategy is deployed to retain managerial staff. They are given a selection of company benefits – flexible working time, holidays, pay rises, performance-related pay, and company-sponsored training.

## Employment relations

ServiceCo has a high staff turnover rate, in part because of the tight job market in the sector. Employees are often leaving for higher pay elsewhere. According to Yang, ServiceCo is seeking ways to reduce labour costs in order to maintain its competitive advantage. One example is the company's avoidance of paying social insurance for its employees. According to a Kunshan municipal regulation, employers can contribute a lower proportion of social insurance for its non-local employees. ServiceCo takes advantage of this regulation by signing contracts with its Kunshan employees in its Shanghai operation. As the social benefit systems in Shanghai and Kunshan are not open to each other, ServiceCo is able to avoid paying social insurance.

According to Yang, poor people management skills among the line managers contribute to the company's retention problem: 'A good relationship between line managers and employees is very important to retain employees. And when they leave, they may sue you on labour regulation issues. I had to pay a 2,000-yuan fine on the spot to one ex-employee who sued us for violation of overtime payment regulations. I had only 1,800 yuan with me after searching all my pockets and handbag. The ex-employee then said, "Oh, just forget about the rest." I was so surprised and asked her, "Isn't the whole point of suing us to get some money from us?" She said, "Not really. I sued because I hated the supervisor. That's why I left the company. I sued in order to get my own back."' Since the enactment of the Labour Contract Law in January 2008, Yang has had at least two tribunal cases each month. She believes that the number of cases will increase in the coming months, when employees become more aware of the new law. Waiving the legal fees makes it much easier for them to sue the company. The lawsuits are mainly to do with overtime payments and social insurance. Normally those who sue have left or are leaving the company. In order to address the staff turnover problem, ServiceCo has introduced employee retention rates as one of the key performance indicators for line managers. This has had some positive effects.

Source: semi-structured interview with Ms Yang, HR director, in 2008.

## Manager case 2.3 Ms Zhu, human resources manager, Company A: privately owned

### Company background

The company (pseudonym Company A) is a speaker manufacturing and wholesale firm established ten years ago by a Chinese entrepreneur, who gained his business and management experience while working for a Japanese MNC. Company A produces high-quality speakers for desktop computers and laptops. Ms Zhu, the HR manager of the company, joined the firm about six years ago.

### Staffing

The majority of the workers are migrant workers and are between the ages of eighteen and twenty-six. Staff turnover is relatively low and many have worked for the firm for a number of years. In the peak period of summer 2008, the firm employed over 600 employees. By April 2009, this had been reduced to about 350 as a result of the credit crunch and reduction of orders. Company A had adopted a no-redundancy and no-reduction-of-wage policy amid the financial turmoil, but had to cut back on overtime. This led to employees leaving the firm to find jobs with higher pay.

### Performance management and reward

Prior to the credit crunch in the second half of 2008, workers earned about 2,500 yuan per month on average, 40 per cent of which was overtime pay. During the credit crunch period, their income dropped to about 1,500 yuan per month as a result of the overtime cut. There is no individual performance-related-pay (PRP) scheme for workers because the CEO holds the view that PRP creates tension between different departments and reduces the quality of production.

### Training and management development

A one-week training course is provided to new workers to teach them how to do their work (mainly product assembly) and on health and safety issues. Mid-ranking managers receive some training, which is mainly conducted in-house by using DVDs purchased for the purpose. There is little management training at the supervisory level. This is in spite of the fact that most of the workplace conflicts and HR problems emerge from workers not getting on with their supervisors. As a result, Ms Zhu and a couple of senior managers have to spend a considerable amount of time counselling the young workers who have emotional or behavioural problems or have disputes with their supervisors. 'The young generation of workers are not like their parents who were able to endure hardship, physically and emotionally. Young people now threaten to commit

continued

suicide when they encounter personal emotional problems or quit very easily if they are unhappy with their supervisor or the company. So we have to manage their emotion.'

## Labour laws and dispute resolutions

As an HR manager, Ms Zhu felt that if the firm observes all the labour regulations, it would make the HR professional's job much easier because there will be fewer labour dispute claims to handle. However, Ms Zhu pointed out that the new Labour Contract Law and Labour Dispute Mediation and Arbitration Law, enacted in 2008, have put Company A in a disadvantageous position *vis-à-vis* workers and the labour authority: 'Sometimes even when we are on the right side, the labour authority will still force us to pay compensation to end the dispute. We are pressurized to resolve dispute claims internally "for the sake of building a harmonious society". The authority does not like to see more cases being submitted and has no capacity or interest to deal with them.'

Source: semi-structured interview with Ms Zhu, HR manager, in 2009.

## Manager case 2.4 Mr Ye, director, Company B: state owned

## Company background

Company B (pseudonym) was set up as an SOE in 1989 and entered a five-year joint venture partnership with P&G (China) in 1994 to produce washing powder and liquid. The partnership ended in 1999 when P&G decided to rationalize its business portfolio and retreat from the detergent production market. Company B was bought by a large stock-listed SOE and became its wholly owned subsidiary. During the JV period, Company B was managed with a series of Western management techniques, including total quality management and a performance management system. A number of local Chinese managers and key professionals were sent to P&G (China) for training and development for six months to one year. Mr Ye went to P&G (China) for one year's training and development in 1996. He became the HR manager of Company B after he had completed the training and returned to the company. He was given the chance to join P&G in Guangzhou when the partnership ended, but he chose to stay with Company B. He became the director of the company in 2005. According to Mr Ye, ten years after the withdrawal of P&G, Company B continues to operate with similar management techniques. 'We are very different from other SOEs. We have a much better management system here which has taken us five years to embed as an enterprise culture. We learned this during the partnership with P&G and continue to improve it each year. It is difficult for other SOEs to try to learn Western management techniques by paying just a few visits.'

## Staffing strategy

Company B deploys a core and peripheral labour strategy. The core workforce consists of 210-plus office staff and skilled production workers who are employees of the company. The peripheral workforce comprises over 180 non/semi-skilled agency workers engaging in product packaging, portering and transportation. This dual labour strategy was adopted in 1998. According to Mr Ye, the main reason for using agency workers is to shift 'all the hassles' of people management from the company to the agency firms. This includes the 'hassle' of monitoring birth control of women workers, as the majority of packaging workers are women. These agency workers receive low wages and limited social security protection.

## Training

Resource constraints mean that there is little external training at Company B apart from sending key staff to participate in the training programmes offered in the headquarters. The majority of the training is provided in-house in two ways. One is to purchase DVDs that are watched by line managers (trainees), usually on a two–six- month basis. The other is to use training courses left by P&G. Managers trained by P&G are asked to do the training.

## Performance management

An annual employee development plan is used with respect to the production employees. This plan emphasizes productivity, safety, quality, cost control and the five 'S's' (sort, straighten, sweep, standardize, sustain). This is supported by monthly performance appraisals. Sharing knowledge about problem solving is emphasized. Workers are required to write up case study reports on the technical problems they have solved and these serve as learning material for other workers. Performance points are given for the case study reports by the line manager, which will be accumulated towards the monthly performance review report of the worker. Peer feedback also forms part of the review but it is not done effectively. There is an end-of-year performance review and performance-related reward. Those who achieve the highest scores will be rewarded with the highest wages and also promotion when vacancies arise. Each month, all points are publicized. This performance management system is very quantitatively oriented. According to Mr Ye, each year, about 4–5 per cent of employees will complain to the higher-level managers about the unfairness of the points allocated by their superior. Complaints are investigated by senior managers and resolved. Usually, only 20 per cent of complaint cases are deemed unfair. Others mainly arise due to personal differences.

Source: semi-structured interview with Mr Ye, ex-HR manager,
now director, in 2009.

## Key challenges

HRM in China faces a number of challenges. These include: skill shortages and related problems in talent management; alignment of HR practices with the demands and needs of the younger generation of employees whose work ethics and career aspirations have diverged from those of previous generations of workers; the tightening of labour laws and regulatory frameworks within which firms need to shape their HR policies; and the need to professionalize the HR function.

## Skill shortages and talent retention

The challenge of recruiting, developing and retaining managerial and professional talent in China has been widely noted (e.g. Björkman and Lu, 1999; Goodall and Warner, 1999; Zhu et al., 2005; Malila, 2007; Tung, 2007; Wang et al., 2007; Dickel & Watkins, 2008). Foreign MNCs and privately owned Chinese firms alike face difficulties in attracting and retaining managerial and professional talent due to the shortage of their supply at national level. Talent shortage has become the bottleneck of business growth for many firms. For example, a study conducted by Manpower in China found that 40 per cent of employers have difficulty in filling senior management positions. While skill shortage for middle managers is slightly less, this has triggered a wage war (Arkless, 2007). McKinsey & Company's study in 2005 predicted that Chinese firms seeking global expansion would need 75,000 leaders who can work effectively in global environments in the next ten–fifteen years (Farrell and Grant, 2005). However, the current stock was only 3,000–5,000 (Grant and Desvaux, 2005, cited in Farrell and Grant, 2005). The same study by McKinsey & Company also reveals that fewer than 10 per cent of the Chinese job candidates were deemed by foreign MNCs operating in China to be qualified for the nine professional occupations, including engineers, accounting and finance workers, medical staff and life science researchers. This study highlights one of the main problems in the Chinese education system – the overemphasis on theory at the expense of application and practical solution and team working (Farrell and Grant, 2005). Similarly, Mercer's recent survey on attraction and retention revealed that 72 per cent of MNC respondents believed that the biggest challenge in recruitment was a lack of qualified candidates in the Chinese market (cited in Wilson, 2008).

Despite the fact that China is now producing some three million university graduates each year at home, in addition to thousands of graduate returnees from abroad, the skill shortage problem is growing. For example, a study of Chinese graduates returning from their overseas education revealed that half of them have no formal work experience – a major constraint for their employment opportunity. Only half of the companies are satisfied with the performance of their overseas returnee employees. Employers from industries that require China-specific knowledge, such as real estate, construction, consultancy, legal, finance and banking, and manufacturing are far less satisfied with their returnee employees than employers in other industries. In addition, foreign-invested companies show a lower level of satisfaction (less than 30 per cent were satisfied) with their returnee employees compared with state-invested firms (over 60 per cent were satisfied) (cited in *Development and Management of Human Resources*, 2008).

Acute skill shortage encourages employers to poach talent and individuals to look outside their company for better opportunities and to become less tolerant with their employer when their demands are not met. A study jointly conducted by DDI and the Society for Human Resource Management (USA) on talent retention issues in China in 2006–07 showed that staff turnover rates in the early 2000s had increased from 6–8 per cent to 14–20 per cent in 2007. Linked to this high staff turnover rate is a relatively high annual wage increase rate of 9–14 per cent, compared with 2–5 per cent in the USA. In addition, 61 per cent of the employees aged between twenty-five and thirty were ready to leave their current employer. Worse still, only 8 per cent of the 862 employees surveyed were 'engaged' with their company. The main reasons reported for turnover are: unhappy relationship with the management and failure to fit in with the company culture (cited in Zhao, 2008). In order to attract and retain talent, many firms have reported that they have to offer job candidates job titles, salaries and responsibilities that are well beyond their current capability and level of experience.

A recent study conducted by Manpower in China revealed that two-thirds of respondents make their job moves for better career development opportunities. Only 15 per cent of respondents indicated that their main reason for leaving was the prospect of better pay and benefits (Arkless, 2007). However, other research studies revealed that pay is far more important in people's job choices and behaviours than we are led to believe and that financial reward is one of the most important factors in retention and motivation in China (e.g. Chiu *et al.*, 2002; Rynes *et al.*,

2004). This is because earning power is a strong indicator not only of the individual's ability to work but of their economic and social status in the new materialistic culture that has developed since the introduction of the 'Open Door' policy in 1978. Nevertheless, it is important to note that career development opportunities, training programmes, mentoring and a positive working environment remain crucial in attracting and retaining talent.

## Training and development

Paradoxically, to train or not to train their key employees is a major challenge that the vast majority of firms face. Many managers interviewed by the author expressed the dilemma of whether to invest in training their key staff. Many firms are cautious about spending money on training for fear of staff turnover. This has resulted in insufficient training for employees. For example, Yang and Li's (2008) study found that a significant proportion of graduate employees in the Beijing area had never received any training from their employer due to the firms' concerns about employee retention. Judging from job advertisements and the recruitment behaviour of firms, we can see clearly that employers prefer to recruit those who are already trained, with at least two or three years of work experience.

Only a small number of firms have a graduate management trainee programme in place to develop their managers in-house. However, the quality of the candidates may be disappointing. For example, the chief executive officer (CEO) of a privately owned real estate firm revealed to the author (interviewed in May 2008) that his company had adopted a new management development method through a management graduate training programme. It set up a partnership with universities to sponsor students and recruit some of them as management graduate trainees. Trainees receive three months' training by job shadowing in any department of their choice, then another three months as follow-up training. Two years ago, the company recruited eighteen management trainees after three rounds of selection. After one year, eight had left, while the remaining ten found positions that they liked in the firm. But only four or five of them are now deemed competent by the CEO who was responsible for the training programme. The CEO believed that the one-child policy enacted in the 1980s by the Chinese government to control the growth of the population has produced a generation of young people (known as the post-'80 generation) who are spoiled by their families, dependent, unwilling to endure hardship and eager for early success.

## Making the HR function strategic and professional

The role of the HR department has a strong bearing on the extent to which the firm views HRM as part of its strategic management. Traditionally, the personnel/HR department of a Chinese firm, particularly an SOE, played a mainly administrative role with little autonomy. As we can see from the case studies reported in the previous section, and those reported elsewhere (e.g. Björkman and Lu, 1999; Cooke 2005; Zhu et al., 2005), HR capacity of firms in China remains relatively low. There is little training and professional development for HR officers. Few of them possess HR qualifications and experience. Most come from a personnel administration background. As a result, HR professionals have little capacity or input in formulating HR strategies and policies, implementing HR initiatives, and aligning HR outcomes with business performance. Instead, HR issues are often dealt with in a fire-fighting approach. In addition, a series of new employment laws and regulations presents new challenges to the HR professionals, who must develop competence to deal with these laws and related dispute and mediation procedures. This is in spite of the fact that firms do not necessarily react to the regulations in a positive way, as we have seen in the case studies.

The absence of a well-developed, nationwide HR professional association in China also means that there is no central influence on HR direction or coordination in the sharing of good HR practice. By contrast, Western countries such as the UK (Chartered Institute for Personnel and Development), the US (Society for Human Resource Management) and Australia (Australian Human Resource Institute) have well-established HR professional associations that have become international bodies to provide effective forums for research and knowledge sharing among the organized HR professional and academic communities (Cooke, 2009). At the national and organizational level, the low capacity of HR is undoubtedly a significant deficiency in the light of the rising number of Chinese-owned national and multinational firms and the important role of strategic HRM in organizational competitiveness.

## Conclusion

This chapter has provided a brief overview of some of the developments in HRM in China and challenges that are encountered by firms. Given the limited scope of the chapter, it is impossible to cover all aspects of HR in detail. When selecting HR issues to discuss, the author has purposefully picked out some relatively new issues that are not addressed elsewhere. These include, for example, work–life balance, mentoring, the role of financial rewards in talent retention, and the implementation of the new labour laws. The omission of other aspects of HR in this chapter does not mean that those issues are less important. Readers are therefore encouraged to read more widely on the topic.

Based on existing evidence, we can conclude that HRM in China has undergone significant changes, although traditional elements remain influential. In particular, it is now evident that Chinese employees are becoming more receptive to performance-oriented rewards and welcome career development opportunities. However, tensions clearly remain in the ability, as well as the willingness, of firms to develop good HR policies, including investing in training and development and providing good employment terms and conditions.

In addition, albeit with low generalizability due to the small sample size, the four case studies reported in this chapter suggest that when we discuss firms' HR practices, we cannot simplistically categorize them by ownership forms and assume that Western MNCs are more progressive than domestic Chinese firms. Instead, we are witnessing the emergence of a diverse range of management practices in which ownership forms, regional variations, industrial sectors, product market and, relatedly, sought-after employees all play important roles. Influences of foreign client firms on labour standards and management outlook/leadership style are also important determinants.

More broadly, HRM is highly context specific in which institutional and cultural factors have enduring influences. Throughout this chapter, the influence of Chinese culture and values has been highlighted. The issue of Chinese characteristics warrants further discussion here. In recent years, enthusiasm for promoting what are perceived to be advanced 'Western' HR techniques has run high in China. HR initiatives are embraced by some firms without being questioned of their utility. Some academics and practitioners blame the lack of systems and procedures for the poor state of HRM in Chinese firms. Recognizing the need for systematic management, Chinese firms are adopting the 'scientific' aspects of HRM developed in Western countries, such as job analysis, e-HR and process management. It is true that having a well-established set of HR policies in place is essential to guide the management function. However, there is a danger that Chinese practitioners are being misguided by the hype of Western HRM and end up forgetting their own roots. It is important to note that Chinese culture emphasizes interpersonal relationships. Relationship management plays a vital role in people management. To a large degree, management is seen as an art rather than a science in China. How to motivate employees and develop their potential is essentially an art in which social value plays an important role. Instead of modelling Western HR theories and practices in an undigested manner, Chinese management needs to develop its own models that are appropriate to the Chinese context. This may mean adopting Western HR techniques to make HRM more systematic and procedural, but implementing them in a humanistic way that is embedded in the Chinese culture.

# Bibliography

Arkless, D. (2007) 'The China talent paradox', *China–Britain Business Review*, June, 14–15.

Bai, X. and Bennington, L. (2005) 'Performance appraisal in the Chinese state-owned coal industry', *International Journal of Business Performance Management*, 7, 3: 275–87.

Bhattacharya, M. and Wright, P. (2005) 'Managing human assets in an uncertain world: applying real options theory to HRM', *International Journal of Human Resource Management*, 16, 6: 929–48.

Björkman, I. and Lu, Y. (1999) 'The management of human resources in Chinese–Western joint ventures', *Journal of World Business,* 34, 3: 306–24.

Child, J. (1996) *Management in China during the Age of Reform* (paperback edition), Cambridge: Cambridge University Press.

*China Statistical Yearbook 2003* and *2007,* Beijing: China Statistics Publishing House.

*China View*, 'Huawei: We're not trying to dodge law', 6 November 2007, http://www.news.xinhuanet.com/english/2007–11/06/content_7019551.htm, accessed on 13 November 2007.

Chiu, R., Luk, W. and Tang, T. (2002) 'Retaining and motivating employees: compensation preferences in Hong Kong and China', *Personnel Review*, 31, 4: 402–31.

Cooke, F. L. (2005) *HRM, Work and Employment in China*, London: Routledge.

Cooke, F. L. (2008) 'Performance management systems in China', in A. Varma and P. Budhwar (eds) *Performance Management Systems around the Globe*, London: Routledge, 193–209.

Cooke, F. L. (2009) 'A decade of transformation of HRM in China: a review of literature and suggestions for future studies', *Asia Pacific Journal of Human Resources*, 47, 1: 6–40.

Development and Management of Human Resources (2008) 'Review', *Development and Management of Human Resources*, 10: 4.

Dickel, T. and Watkins, C. (2008) 'To remain competitive in China's tight labour market, companies must prioritize talent management – and track compensation trends', *China Business Review*, July–August: 20–23.

Ding, D. and Akhtar, S. (2001) 'The organizational choice of human resource management practices: a study of Chinese enterprises in three cities in the PRC', *International Journal of Human Resource Management*, 12, 6: 946–64.

Ding, D., Ge, L. and Warner, M. (2001) 'A new form of Chinese human resource management? Personnel and labour–management relations in Chinese township and village enterprises: a case-study approach', *Industrial Relations Journal*, 32, 4: 328–43.

Farrell, D. and Grant, A. (2005) 'China's looming talent shortage', *The McKinsey Quarterly*, No. 4, http://www.mckinseyquarterly.com/article_page.aspx?ar = 1685, accessed on 3 March 2007.

Gong, Y., Law, K. and Xin, K. (2006) 'The commitment-focused HRM system: adoption and performance implications in domestic private firms', in A. Tsui, Y. Bian and L. Chang (eds), *China's Domestic Private Firms*, Armonk, NY: M. E. Sharpe, 261–76.

Goodall, K. and Warner, M. (1999) 'Enterprise reform, labour–management relations, and human resource management in a multinational context', *International Studies of Management and Organization*, 29, 3: 21–36.

Law, K., Tse, D.K. and Zhou, N. (2003) 'Does human resource management matter in a transitional economy? China as an example', *Journal of International Business Studies,* 34, 3: 255–65.

Lindholm, N. (1999) 'Performance management in MNC subsidiaries in China: a study of host-country managers and professionals', *Asia Pacific Journal of Human Resources*, 37, 3: 18–35.

Malila, J. (2007) 'The great look forward: China's HR evolution', *China Business Review*, 34, 4: 16–19.

Rynes, S., Gerhart, B. and Minette, K. (2004) 'The importance of pay in employee motivation: discrepancies between what people say and what they do', *Human Resource Management*, 43, 4: 381–94.

Tung, R. (2007) 'The human resource challenge to outward foreign direct investment aspirations from emerging economies: the case of China', *International Journal of Human Resource Management*, 18, 5: 868–89.

Wang, X., Bruning, N. and Peng, S. Q. (2007) 'Western high performance HR practices in China: a comparison among public-owned, private and foreign-invested enterprises', *International Journal of Human Resource Management*, 18, 4: 684–701.

Warner, M. (1993) 'Human resource management "with Chinese Characteristics"', *International Journal of Human Resource Management*, 4, 4: 45–65.

Warner, M. (1998) 'China's HRM in transition: towards relative convergence?', in C. Rowley (ed.) *Human Resource Management in the Asia Pacific Region: Convergence Questioned*, London: Frank Cass, 19–33.

Wei, L. and Lau, C. M. (2005) 'Market orientation, HRM importance and competency: determinants of strategic HRM in Chinese firms', *International Journal of Human Resource Management*, 16, 10: 1901–18.

Wilson, B. (2008) 'Hidden dragons', *People Management Magazine Online*, http://www.peoplemanagement.co.uk/pm/articles/2008/08/hidden-dragons.htm, accessed on 4 September 2008.

Yang, H. Q. and Li, J. (2008) 'An empirical study of the employment quality of university graduates', *Labour Economy and Labour Relations*, 2: 87–90.

Zhang, L. H. (2005) 'A case study analysis of the remuneration change strategy of a state-owned enterprise', *Development and Management of Human Resources*, 11: 47–49.

Zhao, G. (2008) 'What to do when employees are not engaged with the company?', *Development and Management of Human Resources*, 2: 35–40.

Zhu, C., Cooper, B., De Cieri, H. and Dowling, P. (2005) 'A problematic transition to a strategic role: human resource management in industrial enterprises in China', *International Journal of Human Resource Management*, 16, 4: 513–31.

Zhu, C. and Dowling, P. (1998) 'Performance appraisal in China', in J. Selmer (ed.) *International Management in China: Cross-Cultural Issues*, London: Routledge, 115–36.

Zhu, C. and Dowling, P. (2002) 'Staffing practices in transition: some empirical evidence from China', *International Journal of Human Resource Management*, 13, 4: 569–97.

# 3 The changing face of marketing management in China

*Yonggui Wang and Hui Feng*

- Introduction
- Context
- Case studies
- Key challenges
- Conclusion

## Introduction

After implementing the Reform and Open Door Policy for thirty years, China has become one of the most dynamic and fastest-growing markets in the world. Between 2003 and 2006, the average annual growth rate of disposable income per capita in China reached over 7 per cent and the average annual income per capita is 29.6 times (urban) and 23.3 times (rural) than thirty years ago (National Bureau of Statistics of China, 2007). At the same time, consumption habits are changing fast. For example, many Chinese consumers today would consider brand names during purchase and they have become more demanding (National Bureau of Statistics of China, 2007). Moreover, local companies are developing fast in building their own brands by improving product and service quality and enhancing brand loyalty to win the market competition. Some local Chinese brands such as Huawei, Lenovo, Haier and TCL even go global and promote their brands overseas with the support of the Chinese government (Zhou, 2006).

Meanwhile, established Western brands also bid aggressively for market share in China. More than 480 firms listed in the *Fortune* 500 had set up affiliates in China by 2006 (UNCTAD, 2006). However, although some global brands such as Coca-Cola and McDonald's have adapted well in the local Chinese market, other famous brands such as Whirlpool, Valentino and NEC left the Chinese market after several years' operation.

Keller and Moorthi (2003) concluded that many powerful global brands failed in developing countries because they failed to deliver what is important to consumers and failed to communicate with them appropriately.

Brand-building strategies in China are different from those practised in the West. Many cultural factors, such as saving face, high uncertainty avoidance, collectivism and the Confucian value system (Hofstede and Bond, 1988), influence consumers' behaviour and brand-building strategies in China (Roth, 1995). Moreover, people living in different parts of China may have totally different values and consumption habits (Zhang, 2007). Therefore, marketers need to develop a deep understanding of local consumption habits and an appropriate marketing strategy for brand building.

This chapter first reviews changes in marketing management that have taken or are taking place in China. Next it puts forward a brand-equity-based marketing strategy framework for China. After that, the chapter provides four case studies to illustrate the characteristics of a successful brand-equity-based marketing management strategy in China from an organizational and a managerial perspective. The chapter also highlights a number of key challenges in marketing management in China before concluding that marketing management in China has moved from a 'manufacturing-capacity-focused' strategy in the 1980s to a 'promotion-and-advertisement-focused' strategy in the 1990s to today's 'customer-focused' strategy. Both local and multinational companies improved their brand-building and marketing management skills in the dynamic market in China during the transition. And both local and multinational firms are facing more challenges in fulfilling consumers' diversified needs and keeping their brands alive today.

## Context

A brand can be defined as 'a name, term, sign, symbol, or design, or a combination of them, intended to identify the goods or services of one seller or group of sellers and to differentiate them from those of competitors' (Kotler, 2003: 418). Customer-based brand equity is 'the differential effect that brand knowledge has on customer response to the marketing of that brand' (Keller, 2002: 7). Aaker (1991) identified five elements of brand equity: brand loyalty, brand awareness, perceived quality, brand associations, and other proprietary brand assets, such as patent, trademark and channel relationships.

As a developing country with a transitional economy, China has a different brand-building market environment. The unique culture and value in China have great impact on brand-building activities. For example, saving face is a very basic and subtle principle in the Chinese mindset (Lin, 1994). Chinese consumers would buy famous brand products mainly to show off their social or economic status (Bond and Kuo, 1986; Tse, 1996). *Guanxi* is another important value in Chinese society. One important function of a famous brand is to facilitate socializing and expanding people's social networks (Eckhardt and Michael, 2001; Tse, 1996). Thus Chinese consumers are more concerned than their Western counterparts with the social value of brands (Tse, 1996). Therefore, the elements of brand equity in China might be different from the construct developed in Western countries.

Scholars have conducted a series of studies on the elements of brand equity in China. For example, Zhao (2005) identified seven elements of brand equity in China: brand loyalty, brand image, brand support, enterpriser image, brand innovation, brand toughness and brand extension. Wang (2006) conducted focus group interviews with consumers in Beijing, Shanghai and Guangzhou and concluded that brand equity consists of corporation ability association, brand awareness, perceived quality and brand resonance. This chapter consolidates previous studies and investigates several key elements of brand equity in China, including perceived quality, brand awareness, brand associations and brand loyalty.

Perceived quality is 'the consumer's judgment about a product or service's overall excellence or superiority' (Zeithaml, 1988: 3). It is therefore the gap between the customers' expectation and the actual perception of quality (Wang and Lo, 2004). In China, due to high uncertainty avoidance (Hofstede and Bond, 1988) and the spread of low-quality products, customers highly value product safety and reliability, service quality, product innovation and value for money (Wang, 2006).

Brand awareness is 'the ability for a buyer to recognize or recall that a brand is a member of a certain product category' (Aaker, 1991: 61). Thus, brand awareness consists of both brand recognition and recall (Keller, 1993). Advertising, especially on TV, is the most effective way of increasing brand awareness among Chinese consumers (Wang, 2006). Official or unofficial news reports are also effective. Moreover, Chinese consumers learn brand names when prime-time advertising sponsorships are reported on China Central Television (CCTV) news, and from official government reports on brands. Therefore, commercial advertising, news reports and public relations are the principal means of communicating with consumers in China (Wang, 2006).

Aaker (1991: 109) defines brand association as 'anything linked in memory to a brand'. It includes information closely associated with brand and secondary associations such as company, country, channels of distribution, spokespeople, sporting or cultural events (Keller, 2001). Chinese consumers tend to associate brand with product quality, corporate image (which includes corporate capability, corporate social responsibility and enterpriser image), country of origin, social status and face (Wang, 2006; Zhao, 2005).

Brand loyalty is 'the attachment that a customer has to a brand' (Aaker, 1991: 39) and is demonstrated by consumers' intention to buy the brand as a primary choice (Oliver, 1997). Chinese consumers tend to recommend the brands they like to their friends and relatives.

## Major changes in marketing management in China

In the past thirty years, China's economy has changed from a state-planned system that was largely closed to international markets to a market-based economy that now plays a major role in the global economy. Marketing practices have developed equally quickly. From 1978 to 1989, the first eleven years of the Reform and Open Door Policy, manufacturing capability was the main concern for most Chinese companies, because almost all supply fell short of demand, and most companies did not have a sales department, let alone a marketing department. Most products were sold to several big department stores as directed or planned. In addition, few companies cared about product quality, customer needs or brand building (Li, 2004).

The 1990s was a painful transforming period for most firms in China. As the market changed from a seller's market to a buyer's market, firms began to compete fiercely by means of personal selling and advertising to increase sales and promote their brands. Many firms employed a great number of salesmen to sell their products across China. For example, Sanzhu Medical's salesmen numbered 150,000, and its sales revenue increased from 100 million RMB to 8 billion RMB in just three years (Li, 2004). In addition, many brands became famous almost overnight when companies invested huge sums in star endorsements and advertising slots during the 'golden time' on CCTV. But many of those brands vanished equally quickly once the companies stopped advertising heavily. The main reason for their failure was that they did not deliver superior service and/or product quality to match their fame. Since then, more companies have become aware of the importance of product quality and after-sales service in brand building.

In the mid-1990s, competition became even more fierce as many multinationals began to enter the Chinese market and customer demands became more diverse. Price wars and advertising-slot bidding wars became white hot. Some leading firms, such as the Haier Group, competed by improving their core competitive advantages in terms of product innovation, service improvement and overseas market expansion to enhance perceived quality and brand awareness (Li, 2004).

The new millennium witnessed a fierce war between foreign and local brands after China entered the WTO in 2001. Many leading local brands, such as Wahaha Drink, NanFu Battery and HuaRun Paints, were acquired by multinationals. However, in the mid-2000s, Chinese consumers, who had previously thought highly of famous foreign brands, began to lose confidence in them after several scandals, particularly in the food industry (Gu and Chen, 2007). During this period, foreign firms became more cautious in their quality-control and crisis management, and learned to market their products in a more Chinese way. Meanwhile, local firms became more experienced in modern marketing management: they learned to provide superior service and product quality to ensure customer satisfaction and implemented customer relationship management to enhance brand loyalty.

## Brand-equity-based marketing strategy framework for China

Researchers suggest that marketing strategies, such as the 4Ps, and non-marketing elements, such as consumer value, lifestyle and market conditions, affect brand equity (Keller, 2003). For example, Simon and Sullivan (1993) list advertising expenditure, sales force, marketing research expenditure and product portfolio as sources of brand equity. Other marketing activities, such as the use of public relations (Aaker, 1991), warranties (Boulding and Kirmani, 1993), company image, country of origin and promotional events (Keller, 1993), are all drivers of brand equity. In light of previous research on the drivers of brand equity in Western countries and in China, the authors propose the following marketing strategies to enhance brand equity in China.

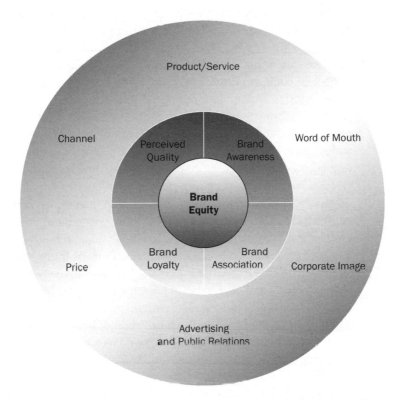

**Figure 3.1** Brand-equity-based marketing strategy framework for China

1 Ensure high product/service quality. Wang's (2006) research shows that Chinese consumers value high product quality. Sixty per cent of Chinese consumers are willing to pay a premium for well-known products because of their high quality (Guo, 2007). Safety and reassurance are the essentials that Chinese consumers seek in branded products as a result of the chaos in the Chinese market. While most products in US and European markets have reached quality and safety standards, that is not the case in China. As the legal system and product quality supervision are not fully mature, low-quality products as well as sham and shoddy commodities are rife in the market. Many consumers have suffered from poor-quality products. Therefore, one important reason why customers buy famous brand products is that they need high-quality products and believe that famous brands guarantee quality. So quality problems may lead to serious brand-equity shrinkage. Therefore, firms must ensure product/service quality to gain consumers' trust and brand loyalty. Companies also need to

explore the various needs of Chinese consumers before innovating and customizing their product/service to gain customer loyalty (Wang, 2006).

2 Pay more attention to word-of-mouth. Word-of-mouth has a significant impact on Chinese consumers' purchasing behaviour. As Chinese people used to live in big family groups, they consider friends and relatives their most reliable sources of information. And Chinese consumers love to exchange purchase experience with their friends and relatives. One survey shows that 39.5 per cent of interviewees often discuss their experience of purchasing or using certain brands (Horizonkey, 2003). Moreover, people trust the information they receive from their relatives and friends more than information they get from any other sources. For example, 59 per cent of people seek product information from friends when they plan to buy a computer, and 40.4 per cent believe the recommendations of friends more than any other sources (Horizonkey, 2003). In addition, many false advertisements and news reports have led consumers to rely even more on word-of-mouth recommendations. It is felt that friends and relatives will only recommend the brand that they truly love. Therefore, companies have to work hard on customer satisfaction to generate more loyal customers and enhance positive word-of-mouth.

3 Enhance brand awareness through advertising and public relations. Most Chinese consumers get to know a new brand from advertising (especially TV advertising), news reports and big events (Wang, 2006). Brand awareness is created by increasing the familiarity of the brand through repeated exposure (Keller, 2001). Many consumers judge a brand and make their purchasing decision according to their familiarity with the brand. Therefore, companies have to take advantage of TV advertising, news and other events to make the brand well known. In addition, according to a study by Roth (1995), strengthening the social image of a brand will enhance brand awareness and win customers in a collectivist society, such as China. So firms need to place more emphasis on public relations and sponsor more activities for the public good. For example, Coca-Cola gains brand awareness by sponsoring the Chinese national football team. Firms also need to develop a good relationship with local and central government to gain state support and media attention and therefore improve brand exposure.

4 Improve corporate image. In Japan, advertisements placed by large-scale and long-established firms tend to gain more trust than those placed by small and new firms (Aaker, 1998). In China, which shares

a similar cultural environment with Japan, consumers also tend to judge the power of brand from the power of corporation: the more powerful the corporation, the better the brand (Wang, 2006). So consumers are more prepared to trust and choose brands from a powerful firm. Corporate capability association has a great impact on consumers' perception of the brand (Brown and Dacin, 1997). Many successful and famous Chinese brands, such as Haier, Lenovo and TCL, stress the importance of corporate image building and corporate brand building. So companies should reinforce their corporate image during brand building by advertising company performance (e.g. annual revenue and growth rate), product innovation and so on to shape a positive corporate image and corporation association with brand.

5 In addition, the international image of a corporation is helpful in improving the overall corporate image. As brands from Western countries represent the value and lifestyle of developed countries, Chinese consumers usually give a higher evaluation towards them than to domestic brands (He, 2006). As many Chinese often joke, 'Even the moon in the foreign countries is bigger than it is in China' – most Chinese consumers are proud to own international brand products and even leave the tags on clothes to show them off (Temporal, 2001). Therefore, multinationals should stress the international image of their brands. For example, Coca-Cola claims to be the American spirit, IKEA represents a North European lifestyle and L'Oréal stands for Paris fashion. Similarly, a local Chinese firm can choose a film star with a global image to be its spokesperson, so as to make its brand look international. For example, Slek shampoo of Hubei-based C-bons Group was considered a global brand because C-bons Group always chose international spokespeople for its adverts (Temporal, 2001). Local companies can also build their international corporate image by investing abroad. For example, Haier Group builds its global brand image by expanding globally. Its global presence has greatly improved its brand equity and fully convinced consumers of its capability.

6 Adopt an appropriate pricing strategy and choose the right distribution channels. China, a vast expanse of land, faces unbalanced economic growth. The economic development levels vary between east and west, south and north, urban and rural areas. Therefore, firms need to investigate local consumption levels in depth before setting the price. Keller and Moorthi (2003) mention that one factor that may lead to the failure of multinationals in developing countries is overpricing.

For example, a McDonald's family meal costs one-sixth of a worker's monthly salary in China. Only by making the price of products affordable by the standards of Chinese people can such brands gain more loyal customers.

Firms also need to set up a vast network of distribution in China. Unlike Americans, who typically buy groceries in bulk from supermarkets once a week by car, most Chinese do not have cars and they prefer to go shopping in nearby stores on foot every day to get fresh vegetables (Mai and Zhao, 2004). Convenience stores often become the centres of distribution in cities, towns and especially in the vast rural areas. Therefore, firms need to have a vast distribution and communication network across the country to reach their customers and make their brands known throughout China.

Several multinationals and local companies have found the right way to manage their brands in China after many years' practice. Table 3.1 shows China's most valuable brands in 2007, according to the World Brand Lab. The next section presents cases from different firms to illustrate successful marketing management practices in China.

**Table 3.1** The top ten brands in 'China's 500 most valuable brands', 2007

| Rank | Brand name | Industry | Brand value (in 100 million RMB) |
|------|-----------|----------|-----------------------------------|
| 1 | China Mobile | Telecommunications | 1100.54 |
| 2 | ICBC | Financial Services | 805.46 |
| 3 | CCTV | Media | 654.34 |
| 4 | Haier | Home Appliances | 640.00 |
| 5 | China Life | Financial Services | 588.67 |
| 6 | Changhong | Home Appliances | 583.25 |
| 7 | Sinochem | Petrochemicals | 582.90 |
| 8 | Lenovo | Communication, Electronics, IT | 580.20 |
| 9 | Baosteel | Steel Processing | 544.86 |
| 10 | China Railway | Railway | 523.12 |

Source: http://brand.icxo.com/meeting2007/brand2007_bd01.htm, accessed on 29 January 2008.

# Case studies

This section provides four case studies of successful marketing management practices in four companies operating in China. The first is a state-owned Chinese multinational company (Haier Group) operating in the home appliance industry. The second is an American-owned multinational company in the fast-food industry – McDonald's (China). Then we will present two other cases from a managerial perspective: one is the Coca-Cola Company and the other is Motorola (China) Electronics Ltd. These four cases have been selected to provide examples of how multinational and local firms operate successfully in marketing management in China's market.

## Organization case 3.1 Haier Group

### Company background

Haier is the world's fourth-largest white goods manufacturer and China's most valuable brand. As of 2007, the Haier Group had established a total of 64 trading companies (19 located overseas), 29 manufacturing plants (24 overseas), 8 design centres (5 overseas) and 16 industrial parks (4 overseas) and employed over 50,000 people around the world. Guided by the branding strategy of CEO Zhang Ruimin, Haier has advanced through the 'brand building', 'diversification' and 'internationalization' stages, and since 2005 has embarked on the fourth stage: 'global branding'.

There are many reasons why Haier became a global brand from a small factory within twenty years. Haier's high-quality products and first-class service, continuous product innovation and effective media communication all contribute to its success. More importantly, Haier has won customers' brand loyalty by delivering what consumers really need and value highly.

### Superior product quality and star service

'The key to building a new strong brand is to ensure high quality,' said Zhang Ruimin when low-quality refrigerators were selling well in the 1980s (because the demand for refrigerators exceeded supply). However, Haier insisted, 'Customer loyalty is built on good reputation. Reputation is more important than sales volume.' Zhang Ruimin asked workers to destroy defective refrigerators in public with sledgehammers to make employees aware that 'a product could be considered tradable merchandise only when its quality satisfies customers, otherwise it is only rubbish'. Haier then deployed 'zero defection' and 'six sigma' quality management to ensure high quality in its products. In addition, Haier was the first local home appliance company to offer after-sale service

continued

during the 1990s. Haier offered a 24-hour service hotline and 24-hour door-to-door service to ensure users' 'zero complaint'. Haier's 'five-star service' has won the company a high reputation and positive word-of-mouth among consumers. Haier also ranked number one in customer satisfaction among Chinese durable product brands during 2003–07 and was the most favoured brand among Chinese consumers in 2005.

## Local-customer-focused marketing strategy

As China is a big country with many ethnic groups, consumers in different areas have quite different needs, attitudes and habits (Zhang, 2007). Haier wins consumers across China and keeps them loyal through its customer-focused marketing strategy: 'Whatever products users demand, we will fulfil their needs and keep a close eye on their new demands,' said Zhang Ruimin (Yan and Hu, 2001: 279). Figure 3.2, from Haier's company website, illustrates its closeness to customers.

**Figure 3.2** Haier: Zero distance with user

Source: http://www.haier.com/abouthaier/CorporateCulture/workforce.asp.

For example, Haier designs bigger refrigerators with greater refrigerating capacity for its northern customers and slim, refined refrigerators to fit the small houses of most Shanghai residents. Haier also designs frost-free refrigerators and washing machines with drying functions for consumers in wet coastal areas. Moreover, appreciating that people in rural China have lower incomes, Haier sells a basic refrigerator at a lower price for rural areas. Haier also redesigned its refrigerators to work efficiently in low-voltage rural China (Yan and Hu, 2001). This local-customer-focused product innovation strategy has kept the Haier brand alive and won the honour of 'China's most valuable brand' each year from 2002 to 2007. 'The core competence of Haier is innovation. In the past, we developed products according to customers' needs, now we have to exceed customers' expectations by producing their desired products even before they realize their needs. Only in this way can we keep our brand alive,' said Zhang Ruimin (Yan and Hu, 2001: 298).

## Public relations

A good relationship with government is vital when doing business in China. It can benefit a company in many ways, such as policy support, media exposure and brand awareness enhancement (Zhang, 2007). In Haier's case, it helps the company build a consistently good brand image. For example, as Haier has kept in close contact with the Consumers' Association, the Bureau of Quality and Technical Supervision and the Administration for Industry and Commerce, whenever a customer complains to these departments about its products, Haier is able to respond quickly to solve the customer's problem before it becomes a negative news report. This helps Haier build its brand image as 'zero complaint' and 'zero defection'. Zhang Ruimin often delivers speeches at the invitation of government departments to gain more media exposure and improve brand image and brand awareness among customers (Zhang, 2007).

Sources: www.haier.com/index.asp and Yan and Hu (2001).

## Organization case 3.2 McDonald's

### Company background

McDonald's is a leading global food service retailer with more than 30,000 local restaurants serving 52 million people in more than 100 countries each day. McDonald's (China) Co. Ltd now owns over 810 restaurants and has 50,000 employees in China. Its first outlet opened in Shenzhen in 1990. McDonald's is one of the world's most well-known and valuable brands. It was ranked fifth among the world's 500 most influential brands by World Brand Lab in 2006, and was listed as one of the 100 most influential world-famous brands in China in 2007 by the World Brand Organization (Wang, 2007).

continued

McDonald's success lies in its good international corporate image, franchising model and localized marketing strategy. It is now a highly recognized brand across China, even in some second-tier cities and remote areas.

## Brand image strategy

As the old Chinese saying goes: people are always prone to trust foreign monks more than local ones. As McDonald's represents the value and lifestyle of the most developed country – America – most Chinese consumers regard having a meal in McDonald's as a way to experience the American lifestyle. McDonald's takes advantage of Chinese consumers' positive attitude towards the American lifestyle, and promotes its American brand image across China to attract more customers. Going to McDonald's has become an important part of people's modern lives. McDonald's defines a fashion and lifestyle for Chinese consumers by associating its brand with American middle-class life. Therefore, McDonald's expanded quickly in China and gained high brand awareness and many loyal customers (Pan, 2006).

## Localization strategy

McDonald's has developed a series of products to cater to the tastes of Chinese people. For example, it offered hot ginger honey tea in the winter of 2007, having learned that most Chinese believe that this could drive away the cold. It also provides its customers with a Chinese-style breakfast. Moreover, McDonald's turns the fast food restaurant into a place for people to socialize, knowing that most Chinese treat having a meal as a social experience. In addition, it attracts parents and children with its 'Learn English with Uncle McDonald' sessions, as most parents want their children to learn English when they are young. Such interactive activities have made McDonald's part of the local community and people's daily life, and they build intimacy between McDonald's and local consumers, which helps to develop customer loyalty towards the company.

McDonald's also decorates its restaurants in a very Chinese way. During the Chinese New Year, it hangs up firecrackers, pastes paper cut-outs on windows and makes its waiters wear traditional costumes (Pan, 2006). These decorations effectively eliminate the cultural gap between McDonald's and its local customers and helps turn McDonald's into a more local restaurant with a place in its customers' hearts. 'An international brand must localize itself. Localization does not mean abandon its original international brand personality. It means it needs to have two faces: an international one and a local one. Each of these two faces . . . should show itself in the appropriate situation,' said Gary Rosen, vice-president of McDonald's (China).

Sources: www.aboutmcdonalds.com/mcd and Pan (2006).

## Manager case 3.3 Ms Zhang (pseudonym), marketing manager, Coca-Cola Company

### Background

Ms Zhang joined Coca-Cola's Nanjing office from an advertising company in 2003 and was appointed the brand manager responsible for devising brand promotion strategies. Now she is the marketing manager for Jiangsu Province and is responsible for the strategic execution of marketing activities, such as advertising and promotion, throughout the province.

The Coca-Cola Company is the largest manufacturer, distributor and marketer of non-alcoholic beverages in the world. It opened its first bottling plants in Tianjin and Shanghai in 1927 and re-entered China in 1979. Today Coca-Cola has thirty-five bottling plants in China and it is the country's leading beverage manufacturer. It has also been the most recognized soft-drink brand in China for the last twenty-five years. Coca-Cola (China) has witnessed double-digit growth in recent years as the Coca-Cola and Sprite brands have become the top two sparkling soft drinks in the country.

### Localized marketing strategy

Many of Coca-Cola's top managers believe that the company's strategy of 'think local, act local' has enabled it to succeed in its overseas markets. Ms Zhang agrees that this is the key to Coca-Cola's success in China, where the diversity of cultures and income levels means there is no unified consumer base. Coca-Cola encourages local managers to develop marketing strategies that are best suited for their areas, and regional offices have the freedom to approve local advertising and promotion plans. For example, in Jiangsu, besides implementing promotional activities that are used elsewhere in China, the marketing team cooperates with local television channels and newspapers to implement some localized promotions. The local marketing team also develops different promotional plans for different parts of Jiangsu Province as the consumption habits and income levels in northern and southern Jiangsu differ greatly.

Coca-Cola has also adjusted its advertising operations for China's unique culture. For example, it has included the twelve Chinese zodiac animals in its television commercials and has used several Chinese pop stars, such as Liu Xiang, S.H.E. and Yao Ming, in its adverts. These localized marketing strategies have greatly reduced the psychological distance between Coca-Cola and its Chinese consumers.

### Localized brand strategy

Besides selling its internationally known drinks – Coke, Fanta and Sprite – in China, Coca-Cola has developed several local brands through its joint venture with the Tianjin Jin Mei Beverage Co. Ltd, such as Tianyudi (Heaven and Earth), a line of

continued

non-carbonated drinks that includes mango and lychee flavours, oolong and jasmine teas, and bottled water; and Xingmu (Smart), a line of carbonated fruit drinks which boasts the top five brands in terms of sales in China's carbonated soft-drink market. Local brands and new beverages such as tea drinks that cater to Chinese drinking habits have minimized the culture gap between Coca-Cola and local consumers, and the company achieved a market share of 60 per cent of the Chinese carbonated soft-drink market in 2008.

## Brand conflict and brand integration

Although multiple brands brought Coca-Cola great profits in China, they also created problems in brand management. Some brands compete with each other for marketing resources and market share. For example, both Qoo and Minute Maid are juice drinks targeting young people, so the promotion of Minute Maid greatly threatened the brand awareness and market share of Qoo, which was a very successful juice brand in China before the launch of Minute Maid. In addition, the multi-brand strategy has reduced Coca-Cola's ability to compete with competitors that specialize in specific markets. For example, compared with some Chinese companies, such as Tongyi, that specialize in tea drinks, Coca-Cola lacks experience and expertise in this sector. 'Coca-Cola needs to integrate its own brands further and improve its multi-brand management ability to continue its success in the Chinese market,' said Ms Zhang.

Sources: www.coca-cola.com and personal interviews with a manager.

## Manager case 3.4 Mr Xu (pseudonym), call centre manager, Motorola Electronics Ltd

### Background

Mr Xu joined Motorola (China)'s Shanghai office in 2008 as a call centre manager. Before joining the company, he had worked as a sales manager for Dell (China). Now his main responsibility is to build up a customer database, explore new sales opportunities in existing and new customers, and build up and train the call centre sales team.

Motorola entered the Chinese market in 1987 when it opened a representative office in Beijing. In 1992, Motorola (China) Electronics Ltd was established in Tianjin, which is one of the world's major manufacturing centres for communications equipment today. Now China is Motorola's top market outside the United States. Motorola (China) has 8 joint ventures and 24 subsidiaries, with more than 10,000 employees in China.

## Superior product quality and after-sale service

Motorola was the first foreign wireless communication brand known by many Chinese consumers during the 1990s. At that time, the pager market in China was just beginning. Motorola highlighted its high-quality brand image in advertisements and created an association between the brand name 'Motorola' and high quality. In addition, it enhanced brand awareness quickly by advertising heavily. In the late 1990s, most Chinese equated Motorola with mobile phones, and 92 per cent of Chinese knew the brand by 1998 (a massive increase from only 11 per cent in 1994).

Motorola's after-sale service is also highly respected by its Chinese customers for being professional and fast. Motorola set up hundreds of service stores to ensure fast repair of mobile phones. It also set up a 'total customer satisfaction' group to analyse service defection and improve service efficiency. Motorola's after-sale service is regarded as the leading brand in the after-sale service market in China.

## Public relations

Motorola is also good at building a positive brand image through public relations. For example, it launched the 'Green China' programme in six major cities to collect used phones and batteries. In addition, it has donated 27 million RMB, set up over 60 'Project Hope' primary schools and funded 12,000 poverty-stricken children to return to school in the past nine years. These activities have built up a good corporate image for Motorola, and thus have helped to create positive word-of-mouth and enhanced its brand loyalty.

## Brand renewal

Motorola's long history in China has left an old brand image in Chinese consumers' minds. Now it is facing the problem of brand aging. A survey showed that most Chinese consumers considered Motorola a traditional, technology-focused brand. Motorola's brand is now rivalled by new market entrants such as Nokia and Samsung, both of which place more emphasis on fashion and individuality than on technology. As such, they have a modern and young brand image. Therefore, Motorola needs to renew its brand image by digging deep into its customer database and anticipating consumer needs to create new markets and keep its brand young and vibrant.

Sources: www.motorola.com.cn/en/about/inchina/default.asp and personal interviews with a manager.

## Key challenges

The brand-building environment is changing quickly with the fast development of China's economy. After several rounds of brand mergers and acquisitions, many strong brands in several sectors – such as Wal-Mart and Carrefour in retailing, and Danone and Coca-Cola in the beverage industry – have carved up the markets and brand competition has become fiercer. Meantime, the central government has provided credit funds to local brands in the hope of building several strong made-in-China brands in different industries (Zhou, 2006). Many local companies, such as Haier, TCL, Huawei, Zhongxing, Chery Automobile and Lenovo, have grown up quickly and compete with global brands in the Chinese and overseas markets. Additionally, Chinese consumers have become more demanding as more brands and products become available. The booming of the Internet has also empowered customers with more information and options. Consumers' purchasing and consuming habits are changing and their needs are becoming more diversified. Both multinational companies and local firms are facing more challenges than ever before.

## Regional differences

As China is a big country with fifty-six ethnic groups, consuming habits are quite different for consumers living in urban and rural areas, southern and northern China, eastern and western China. And the country's fast economic development has made the income gap between east and west, urban and rural even bigger. So firms need to do in-depth investigations of local customers' income levels, consumption habits and environments to adjust their marketing strategies and win them over. For example, learning that consumers in southeast China love seafood, Wal-Mart expanded its seafood section in its supermarkets in the southern provinces. In addition, the income structure and consumption habits of people in rural areas are quite different from those of people living in cities. Urban Chinese earn about three times as much as rural Chinese, according to a survey by Gallup (McEwen *et al.*, 2006). So firms need to adjust their marketing strategies when exploring rural markets. Sanzhu Medical set a good example in this. As television was not very prevalent in rural areas, it sent out many salesmen to put up posters and hand out leaflets in even the remotest villages to advertise its products. The company also hired many doctors to carry out no-benefit clinics in communities, towns and villages. This made Sanzhu well known in every corner of China and gained the company a good reputation (Li, 2004). By contrast, although powerful foreign supermarkets, which thrive on large-volume sales and lower prices, are successful in big cities, they struggle to survive in rural areas due to minuscule demand and high prices (Euromonitor, 2006). Therefore, firms need to study local market conditions carefully and adjust their marketing plans before entering different regions.

## Stricter legal and media supervision

In 2007, the State Council set up a special committee for product quality and food safety inspection. A nationwide quality inspection is in process to ensure high quality of products. At the same time, as environmental protection grows, the central government is promoting a resource-saving and environment-friendly society. Enterprises should not disregard the environmental protection policy in manufacturing or even in advertising. For example, one advert by the clothes brand Semir was banned because it stated: 'We do not care about global warming'.

In addition, 'brand scandals' now receive more attention from the media. Negative news can generate nationwide discussion and condemnation very quickly. And scandals spread even faster via the Internet. Any minor decline in quality or service will spread quickly and severely damage customers' trust in the brand. For example, Sanzhu Medical – whose sales revenue had increased by eighty times and reached eight billion RMB in just three years due to its 150,000 salesmen's efforts – went bankrupt in three months after a local newspaper released a report headlined: 'Eight Bottles of Sanzhu Liquid Medicine Led to Death of an Old Man' (Zhang, 2007).

## Crises of customer confidence towards brands

Many famous brands have encountered crises of customer confidence since 2005. For example, the carcinogenic Sudan I was found in Heinz–Meiweiyuan pepper sauce; KFC was also found using Sudan I in its sauce; unacceptably high levels of iodine were detected in Nestlé Jin Pai Growing 3+ milk powder; and Evian mineral water was found to contain excessive bacteria (Gu and Chen, 2007). All of these crises made Chinese consumers more cautious about branded products, and many now distrust them. For example, Chinese consumers' trust level towards brands in the food and beverage industry is currently less than 50 per cent (Gu and Chen, 2007).

## Stronger patriotism

Chinese are very proud of their 5000-year history and culture. People are very sensitive towards anything that offends their national pride. Companies have to respect the traditional Chinese culture and be careful not to hurt patriotic feelings during communications, or they will suffer the consequences. For example, a Nike advertisement titled 'Chamber of Fear' was criticized and ultimately banned because it did not show respect for symbols representing China. Nike's sales in China fell for a period of time because of this advertisement. Likewise, a Nippon Paint (China) advertisement featuring a 'fallen dragon' caused great anger among Chinese consumers as the dragon is a symbol of China. In another instance, Starbucks moved out of the Imperial Palace in Beijing because the company represents American culture while the Imperial Palace symbolizes the essence of Chinese historical heritage. Opening a coffee shop in the Imperial Palace was considered a cultural offence.

## Brand loyalty to be established

Research by Coulter, Price and Feick (2003) shows that consumers in transitional economies experience a short period from no brands to lots of brands (cited in He, 2006). Consumers do not use a particular brand for a long time and so are unlikely to become loyal to a brand. Most consumers buy branded products whose names sound familiar. Chinese people are keen on a fair return: they are very price sensitive and shift easily between brands when convinced to do so by promotional activities. So firms need to devote more resources to cultivate brand loyalty. In addition, although at the moment most Chinese consumers prefer foreign brands to local ones, this may change over time. The symbolic function of foreign brands is weakened when the local economy develops, and people become more rational towards foreign brands (He, 2006). Therefore, the global brands need to provide high-quality products, superior service and localized communication to win brand loyalty from Chinese consumers.

# Conclusion

China's economy has moved from a centrally planned system that was largely closed to international markets to a market-based economy that has a rapidly growing private sector and plays a major role in the global economy. Accordingly, local marketing practices have developed from a 'manufacturing-capacity-focused' strategy in the 1980s to a 'promotion-and-advertisement-focused' strategy in the 1990s to today's 'customer-focused' strategy. Local firms gradually began to realize the value of brand and made great efforts to enhance their brand equity by improving product quality, providing superior service and building a good corporate image through public relations. They compete fiercely with foreign brands and have gained knowledge and experience in marketing management and brand-building issues during the brand war. Many leading local brands, such as Wahaha and NanFu, were acquired by foreign brands during the competition, while some others, such as Haier and Huawei, began to expand their markets abroad and promote their brands globally. And foreign brands also learned fast to adapt their brand-building and marketing management strategies in the diversified market of China.

Meanwhile, the brand-building environment is changing quickly. Both multinational companies and local firms are facing more challenges than ever before. As the seller's market became a buyer's market, Chinese consumers became more demanding as more brands and products became available, and their purchasing and consuming habits continue to change quickly. Chinese consumers no longer have blind faith that famous brands are always of good quality in the aftermath of so many scandals. Therefore, firms need to provide high-quality products, superior service and localized communication to improve brand equity and win loyal customers. They also need to study the local market environment and consumer habits before they enter second-tier cities and rural areas.

In addition, with 210 million netizens (Internet users) – about 16 per cent of the population – China had the second-largest online population in the world by the end of December 2007 (CNNIC, 2008). The fast development of the Internet has opened a new era of marketing by empowering customers with more information and options and equipping firms with new marketing tools. The 2008 Beijing Olympics also brought new opportunities for more China brands to go global. Retailers, such as GOME, Wal-Mart and IKEA, are becoming more powerful. Firms need to dig deeper into their customer databases and anticipate consumer needs to create new markets and keep their brands alive.

## Acknowledgement

The authors acknowledge the financial support given by the National Natural Science Foundation of China (706720180 and 70472052), the Leading Academic Discipline Program of 211 Project for University of International Business and Economics (3rd phase) and the Research Project of the University of International Business and Economics.

## Bibliography

Aaker, D. A. (1991) *Managing Brand Equity: Capitalizing on the Value of a Brand Name*, New York: Free Press.
—— (1998) *Building Strong Brands*, New York: Free Press
Bond, M. H. and Hwang, K. (1986) 'The social psychology of the Chinese people', in M. Harris (ed.) *The Psychology of the Chinese People*, New York: Oxford University Press, 213–66.
Boulding, W. and Kirmani, A. (1993) 'A consumer-side experimental examination of signaling theory: do consumers perceive warranties as signals of quality', *Journal of Consumer Research*, 20: 111–23.
Brown, T. and Dacin, A. (1997) 'The company and the product: corporate associations and consumer product responses', *Journal of Marketing*, 61, 1: 68–84.
CNNIC, 'Netizens in China reach 0.21 billion and the Internet spreads to various levels', http://www.cnnic.cn/html/Dir/2008/02/29/4999.htm, accessed on 4 June 2008.
Eckhardt, G. M. and Michael, J. H. (2001) 'Cultural paradoxes reflected in brand meaning: McDonald's in Shanghai, China', *Journal of International Marketing*, 10, 2: 68–82.
Euromonitor, 'Retailing in China', http://www.gmid.euromonitor.com/HitList.aspx, accessed on 3 November 2006.
Gu, H. Y. and Chen, Z. (2007) 'Overview of brand crises in 2005', *Effective Marketing*, http://www.em-cn.com/Article/200701/101623.html, accessed on 3 June 2008.
Guo, X. L. (2007) *Consumer Brand Sensitivity: Theoretical Models and Empirical Tests*, Beijing: University of International Business and Economics Press.

Haier Group, 'Company background', http://www.haier.cn/about/honor.shtml, accessed on 27 January 2008.

He, J. X. (2006) 'Advance on measures of customer-based brand equity-scale development, validation and cross-cultural approach', *Business Economics and Administration*, 4, 174: 53–58.

Hofstede, G. and Bond, M. H. (1988) 'The Confucius connection: from cultural roots to economic growth', *Organizational Dynamics*, 16, 4: 5–21.

Horizonkey, 'Gold in word of mouth communication', 12 November 2003, http://www.horizonkey.com/showart.asp?art_id = 89&cat_id = 5, accessed on 25 January 2008.

Keller, K. (1993) 'Conceptualizing measuring and managing customer-based brand equity', *Journal of Marketing*, 57, 1: 1–22.

—— (2001) 'Building customer-based brand equity', *Marketing Management*, 10, 2: 14–19.

—— (2002) *Branding and Brand Equity*, Cambridge, MA: Marketing Science Institute.

Keller, K. and Moorthi, Y. (2003) 'Branding in developing markets', *Business Horizons*, May–June: 49–59.

Keller, K. (2003) 'Brand synthesis: the multidimensionality of brand knowledge', *Journal of Consumer Research*, 29, 4: 595–600.

Kotler, P. (2003) *Marketing Management* (11th edition), New Jersey: Prentice-Hall.

Li, Z. Q. (2004) 'The cost of self-support channels', *Globrand.com*, http://www.globrand.com/2004/5106.shtml, accessed on 30 May 2008.

Lin, Y. (1994) *The Chinese People*, Shanghai: Shanghai Xuelin Press.

Mai, L. and Zhao, H. (2004) 'The characteristics of supermarket shoppers in Beijing', *International Journal of Retail and Distribution Management*, 32, 1: 56–62.

McDonald's, 'About McDonald's', http://www.mcdonalds.com/corp/about.html, accessed on 27 January 2008.

McEwen, W., Fang, X., Zhang, C. and Burkholder, R. (2006) 'Inside the mind of the Chinese consumer', *Harvard Business Review*, 84, 3: 68–76.

National Bureau of Statistics of China (2007) 'China Development Review Report Series 1: Open, develop and crossover', 18 September, http://www.stats.gov.cn/tjfx/ztfx/sqd/t20070918_402433210.htm, accessed on 24 January 2008.

Oliver, R. (1997) *Satisfaction: A Behavioural Perspective on the Consumer*, New York: McGraw Hill.

Pan, H. L. (2006) *Harvard Brand Strategy Decision Analysis and Classic Case Study*, Beijing: Renmin Press.

Roth, M. S. (1995) 'The effects of culture and socioeconomics on the performance of global brand image strategies', *Journal of Marketing Research*, 32, 2: 163–75.

Simon, C. J. and Sullivan, M. W. (1993) 'The measurement and determinants of brand equity: a financial approach', *Marketing Science*, 12, 1: 28–52.

Temporal, P. (2001) *The Creation, Development, and Management of Asia Brands for the Global Market*, Shanghai: Shanghai Communication Press.

Tse, D. (1996) 'Understanding Chinese people as consumers: past findings and future propositions', in M. Bond (ed.) *The Handbook of Chinese Psychology*, Hong Kong: Oxford University Press, 352–63.

UNCTAD (2006) 'World Investment Report 2006', http://www.unctad.org/Templates/webflyer.asp?docid = 7431&intItemID = 3968&lang = 1&mode = downloads, accessed on 25 January 2008.

Wang, H. Z. (2006) *Brand Equity in China, from Measurement Model to Implementation Strategies*, Beijing: Tsinghua University Press.

Wang, L. W. (2007) 'The 100 most influential world-famous brands in China in 2007', http://news.sohu.com/20071130/n253720042.shtml, accessed on 10 December 2009.

Wang, Y. G. and Lo, H. P. (2004) 'An integrated framework for customer value and customer relationship management performance', *Managing Service Quality*, 14, 2/3: 169–82.

Yan, J. J. and Hu, Y. (2001) *Haier Made in China*, Haikou: Hainan Press.

Zeithaml, V. A. (1988) 'Consumer perceptions of price, quality, and value: a means–end model and synthesis of evidence', *Journal of Marketing*, 52, 3: 2–22.

Zhang, S. X. (2007) *Modern Brand Strategy*, Beijing: Economy and Management Publishing House.

Zhao, Z. B. (2005) 'An empirical study of brand equity dimensions', *Management Sciences in China*, 18, 5: 10–16.

Zhou, X. (2006) 'Proposal on China's foreign direct investment policy, transformation characteristics and future improvements', http://magazine.moneychina.cn/d/2006/08/13/1155438021216.html, accessed on 3 June 2008.

# 4 The changing face of accounting management in China

*Richard Chamblin, J. Mark Munoz and Xiu Ying Zheng-Pratt*

- Introduction
- Context
- Case studies
- Key challenges
- Conclusion

## Introduction

As companies around the world expand internationally in a globalized environment, various strategies have been employed to establish overseas presence successfully. While the phrase 'international expansion and China' used to denote foreign direct investment into China, it now implies overseas expansion of Chinese companies. Media have featured numerous stories of Chinese companies participating in a project bid, international investment, acquisition, joint venture, or even strategic alliances. For example, Chinese companies or government agencies have announced investments in Barclays, Bear Stearns and Blackstone – three of the best-known names in international finance. Chinese mining and energy companies have invested in copper mines in Afghanistan and tungsten mines in Tasmania (Dyer and Tucker, 2007).

With the internationalization of Chinese enterprises, it becomes imperative for executives to understand the differences in the operational environments of the home and host countries. While there exist several cultural, business, economic and management differences across countries, an important area of examination is the accounting practice. This chapter describes the current state of accounting in the People's Republic of China (PRC), identifies differences between China and countries such as the United States, and discusses business implications for the internationalizing Chinese enterprises.

Many Chinese companies have succeeded in international expansions. For instance, Haier, Lenovo and TCL have all made their mark on foreign shores due to their ability to overcome barriers and select viable strategies.

Chinese companies have shown adaptability and creativity in their strategies. One methodology used by TCL is the purchasing strategy, or the acquisition of a well-known overseas enterprise as an entry point into foreign markets. A strategy used by Galanz is the private-label original equipment manufacturer (OEM) manufacturing for global brands. Another approach entails filling a niche through the provision of specialized products, such as the supply of parts, microchips and related lines. An equally important method of global expansion is establishing manufacturing capabilities outside of China. The Haier Group has successfully established fourteen factories around the world (Han, 2006).

However, while there have been several cases of successful Chinese overseas expansion, failures abound. Even with domestic success, internationalizing Chinese firms face difficulties overseas. Failures arise from cultural and business disparities and the diversity of operational environments. Operational challenges include: lack of familiarity in international trade practices, inexperience in the demands and expectations of foreign environments, product/brand management approaches, business development strategies, human resource management, and financial management – such as the management of cross-border accounting disparities, policies and procedures (Munoz et al., 2008).

For Chinese companies expanding overseas, accounting adaptability is the key. In order to raise equity in the overseas stock market or acquire debt from an overseas financial institution, Chinese companies need to implement accounting policies and reporting standards that are accepted internationally (i.e. International Financial Reporting Standards (IFRS) or US generally accepted accounting principles (GAAP)). Some Chinese companies hesitate in listing on the US stock exchange due to perceived legal liability and the need to comply with regulations such as the Sarbanes-Oxley Act of 2002. The management of accounting disparities requires adaptability from Chinese companies as they deal with more stringent internal controls, divergence of corporate governance principles, and procedural differences in foreign venues.

# Context

In an effort to characterize China's current accounting landscape, the authors identify attributes of the Chinese accounting system and how it differs from the US and other Western approaches. In addition, problems in the Chinese accounting system which might create barriers and challenges to internationalizing Chinese firms are discussed. The authors offer a seven-step system that could be helpful in managing these accounting issues.

## Differences in accounting practices – US vs. China

In China, while many businesses maintain proper accounting records, some of the systems used require thick manuals and incorporate confusing provisions (*The Economist*, 2007). In addition, the business landscape has been characterized by documented cases of corruption, poor planning, little regard for shareholder rights, and even market manipulation (Tam, 2002; Chandler, 2004). Information accuracy is an issue in China. One accounting challenge that exists in the country relates to the availability of adequate and reliable information to make informed decisions (Chang, 2001). Another challenge exists in auditing systems, where ill-defined viewpoints from auditors were noted (Tang *et al.*, 2000).

In order to craft and implement efficient accounting approaches, it is important for internationalizing Chinese enterprises to understand the differences between the accounting practices in China and those of the US GAAP.

In the Chinese culture, the emphasis on relationship building or *guanxi* (Li and Wright, 2000) can lead to business approaches that are divergent from Western practices. *Guanxi* is often utilized to further one's position or business (Xin and Pearce, 1996; Leung and Wong, 2001). It might lead to the release of private information, expedited work, and even faster debt collection (Barnathan *et al.*, 1996).

Szeto, Wright and Cheng (2006) depicted the Chinese environment as one where business ethics and *guanxi* clash, especially with the integration of Western appraisal systems and more complex technology. In fact, Tsui and Windsor (2001) observed that ethical reasoning scores of Chinese auditors were lower than those of their Australian counterparts.

Aside from culture, the Chinese accounting environment is unique due to differences in the accounting treatment and the economic environment (Choi and Levich, 1992). In addition, differences in currencies can be factors in accounting. While the Chinese currency – the yuan – has been relatively stable in recent years, confusion in conversions can easily arise, especially among inexperienced practitioners (Munoz et al., 2008).

Government policies and procedures can also play a hand in accounting practices. In 2005, the Chinese government decided to implement measures to converge their systems with the IFRS. In February 2006, China's Ministry of Finance released new accounting guidelines that moved the PRC's GAAP closer to IFRS standards. These new standards became effective in 2007 and were adopted primarily for designated entities, such as stock exchange listed companies (KPMG Primer, 2006). Small business enterprises that are not listed on a stock exchange may not have adopted these new standards.

Many Chinese managers are making efforts to implement international accounting standards (Miller, 2001). While the standardized guidelines and framework of GAAP exists in China, implementation challenges abound. Accounting system enhancements are needed to aid implementation (Chen et al., 2001).

The accounting system in China is in a state of flux. The recent adoption of most international accounting standards appears to mitigate the problems of comparability and disclosure. In some cases, this has reduced the usefulness of Chinese financial reports issued to out-of-country stakeholders in the past. However, Chinese financial reporting still displays a troubling lack of consistency, reliability, timeliness and full disclosure due to a shortage of trained accountants (Munoz et al., 2008).

## Twelve significant accounting issues

Chinese companies expanding overseas face a broad range of accounting differences. For instance, in spite of China's convergence with IFRS, significant accounting issues remain between PRC GAAP and US GAAP. A Chinese company expanding into the US versus any other overseas markets will have more accounting-related issues to consider. Table 4.1 lists twelve significant accounting issues that are important for Chinese companies to consider prior to expansion into the US (Munoz et al., 2008).

**Table 4.1**  Twelve key accounting issues in China

| Issue | Explanation | Business implication |
|---|---|---|
| Revenue Recognition: Warranty Costs Multi-Element Sales Contracts | PRC GAAP does not provide detailed guidance for the accounting treatment of specific types of revenue transactions. | Revenue may be overstated when compared to an identical economic transaction reported in the US. |
| Disclosure of Related Party Transactions – Transfer Pricing | Disclosure of related party transactions is required; however, PRC GAAP does not consider state-owned enterprises as related parties. | Lack of transparency can lead outsiders to misinterpretation of financial information. |
| Cash Flow Statements – Disclosure | PRC GAAP allows for the inclusion of bank overdrafts in cash and interest received or paid is classified as either operating or financing activities. | Comparability of cash flows of operating and financing activities is diminished. |
| Intangible Assets | PRC GAAP recognizes internally developed intangible assets while in the US internally developed intangibles are written off immediately against earnings. | Intangible assets and income may be overstated under PRC GAAP. |
| Borrowing Costs Classification of Costs and Timing of Expenses | PRC GAAP requires the capitalization approach when the capitalization criteria are satisfied. IFRS provides a choice to expense as incurred or capitalize. | Comparability of net assets and income is affected if not disclosed. |
| Leases – Capitalization, Land Rights | Land rights in China have changed and allow entities to possess rights of land permanently. Rights are capitalized. | PRC still effectively owns the land itself, so the possibility of the revocation of land rights exists. |
| Inventories – Valuation and Effect on Cost of Goods Sold | PRC GAAP does not have guidance for inventory valuation reserves. | The future decline in price of inventory is not recorded and disclosed. |

continued

**Table 4.1 (contd)** Twelve key accounting issues in China

| Issue | Explanation | Business Implication |
|---|---|---|
| Fixed Assets – Valuation and Expensing | Fixed assets are generally accounted for in the same manner as elsewhere in the world. | Generally, questions regarding fixed assets arise concerning the existence of the asset. |
| Research & Development (R&D) Costs | Research is expensed when incurred. Development costs are capitalized when the project is deemed to be viable. | The differences in accounting treatment can result in expense reporting that could vary significantly from practices outside PRC. |
| Accounts Receivable (A/R) – Valuation and Timing of Bad Debt Expense | A/R typically aged in PRC based upon years rather than thirty-day increments. Doubtful accounts are not based on experience and are typically undervalued. | As companies move towards privatization, A/R becomes more important in terms of valid assets and cash flow. |
| Effects of Currency Conversion Methods on Income | Exchange rate is held artificially constant by the PRC government, but forces international participants to anticipate PRC actions, rather than relying on market forces. | Unpredictability in the valuation of financial activities reduces comparability. |
| Income Taxation | PRC GAAP adopts the balance sheet liability method to determine deferred tax of temporary difference. The accounting treatment for taxation of income is similar between PRC GAAP and US GAAP. | China has a very complicated tax system, involving national, provincial, city and district laws and tax officials. Each taxing body has its own regulations on income taxes. For example, China has a number of tax zones, and each may offer a different corporate income tax rate ranging from 15 to 33 per cent. |

# The Management of International Accounting Disparities (MIAD) model

While there are several other issues that could be considered by a Chinese company expanding overseas, the twelve listed here are the most critical. As a result of significant variations in accounting practices, we recommend a seven-step process that would help internationalizing enterprises in identifying, reconciling and managing accounting differences in foreign locations. These steps are presented in Table 4.2.

**Table 4.2** A seven-step process for the MIAD model

| Recommended process | Description |
| --- | --- |
| 1 Market environment assessment | Research, analysis and evaluation of the business, economic, political and cultural landscape of the international location |
| 2 Accounting system evaluation | Research and assessment of the accounting system of the international location |
| 3 Identification of key accounting differences | Identification of key areas where accounting standards and practice differences exist |
| 4 Assessment of business impact of differences | Analysis and evaluation of business implications of the accounting differences |
| 5 Implementation of selected measures | Implement measures that will mitigate business risk and increase efficiencies |
| 6 Evaluation and monitoring | Track and monitor actions taken and gauge their results and efficiencies |
| 7 Review and update | Review performance and reconcile with changing business, economic and political conditions |

It is important to note that inherent factors such as the economic environment and competitive intensity play large roles in determining viable accounting approaches in foreign markets. Nevertheless, a well-conceived set of strategies can be helpful in preventing and steering away from potential business obstacles. We discuss the seven-step process for the Management of International Accounting Disparities (MIAD) model below (also see Figure 4.1).

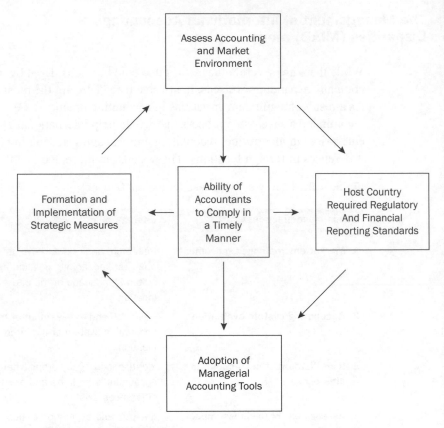

**Figure 4.1** A model for MIAD

1 *Market environment assessment.* Environmental assessment and scanning need to be conducted with emphasis on key business functions such as accounting and marketing. Furthermore, the use of several industry sources is recommended. Useful pointers include the following:

a) Analysis of the financial activity of companies operating in the targeted industry can be obtained from reliable and independent sources, such as Dun & Bradstreet and Robert Morris & Associates. These sources provide industry-related ratio analysis data including common-sized income statements that can be used to compare operating results to industry averages.

b) Analysis of market potential and the competitive environment can be obtained from primary sources, such as market research surveys conducted by a market research firm. Secondary sources from industry trade journals, magazines and newsletters, and federal government agencies would also be useful.

2 *Accounting system evaluation.* In assessing the accounting system in a new location, industry-specific, reliable and timely information is needed.

   a) Financial information should be in recognized formats (such as US GAAP or IFRS) and should be suitable for presentation to stakeholders.
   b) Internal reports should facilitate management decision-making on aspects such as pricing, mark-up, product continuation, use of resources, resource requirements and accountability.
   c) The system should provide accessible, reliable and detailed information needed for the preparation and submission of all required regulatory reports. These reports include the submission of income tax returns, sales tax returns, employee payroll tax returns and employee benefits reports.

   Assistance in identification of appropriate accounting systems may be obtained from business schools, business consultants and accounting program suppliers.

3 *Identification of key accounting differences.* Many countries struggle in the alignment and reconciliation of their own GAAP to international standards. In China, the financial reporting principles used by some companies may differ from IFRS standards adopted by the PRC. Since accounting principles are industry-specific, it is important for Chinese companies entering foreign locations to obtain an analysis of the accounting differences from recognized professional accounting firms.

4 *Assessment of business impact of accounting differences.* The use of accounting standards that differ from US GAAP may lead users of financial statements and internal reports to incorrect conclusions. Revenue recognition standards affect the income statement and the contribution margin of a product. If the revenue recognition standard used reports revenue in excess of that which would be produced using a US standard, the resulting relationship of revenue to variable costs would be affected. External and internal stakeholders schooled in the use of US standards could be misled by the information.

5 *Implementation of selected measures.* An accounting system should require minimal operator training and produce financial reports in a timely manner. For instance, an operating statement must be

available to management quickly enough to act within the 'window of opportunity'. The system must produce internal, external and regulatory reports that allow management the opportunity to act in a timely manner to avoid regulatory penalties, provide external stakeholders with expected reports, and allow management to compare actual results with company goals.

6 *Evaluation and monitoring.* Accounting program design should provide a trail of evidence that allows internal and external auditors to track transactions from the initial event to the required reports. This trail provides evidence useful in measuring the reliability of the output information and can be used as an accounting training tool.

7 *Review and update.* The resulting reports can be used to compare actual results to company goals and expectations to aid in improving efficiencies. The reports can also be used to implement the analysis indicated in Step 1 to measure operating efficiency and competitiveness.

In clarifying how these factors affect the accounting practice, a case study on an internationalizing Chinese company is presented below.

# Case studies

## Organization case 4.1 Haier

### Company background

The viability of the model introduced by the authors is illustrated by using the case of a Chinese company called Haier. Case facts have been obtained from the company's website. Haier is a company that built on the framework of its local success to pursue a dynamic international expansion strategy. In the process of global expansion, the company faced significant challenges. The challenges were shaped by both internal and external business factors. As the company grew and expanded overseas, it addressed these challenges by implementing innovative and effective management approaches. The implemented strategies had an impact on diverse management functions such as marketing, finance, operations and accounting. The company's accounting approach helped define its future.

In this case, Haier's accounting approach and our proposed accounting model, called the MIAD, will be discussed.

## Haier in America

Haier's entry into the US was marked by the opening of the American Haier Industrial Park in South Carolina on 30 April 1999. Since then, Haier has opened several other companies, such as the Haier Holding Company (US), Haier Real Estate Ltd, Haier America Trading Company in New York, and R&D and design centres in Los Angeles, New York and South Carolina. Presently, more than 95 per cent of Haier's employees in the US are local residents.

Haier has developed strong relationships with major US retailers. Haier products are currently sold by Best Buy, Wal-Mart and other top North American retailers. The main products sold in the US market include: refrigerators, freezers, top-load washers, home air-conditioners, commercial air-conditioning systems, microwave ovens, dishwashers, televisions and cell phones.

The company's success in the US has been attributed to its innovative spirit and desire to satisfy the needs of local consumers. In recent years, Haier has rolled out innovative products such as the Michael Freezer, the Frog Television and the Computer Desk Refrigerators. The Michael Freezer was first proposed by Michael Jemal, chairman of the board for Haier America Trading Company. It took the Haier design team less than seventeen hours to develop Jemal's original proposal into a working prototype. Another product, the Frog Television, has become a popular gift for special occasions such as Christmas, New Year and Valentine's Day. Haier's Computer Desk Refrigerators are a huge hit on university campuses throughout the US.

The company's growth and competitive pricing have been partly supported by the US government. Haier recognized that the US government subsidizes environmentally friendly products and started innovating in that direction to assist in the development of competitive pricing. For instance, since 2007, US consumers have received rebates of US$40–100 when they purchase Haier Double Drive washing machines. The US government's support allowed Haier to implement an aggressive pricing strategy.

Haier's success in the US may be attributed to several factors. The effective use of its accounting system should be one of them. The company's fast and successful entry into the US market suggests that its business information system and financial reporting platform had to be nimble, flexible and in a position to evolve. These characteristics are necessary for relevant tasks such as promptly retrieving the relevant financial information needed to support the decision to produce the Michael Freezer in a short period of time. Similarly, the same characteristics are needed when financial reports in a widely accepted accounting standard had to be promptly prepared in order to attract local investors. It may be inferred that Haier's success in the US market is attributable not only to the company's right set of operational growth strategies, but to its effective use of accounting.

continued

## Haier and the MIAD model

It is evident that Haier has made a successful entry into the US market. In its international expansion, the company has effectively utilized the seven steps of the MIAD model, as depicted in Table 4.2 on p. 81.

### Market environment assessment

In the late twentieth century, globalization provided opportunities for Chinese companies to earn foreign exchange by leveraging lower production costs and functioning as an OEM for multinational corporations (MNCs). This is the entry strategy Haier employed when venturing into the US market in 1995. Haier noted the continued economic growth in the US and pursued the opportunity to expand into this market. Haier's move into the US market was initially cautious with emphasis placed on niche markets such as computer desk refrigerators and electric wine cellars. Both markets were largely neglected by American manufacturers and Haier saw a large potential return. The company's sales figures soon proved this belief to be correct, and allowed Haier to establish itself firmly in niche segments in the US. With this success, Haier looked to make further inroads in the North American market by moving into the full-size refrigerator category. This brought it into direct competition with established American giants including GE, Whirlpool, Frigidaire and Maytag. As part of its strategy, Haier decided to build a production facility in the US at Camden, South Carolina. The initiative started in 1999 and the first refrigerator rolled off the production line in 2000. By 2002, US revenues had reached US$200 million. As Russell Brown, managing partner at LehmanBrown noted: 'The CEO of the Haier Group believes that his company can extend its strong domestic brand reputation into the West by introducing innovative products for specific consumer markets and then expanding into bigger ones, a strategy that would enable the company to enjoy the higher margins that come with brand sales instead of slugging it out as a low-cost supplier to western companies' (Brown, 2004).

### Accounting system evaluation

Throughout the 1990s Haier developed and implemented its three-stage business strategy. In addition, it built on management control systems such as corporate culture, OEC management and market chains based on business process re-engineering in order to achieve competitive advantage and success. From mid-August to October 1999, Haier implemented the final part of the first phase business process re-engineering system through a revolutionary organizational change, which involved reorganizing the accounting structure. Instead of having an accounting department at each product line division, a more centralized accounting division was formed to develop a core process for the company. The various organizational changes, along with the modification in the accounting function, would have required Haier to revamp its accounting system to satisfy the information needs under the new structure. This new business process re-engineering, along with a corporate culture that emphasizes excellence, provided the framework that allowed Haier to turn around from near bankruptcy to high profitability.

## Identification of key accounting differences and assessment of business impact

Prior to expanding into the US market, ideally Haier would wish to identify key accounting differences between PRC GAAP and US GAAP. In this process, the twelve key accounting differences listed in Table 4.1 on pp. 79–80 would have surfaced. Identifying these differences early will minimize misinterpretation of financial information (disclosure of related party transactions – transfer pricing), clarify comparability of financial information (cash flow statements – disclosure; borrowing costs – classification of costs and timing of expenses), and prevent overstatement of assets and income (intangible assets; revenue recognition – warranty costs and multi-element sales contracts). Without clarity and with the lack of proper articulation on the impact of these differences on business, potential investors may be discouraged from investing in a company like Haier.

## Implementation of selected measures

Cognizant of the challenges of thriving in the US market and dealing with the accounting reporting differences between PRC GAAP and US GAAP, Haier has opted to prepare all of its financial statements in accordance with Hong Kong Accounting Standards (HKAS) in order to narrow the gap of reporting differences. Since their inception in 2005, the Hong Kong Financial Reporting Standards (HKFRS) are identical to the International Financial Reporting Standards (IFRS). While there are still various differences between IFRS and US GAAP reporting standards, the disparity is minimal when compared to PRC GAAP vs. US GAAP. With the continual push to converge the US GAAP and IFRS systems completely in the near future, reporting in accordance with HKAS is a move in the right direction for Haier. Another effective approach was choosing Ernst and Young (E&Y) as its external auditors. E&Y is one of the largest professional services firms in the world and one of the Big Four auditors, along with PricewaterhouseCoopers (PwC), Deloitte Touche Tohmatsu (Deloitte) and KPMG. E&Y is a well-known auditing firm in the US and its roots can be traced back well over a hundred years to the formation of the auditing business and the development of the generally accepted accounting practices (International Directory of Company Histories, 1999). Having E&Y as an external auditor should boost US investors' confidence in Haier's published financial information.

## Evaluation and monitoring, and review and update

Haier needs to track and monitor the success it currently enjoys in the US market. For instance, it should examine its US and North American sales and profit growth since

continued

its entry into the market in 1995. Another area Haier should monitor is the growth and expansion of the number of its US investors. Understanding the driving force behind this growth can play a crucial role in attracting further investment and growing the business in the US market.

Continually tracking environmental changes would be an effective strategy for Haier. External factors such as economic, political and technological changes continually impact business in profound ways. Haier needs to track the market evolution, review its strategies and implement necessary updates to stay aligned with market trends and business expectations.

Haier has made good business decisions. Among these is the selection of an accounting strategy that fits the market environment and is in tune with the needs of stakeholders. Having a well-planned international accounting framework sets the stage for companies to overcome potential challenges and allows them the flexibility to adjust and fine-tune their business strategies.

Many Chinese companies will likely follow the path of Haier. A close examination of the lessons learned would be useful for international entrepreneurs, corporate executives and accounting practitioners worldwide. While Haier is certainly an excellent example of a Chinese company that has successfully internationalized, several other companies are also worth examining. For instance, Lenovo and TCL are making inroads around the world. Successful international companies could be excellent role models and mentors for other Chinese firms posed for international growth.

Sources: Haier company documents.

## Organization case 4.2 Firm X

In this section, the authors discuss a real-life case of a US-based company called Firm X (pseudonym). The case facts are accurate and have been gathered through an interview with one of the company's managers. The firm's real name is withheld for reasons of confidentiality.

In this case, the firm's management implemented six steps as it embarked on business expansion into China.

### Market environment assessment

A conservative and mature US firm, Firm X recently experienced a flattening revenue growth curve and realized that it needed to pursue a more innovative growth strategy. It decided to look at international markets to expand revenue. Its industry analysis indicated that the sector was headed towards a growth path. Feasibility studies suggested that production costs needed to remain at the firm's current level (percentage of cost of goods sold to sales) in order to allow viable expansion.

Firm X decided to explore the acquisition of a Hong Kong-based vendor that had been a supplier to the firm for over ten years. The vendor's quality and delivery were reliable. Further assessment of gathered information indicated that the vendor served a lucrative market and that significant production capacity was available. Firm X's management team decided to acquire the vendor.

## Accounting system evaluation

Firm X was aware that the vendor's several production facilities were located in mainland China. Due to the fact that the firm had no direct experience with the production facilities, it organized a team to evaluate financial/managerial reporting practices, production methods and human resource conditions in the country.

## Identification of key accounting differences

The team found that the production facilities in China required employees to work overtime but the financial reports to the PRC did not reflect the total wages incurred. Further investigation revealed that the overtime wages were routinely recorded in various operating expense accounts.

## Assessment of business impact of accounting differences

Firm X determined that the misclassification would understate the vendor's cost of goods sold and overstate period costs in their financial reports. The misclassifications would reduce the comparability of firm results from period to period and to industry averages. Some ratio analysis results would also be distorted.

In addition, managerial reports in Contribution Margin format would understate variable costs (overtime wages) and overstate fixed costs (some operating expenses). The result would lead to a distorted cost–volume–profit analysis for each production facility.

The use of this information may result in incorrect internal decisions on management issues such as the break-even point due to variances in revenue volume, pricing, make vs. buy, keep vs. drop, and other cost–volume–profit information.

In addition, Firm X recognized that there were significant unrecorded liabilities for unpaid payroll taxes and penalties.

## Implementation of selected measures

The chief executive officer (CEO) of Firm X issued a lengthy email to the managers of the production facilities. The email pointed out the problems associated with the practice

continued

and instructed the managers to adjust their accounts accordingly and to record overtime as a labour cost in the future. The CEO also ordered the determination and payment of all back taxes and penalties. The managers all reacted to the email by shutting down their plants. Their view of the order was that they were being set up for imprisonment or worse.

The US managers of the firm were unaware that PRC law discourages overtime pay to employees by imposing extensive taxes and penalties. Managers viewed these taxes and penalties as obstacles to their ability to meet delivery and pricing requirements imposed by their US customers. Local governmental officials are responsible for monitoring compliance. Local plant managers secured relief from the law by paying local officials to 'look the other way'.

Plant employees and local governmental officials learned of the contents of the email issued by the CEO. (Email accounts were not secure in the locations involved.) Government officials were terrified because a cabinet-level governmental official had recently been executed for bribery. The employees were upset by the uncertainty of their fate. The prevailing culture accepted such activity as illegal but necessary to facilitate business.

Firm X's comfort level with the vendor had caused management to neglect due diligence regarding the laws and customs in the PRC business environment.

Although it would seem prudent for the firm to buy the assets of the vendor to avoid undisclosed liabilities, Firm X chose to buy the stock of the vendor to avoid the problem of obtaining title to the personal property and the licence to use the land occupied by the production facilities.

After learning the whole story, the CEO of Firm X rescinded the order. Local governmental officials apparently contained the spread of the information and all Chinese parties returned to their normal activities.

## Assessment of business impact of accounting differences revisited

Firm X's management team would have discovered the political and cultural landscape of the production facilities located in China prior to the acquisition of the vendor if they had employed the seven-step process for the MIAD model. This case provides an example of the problems that can arise if an early evaluation of the target country's accounting system is ignored.

The existence of a potential liability for taxes and penalties was not reflected on the balance sheet of the vendor at the time of the acquisition. Therefore, equity was overstated. The overstatement of equity is one element of valuation that would tend to overvalue the vendor.

The continued existence of a potential liability is the overstatement of equity on the combined balance sheet of the firm. Potential stakeholders such as lenders and investors are misinformed when the misstatement is material. Materiality of the misstatement is not limited to the dollar amount. The liability causes broader business risks, such as possible imprisonment or execution of company personnel and loss of land-right licences.

The relationship between the US management team and the production facility managers is also affected by this situation. The US management team's poor due diligence coupled with the agreement to continue the fraudulent practice does not provide a sound foundation for building long-term success.

While this case indicates the challenges faced by a US company when expanding into China, it is likewise apparent that Chinese companies accustomed to Chinese accounting practices would be confused when dealing with Western and other international systems.

Sources: interviews with managers of Firm X in 2009.

## Manager case 4.3 Mr Wang, partner, Hendersen Consulting

### Background

Hendersen Consulting consists of a group of experienced professionals who used to work for *Fortune* 100 companies and the Big Four accounting firms. Hendersen is committed to adding value to their clients by providing top quality information and strategy. The firm's mission is to become the consummate adviser with the ability to provide world-class consulting services to multinationals and companies of all sizes.

Kevin Wang is a partner at Hendersen Taxand. He was interviewed by the authors in May 2009 to determine accounting challenges and viable strategies when doing business in China. His viewpoints are expressed below.

### Identification of key accounting differences and challenges

Various accounting-related issues are encountered by multinational companies when doing merger and acquisition (M&A) transactions in China. Some common issues observed by Hendersen Consulting include insufficient financial information for business valuation, and variations in the GAAP interpretation and application. In some cases, the M&A target uses two set of books – one for management reporting, and one for tax reporting. Mr Wang indicated that although Chinese accounting rules are getting closer to international standards, policies regarding turnover tax and income tax pose challenges as they are changing and evolving. Companies may need to adjust their books from time to time to remain compliant with the most recent tax rules. Mr Wang elaborated that though Chinese accounting rules are getting closer to international standards, turnover tax and income tax are challenges to international managers as Chinese tax rules are always changing and the changes are sometimes retroactive. This

continued

often means that companies may need to adjust their books from time to time to remain compliant with the most current tax rules.

## Implementation of viable strategies

Due to the numerous challenges of a multinational company entering China, it is critical to implement the right measures to ensure the long-term success of an M&A. Mr Wang suggested that to reduce risks of managing accounting disparities across borders, many multinational companies rely on the advisory work of consulting firms such as the Big Four, accounting consulting firms and local audit firms. He also indicated that international managers prefer to use big-name firms to reduce their risk.

Source: interview with Mr Kevin Wang, a partner at Hendersen Taxand, in 2009.

## Manager case 4.4 Mrs A, accounting manager, XYZ Corp

### Background

XYZ Corp is among the world's leading manufacturers. The company began accelerating its expansion in China in the early 1990s with the establishment of a significant local production strategy. It increased its presence in China aggressively, and subsequently reaped unprecedented growth and profit in the country. With the company's renowned global product brands and strategic local commitment, it is poised to take advantage of long-term growth in China.

Mrs A is an accounting manager at XYZ Corp. She was interviewed by the authors in May 2009 to determine accounting challenges and viable strategies when doing business in China. Her viewpoints are summarized below.

### Identification of key accounting differences and challenges

Although China is slowly converging to the International Accounting Standards (IAS), there are still significant differences between US GAAP and PRC GAAP that any multinational corporation will need to be conscious of while doing business in China. One example is modification of travel expense reporting due to differences in PRC tax regulations. XYZ Corp had to modify its typical US policy for receipt requirements for reporting of travel expenses to a much lower threshold (ten yuan) in order to satisfy the Chinese tax laws. Failure to produce receipts for expenditures above the threshold amount could result in deductions being disallowed by the Chinese tax authorities. Another difference is the threshold for when an equipment purchase is to be expensed or capitalized.

## Implementation of viable strategies

To ensure continued success in China, making sure the company adheres to local accounting reporting requirements is crucial. In response to the lower threshold of receipt requirement for travel expense reporting, XYZ Corp implemented the requirement for supervisors to sign off all expenses reported with missing receipts. To address other differences, XYZ Corp had to design its accounting reporting system in China to conform with *both* US GAAP and PRC GAAP in order to satisfy local reporting and corporate consolidated reporting. The company also has a centrally established tax and legal team in the Asian region to help the accounting reporting group at each location with specific assistance in handling any reporting discrepancies.

Source: interview with Mrs A, accounting manager of XYZ Corp, in 2009.

# Key challenges

While there are several accounting considerations that need to be considered by globalizing Chinese enterprises, two issues are of high relevance: revenue recognition; and disclosure of related party transactions – transfer pricing. This section discusses the challenges associated with these accounting disparities.

# Revenue recognition

In the case of the manufacturing industry, revenue recognition is similar in the PRC GAAP and the US GAAP (KPMG Primer, 2006). The PRC GAAP provides no guidance concerning the timing of revenue recognition when rights of return, warranties, installation charges and post-support services are elements of the transaction. US GAAP has very specific guidance (KPMG Primer, 2006). Converting from PRC GAAP to US GAAP can result in the deferral of revenue recognition until substantially all elements are accounted for. The conversion would result in the recognition of less net income. For example, Company US and Company PRC each has a gross revenue of US$1 million and has experienced identical warranty costs to sales ratios in the past. Company US uses past experience to determine the ratio of warranty cost to sales (in compliance with US GAAP) that it has determined to be 5 per cent of sales. Company PRC decides to use only US$10,000 as the expected warranty costs on its revenue in order to show a larger net income. The results are depicted in Table 4.3.

**Table 4.3** Differences in revenue recognition between US and PRC

| Account | Company US | | Company PRC | |
|---|---|---|---|---|
| | $ | C-S | $ | C-S |
| Revenue | 1,000,000 | 100% | 1,000,000 | 100% |
| Warranty expense | 50,000 | 5% | 10,000 | 1% |
| Net income | 950,000 | 95% | 990,000 | 99% |

Note: C-S = common-size percentage

In this example, when a Chinese company converts from reporting under PRC GAAP to US GAAP it will show a lower profit because it will no longer be allowed to pick an arbitrary amount for expected warranty expense under the US GAAP and will be unable to defer the recording of the warranty expense to a later period.

A similar difference exists concerning multi-element contracts that specify the delivery of the various elements of a system in stages. US GAAP defers revenue recognition until all elements are delivered unless the separate stages have stand-alone value that can be determined. An example of a possible multi-element contract would be for a vendor to install computer hardware and software in stages and provide training as needed. PRC GAAP provides no guidance, which may result in the recognition of the entire contract revenue at the time when the contract is signed. Under US GAAP a venture may recognize the revenue pertaining to each element as that element is accepted by the customer, or defer recognition of all revenue until the time when the entire contract is satisfied, depending on the terms of the contract. If the contract is performed in one accounting period, there would be no difference between the two standards. If performance of the terms of the contract covers more than one period, conversion of Chinese accounting for such a transaction to US GAAP may result in the recognition of less net income by the venture during the period that it takes to satisfy US GAAP rules.

The US GAAP provides for the recognition of agency commission revenue while PRC GAAP provides for the recognition of the gross revenue and expense elements of the transaction. While the net income from the transaction will be the same under both accounting systems, the gross revenue and expense will be reduced by the same amount if the transaction is converted to US GAAP. The use of gross versus net

**Table 4.4** Net revenue approach of US v. gross revenue approach of PRC to reporting commissions earned

| Account | Company US $ | Company US C-S | Company PRC $ | Company PRC C-S |
|---------|---------|---------|---------|---------|
| Revenue | 50,000 | 100% | 10,000 | 100% |
| Expenses | 48,000 | 96% | 8,000 | 80% |
| Net income | 2,000 | 4% | 2,000 | 20% |

Note: C-S = common-size percentage

revenues will change the ratios obtained when using common-sized statements. For example, Company US uses the net revenue approach and Company PRC uses the gross revenue approach to reporting commissions earned as agents as shown in Table 4.4.

As depicted above, if a Chinese company converted to reporting under US GAAP rules, it would report earnings of 4 per cent of revenue instead of 20 per cent as previously under PRC GAAP. The use of PRC GAAP would impair comparability with industry averages using US GAAP.

## Disclosure of related party transactions – transfer pricing

Under international accounting standards, economic transactions between companies with overlapping ownership are supposed to be clearly disclosed (*The Economist*, 2007). This rule applies to transactions between owners and the company they own, individual companies with common ownership, and vendors.

The related party rule usually applies to materially significant transactions, measured in monetary terms, between parties that can benefit from the transaction(s) and have the influence to manipulate the economic terms of the contract. The economic terms of related party transactions cannot be presumed to be at 'arm's length'. A transaction is deemed not to be at arm's length if it deviates from terms offered to customers or the fair market value (FMV) of the product or service involved.

Disclosure is accomplished by providing the details of the related party transactions in the footnotes that accompany the financial statements.

Related party disclosure is intended to facilitate financial statement readers' understanding of the nature and extent of the related party transactions. Such disclosure is intended to prevent companies from window-dressing their financial position.

The following are examples of related party transactions that should be disclosed:

> A company with the equivalent of US$1 million in total assets sells an unused warehouse (FMV of US$100,000) to an owner for US$100,000. This is a related party transaction that should be disclosed in the footnotes of the financial statements. Stakeholders would be informed that the transaction occurred in a proper manner.

> If the same owner had paid less than the FMV for the purchase of the warehouse, the terms of that transaction would be disclosed and the readers would be warned that an improper transaction had occurred.

Transfer pricing is another type of related party transaction. Transfer pricing involves economic transactions between commonly controlled enterprises at prices that do not reflect arm's-length negotiation. An example of transfer pricing is:

> Company A is located in a 33 per cent tax region and Company B is located in a 20 per cent tax region. If both companies are under common control, the situation provides an opportunity for the two companies to agree to economic transaction terms that decrease the selling price of any products sold only to Company B.

Tables 4.5 and 4.6 illustrate the impact of transfer pricing on the following transaction: Company A sells a product with an FMV of US$100 to a related company.

**Table 4.5** Transfer pricing transaction that does not reflect FMV

|  | Company A | Company B | Combined | % |
|---|---|---|---|---|
| Sales | 50 | 100 | 150 | 100.0 |
| Cost of sales | 50 | 50 | 100 | 66.7 |
| Gross margin | 0 | 50 | 50 | 33.3 |
| Income tax | 0 | 10 | 10 | 7.5 |
| Net income | 0 | 40 | 40 | 25.8 |

**Table 4.6** Transfer pricing transaction that reflects FMV

|  | Company A | Company B | Combined | % |
|---|---|---|---|---|
| Sales | 100 | 100 | 200 | 100.0 |
| Cost of sales | 50 | 100 | 150 | 75.0 |
| Gross margin | 50 | 0 | 50 | 25.0 |
| Income tax | 17 | 0 | 17 | 9.0 |
| Net income | 33 | 0 | 33 | 17.0 |

The effect of the arrangement not reflecting FMV is to reduce the taxable income of Company A and increase the taxable income of Company B, thereby providing a decrease in the combined tax rate of the two enterprises.

A transfer pricing arrangement that does not reflect FMV is deemed an illegal avoidance of tax under US tax laws. It creates an unrecorded and undisclosed liability for the unpaid taxes and related penalties that may be assessed against both companies and does not comply with US GAAP. PRC tax law does not sanction avoidance but enforcement is not uniform.

A different (but not arm's-length) transfer pricing arrangement is sometimes entered into to provide window-dressing for the benefit of prospective investors or out-of-country partners. This arrangement involves the sale of products to a controlled enterprise at inflated prices to overstate net income and thereby increase the stockholders' equity in the firm. This kind of arrangement involves the sale of non-existent goods or goods not delivered to the buyer. Another form of transfer pricing involves selling products to a controlled firm at discounted prices to enhance the profits of the transferee firm.

Unfortunately, unethical and illegal transfer pricing is a significant problem in China because of its history of overlapping ownership by the government and by businessmen. A Chinese company needs to be aware that when financial reports are converted to reporting under US GAAP, proper disclosure of related party transactions is required.

# Conclusion

The case studies and examples illustrate that sensitivity to cross-border accounting disparities is essential for internationalizing organizations.

The more systematic and well planned the methodology to address accounting differences, the greater the likelihood of success. The MIAD model proposed by the authors is a helpful tool in dealing with international accounting challenges.

In order to enhance the accounting practices, we offer some specific suggestions. First, Chinese firms need to consider the differences in accounting policies and reporting standards between PRC GAAP and US GAAP and/or IFRS. Areas where operational disparities exist include: required regulatory and financial accounting reporting standards, sophistication of accounting tools, business costs, and extent of collaboration with public accounting firms. Second, due consideration needs to be given to implementation time. There are often delays in the implementation process. Firms need to provide adequate time for projects, and task prioritization is the key. Third, firms need to ensure reliability of information. Accurate information is not always easy to gather. Double-check the information source and quality. Fourth, regular assessments help in the attainment of optimal performance. Firms need to understand strengths and build on organizational attributes to succeed (Hott *et al.*, 1998). Fifth, anticipate organizational disparity and adapt. Level of development, national and organizational culture, and perspectives are different across countries. For example, investors in developed nations tend to be more proactive and long-term-focused when compared with those in emerging nations (Luo, 1998). Chinese firms need to prepare for organizational disparities. Sixth, understand legal and contractual obligations well. There is a diversity of laws and systems. Legal frameworks for business in China are categorized by some as underdeveloped (Xin and Pearce, 1996). Chinese firms should be aware that legal approaches in foreign locations may be more elaborate. Seventh, utilize the service of an experienced Hong Kong accounting firm. If cultural sensitivity is a concern, Chinese firms should engage Hong Kong accounting firms with broad international experience.

The internationalization of Chinese enterprises will continue and intensify in coming years. Efforts are under way to harmonize accounting systems worldwide. Meanwhile, accounting disparities exist between China, the US and other countries. International managers would be well served by understanding accounting challenges and in planning ahead.

# Bibliography

Barnathan, J., Crock, S., Einhorn, B., Engardio, P., Roberts, D. and Borrus, A. (1996) 'Rethinking China', *Business Week*, 4 March, 13–20.

Brown, Russell (2004) 'The changing role of CFOs and accountants in China', http://www.lehmanbrown.com/Newsletters/PTO/LB14.htm, accessed on 3 December 2008.

Chandler, C. (2004) 'Inside the new China', *Fortune*, 150: 84–98.

Chang, G. G. (2001) *Coming Collapse of China*, New York: Random House.

Chen, C., Chen, S. and Su, X. (2001) 'Profitability regulation, earnings management, and modified audit opinions: evidence from China', *Auditing*, 20, 2: 9–31.

Choi, F. and Levich, R. (1992) 'International accounting diversity and capital market decisions', in E. Frederick and F. Choi (eds) *The Handbook of International Accounting*, New York: Wiley & Sons.

Dyer, G. and Tucker, S. (2007) 'In search of illumination: Chinese companies expand overseas', *Financial Times*, 3 December, http://www.ft.com/cms/s/0/176f01c2-a1d6-11dc-a13b-0000779fd2ac.html?nclick_check = 1, accessed on 3 May 2008.

*Economist, The* (2004) 'China's Growing Pains', 21 August, 11.

—— (2007) 'Finance and economics: cultural revolution: Chinese accounting', 13 January, 63.

Han, V. (2006) 'Overseas strategies of Chinese companies', *Appliance Magazine*, April, http://www.appliancemagazine.com/editorial.php?article = 1396&zone = 1&first = 1, accessed on 8 December 2008.

Hott, M., Keats, B. and DeMarie, S. (1998) 'Navigating in the new competitive landscape: building strategic flexibility and competitive advantage in the 21st century', *Academy of Management Executive*, 12, 4: 22–42.

International Directory of Company Histories (1999) 'Ernst & Young', http://www.fundinguniverse.com/company-histories/Ernst-amp;-Young-Company-History.html, accessed on 8 December 2008.

KPMG Primer (2006) *Investment in People's Republic of China*, Fall, Hong Kong: KPMG International.

Leung, T. and Wong, Y. (2001) 'The ethics and positioning of *guanxi* in China', *Marketing Intelligence and Planning*, 19, 1: 55–64.

Li, J. and Wright, P. (2000) '*Guanxi* and the realities of career development: a Chinese perspective', *Career Development International*, 5, 7: 369–78.

Luo, Y. (1998) 'Strategic traits of foreign direct investment in China: a country of origin perspective', *Management International Review*, 38, 2: 109–32.

Miller, A. (2001) 'Beijing confirms commitment to IAS/Eastern promise', *Accountancy Age*, 26 July, 17–20.

Munoz, J. M., Chamblin, R. and Hinkamper, R. (2008) 'Issues relating to accounting practices in China: implications to international entrepreneurs',

Paper presented at the United States Association for Small Business and Entrepreneurship (USASBE) Conference in San Antonio, TX, 10–13 January.

PricewaterhouseCoopers (March 2007) 'Transfer pricing implications of China's new corporate income tax law', *China Tax/Business News Flash*, Issue 7.

Szeto, R., Wright, P. and Cheng, E. (2006) 'Business networking in the Chinese context', *Management Research News*, 29, 7: 425–38.

Tam, O. (2002) 'Ethical issues in the evolution of corporate governance in China', *Journal of Business Ethics*, 31: 143–50.

Tang, Q., Kilgore, A., Yang, Y. and Hong, J. (2000) *Auditor Government Associations and Auditor Independence in China*, EAA 2000 Abstracts, http://www.bham.ac.uk/EAA/eaa2000/tang_kil.htm, accessed on 8 December 2008.

Tsui, J. and Windsor, C. (2001) 'Some cross-cultural evidence on ethical reasoning', *Journal of Business Ethics*, 31, 2: 143–51.

Xin, K. and Pearce, J. (1996) '*Guanxi*: connections as substitutes for formal institutional support', *Academy of Management Journal*, 39, 6: 1641–58.

# 5 The changing face of state-owned enterprise management in China

## Russell Smyth and Qingguo Zhai

- Introduction
- Context
- Case studies
- Key challenges
- Conclusion

## Introduction

China's economic reforms commenced in December 1978 when the Third Plenum of the Eleventh Central Committee issued a communiqué calling for a reduction in the degree of centralization of economic management and reform of the commune structure. The initial reforms focused on agriculture, but in the 1980s they spread to the state-owned enterprise (SOE) sector. In the first period of SOE reform, lasting from 1984 to 1993, SOEs were made responsible for profits and losses in the market and contract arrangements were introduced that rewarded managers for meeting specified performance targets. These reforms had some success in reducing government intervention in the management of SOEs, but the rights and responsibilities of SOE managers remained ill-defined. The second period of SOE reform, which commenced in 1993 and is ongoing, has focused on establishing a modern corporate governance structure in China's large and medium-sized SOEs and enterprise groups.

After a decade of havoc wreaked by the Cultural Revolution (1966–76), when the Third Plenum of the Eleventh Central Committee met in 1978 China was on its knees. In the period since, the country's economic landscape has undergone substantial change. The reforms initiated by Deng Xiaoping have generated a massive improvement in the living standards of the Chinese people. Estimates by the consulting group Consensus Economics, published in 2005, suggest that by 2015 China will overtake the United States as the world's largest economy (Eslake, 2006). This is just the beginning. An article in the *New York Times* predicted that the twenty-first century would be China's century, given its potential to evolve into a major economic superpower (Fishman, 2004). However, in spite of what the reforms have thus far achieved, and the promise for the future, China's SOE reforms are at a critical stage as the central government embarks on restructuring its large and medium-sized SOEs and privatizing its smaller SOEs.

The purpose of this chapter is to examine the outcomes of the latest stage of China's attempts to corporatize its SOE sector and consider some of the major challenges that exist for further economic restructuring of China's large SOEs three decades on from the Third Plenum. To realize our objective, we draw on a case study of the Fushun Petrochemical Company (FPC) – a large state-owned enterprise in Liaoning Province under the control of the China National Petroleum Corporation (CNPC). Drawing on interviews with managers and local government officials, we use the economic restructuring of FPC that commenced in 1999 to illustrate how the reforms have been implemented on the ground and some of the major difficulties that further economic restructuring poses. We also examine how Li Ruoping, the current general manager of FPC and an example of a successful manager in a large SOE, used an emerging environmental awareness in China in the lead-up to the Beijing Olympics to promote a positive image of FPC.

## Context

### Enterprise and industrial restructuring

Following the Fourteenth Communist Party Congress in 1993, the Chinese government commenced transforming large and medium-sized SOEs into joint stock companies (*gufen youxian gongsi*) and limited liability companies (*youxian zeren gongsi*) on a trial basis. The government also started divesting small SOEs on an experimental basis in pilot areas. These ownership reforms gathered momentum at the Fifteenth Communist Party Congress in 1997, when the Chinese government endorsed the slogan *zhuada fangxiao* ('grasp the big and let go of the small'). The result was the establishment of several large enterprises and business groups (*qiye jituan*), formed through mergers and acquisitions. Senior government officials sometimes spoke in terms of 'grasping' 500 or 1000 large enterprises, but in the end settled for 520 'key-point' enterprises (Yusuf *et al.,* 2006). Many of these 'key-point' enterprises were members of fifty-seven business groups promoted by the central government (Nolan, 2001). The structure of these business groups varies, but tends to fall somewhere between a highly integrated conglomerate and a more loosely connected series of firms similar to the Japanese *keiretsu* (Nolan, 2001; Yusuf *et al.*, 2006).

Foreign investors have participated in the mergers and acquisitions process (Norton and Chao, 2001), although at the end of 2006 the chair of the State Assets Supervision and Administration Commission of the State Council (SASAC), Li Rongrong, identified seven industries of strategic importance where the central government would maintain sole ownership or an absolute controlling stake. These seven industries – defence, power generation and distribution, oil and petrochemicals, telecommunications, coal, aviation and shipping – contain many of the largest and most profitable SOEs and state-controlled business groups. In these industries, foreign investors and the private sector will be restricted to either participating in developing downstream products, such as petrochemicals, or value-added services, such as telecom products (Mattlin, 2007). Outside of the 520 key-point enterprises, an estimated 8,700 large and medium-sized enterprises have had to fend for themselves or seek assistance from provincial-level governments (Hovey and Naughton, 2007). Several provincial-level governments have promoted smaller enterprise groups at the sub-national level. Meanwhile, small SOEs were closed, sold outright, leased or converted into shareholding cooperatives. In the decade following the Fifteenth Communist Party Congress an estimated 120,000 small SOEs were privatized, closed or otherwise divested (Hovey and Naughton, 2007; Yang, 2008; Yusuf and Nabeshima, 2006).

Running parallel with the creation of large business groups, in the late 1990s, several large state-owned conglomerates in strategic sectors were reorganized. For example, in aircraft manufacturing, Aviation Industries of China (AVIC) was split into two fully integrated conglomerates: AVIC I and AVIC II (Goldstein, 2006). Other restructuring occurred along geographical lines. In the steel sector, the central government orchestrated a number of takeovers with the aim of having Baosteel, Angang, Wugang and Pangang as the four 'national champions' in east China, northeast China, central China and southwest China (Sun, 2007). In the oil and petrochemical sector, prior to restructuring SINOPEC was mainly engaged in oil processing while CNPC was mainly engaged in oil production. Following restructuring, both state-owned business groups integrated development, drilling and refinement of petroleum with production of petrochemical products. CNPC has a number of oil and petrochemical subsidiaries in the north and west of China, while SINOPEC oversees the oil and petrochemical sector in the south and east (Smyth and Zhai, 2001). In the shipping industry, China State Shipbuilding Corporation (CSSC) was restructured into two large state-owned groups – CSSC and China Shipbuilding Industry Corporation (CSIC) – with CSIC controlling the shipyards in the north of China and CSSC those in the south (Smyth *et al.*, 2004a).

The reorganization of strategic sectors paved the way for separation of production and service companies and equity-for-debt swaps (EDS). This also commenced in the late 1990s, in preparation for listing large SOEs on the stock market. The separation of production and service companies in core enterprises or subsidiaries within business groups such as CNPC and CSIC was a means to divest the core enterprise of non-core businesses together with large swaths of surplus labour. The non-core businesses and surplus labour were hived off to service companies. There were two main categories of service companies: namely, companies with independent accounting arrangements that were to be responsible for their own profits and losses; and companies with internal accounting arrangements that were not capable of surviving in the market on their own. The production company was typically given the enterprise's best assets following the separation to make it attractive to potential investors with the objective of listing the production company on the stock market.

The EDS reforms were allied with the separation of production and service companies and were designed to prepare the production companies for listing. The EDS was announced in 1999 and the first swap occurred in 2001. Under this scheme, the long-term debt of selected SOEs owed to the state-owned banks was swapped for equity controlled by four asset management companies (AMCs) affiliated with each of the banks. Ostensibly the EDS had two objectives. One was to improve the debt–asset ratio of participating SOEs and reduce the bad debts of the state-owned banks. The other was to improve the decision-making structures within the SOEs. The first objective was realized, at least initially. In the first EDS, 601 selected enterprises swapped 400–500 billion RMB, which was equivalent to about 50 per cent of the out-standing loans of the banking sector at the end of 1997 (Huang, 2001), although bad debts have since started to accumulate again. Case studies conducted between 2000 and 2003 suggested that the second objective was not being realized, with the AMCs reluctant to interfere with the management of the firm even when they had the controlling shares (Smyth *et al.*, 2004b; Steinfeld, 2001).

## Reduction in surplus labour

In 1997, the State Commission for Economic Restructuring estimated that the number of surplus workers in SOEs was 54 million, close to half the total workforce (*South China Morning Post*, 7 May 1997, cited in Morris *et al.*, 2001: 69). Fieldwork conducted between 1995 and 1997 suggested that firms intended to reduce their core workforce by between 15 and 50 per cent over the course of the Ninth Five-Year Plan (1996–2000) (Hassard *et al.*, 2006). However, the reduction in surplus labour has been far less than these forecasts (Dong and Xu, 2008, 2009; Hovey and Naughton, 2007). Case studies of large SOEs in the southwest and northeast of China in the late 1990s and early 2000s suggested surplus labour was still between 20 per cent and 60 per cent of total employees (Morris *et al.*, 2001; Smyth *et al.*, 2004a; Smyth and Zhai, 2003). The government and trade union movement have been reluctant to let SOEs cut ties with their surplus workers because of the potential for demonstrations and social unrest, the lack of alternative employment opportunities, particularly in smaller cities, and the embryonic nature of the social security system (Yang, 2008).

Instead, SOEs have taken measures to disguise the true reduction in surplus labour. One common approach has been to give surplus workers the administrative label *xiagang*, meaning they are 'on leave' from the enterprise. These *xiagang* workers retain their ties to the SOE and the SOE is obliged to pay them a subsistence allowance. Sometimes, alternative labels to *xiagang*, such as *changxiu* ('long-term rest') or *li gang* ('left their posts'), are used. At the municipal and district levels these terms are often used interchangeably to mean the same thing. In Fushun, where our case study is located, the municipal labour bureau uses the term *xiagang*, while the district-level bureaux use myriad categories, including *changxiu* and *li gang*, to mean the same thing. According to official figures, 26 million employees were given these labels between 1998 and 2002 (Armitage, 2003).

Another approach to reducing the workforce is to ask workers to take semi-retirement (*neitui*) (Morris *et al.*, 2001). The arrangement for semi-retirement varies across industries and locales. However, in one large shipbuilding SOE in the northeast males aged fifty-five and females aged fifty can apply for semi-retirement. In this SOE, workers who are semi-retired receive 50–70 per cent of their position wage, but no bonuses (Smyth *et al.*, 2004a). Following separation of production and service companies, a third approach to reducing surplus labour was to shift employees off the books of the production company into one of the service companies. Some large SOEs have gone further and created a diversified network of subsidiaries to employ redundant workers. For example, the Shougang Group set up businesses in real estate and the service sector in order to minimize lay-offs and repair eroding profit margins (Nolan and Yeung, 2001). Other leading Chinese companies such as Haier and Lenovo have followed a similar approach to stem falling profit margins (Yusuf and Nabeshima, 2006). Steinfeld (2004) criticizes this tendency, arguing that by investing in commodified products where profit margins are already thin, these leading manufacturers are not building corporate strength. The alternative argument, though, which has its origins in the late industrialization literature, is that the technological stage of China's development forces firms to operate in markets for commodified products with narrow profit margins (Khanna and Palepu, 2007).

## Managerial reform

Studies of SOE management up to the mid-1990s suggested that political interference in managerial decisions was a persistent phenomenon (Chen, 1995; Child, 1994). More recent studies have reported that managers in SOEs continue to complain about political interference in forcing unwanted mergers with loss-making firms and putting caps on forced redundancies (Hassard *et al.*, 2006). However, there is evidence that the level of political interference in senior and middle-level management has declined over time. Our previous research, based on case studies of large SOEs in Liaoning, suggests that increasingly it is the general manager who is responsible for the success or failure of the enterprise, rather than party committees (Smyth and Zhai, 2003). The proportion of managers with tertiary qualifications in SOEs has increased over time and the criteria for promotion have become more performance based (Smyth *et al.*, 2004a). The bonus system, which had been abolished in the Cultural Revolution, has had a positive effect on managerial performance. Several econometric studies using data since the 1980s suggest that bonuses for managers are positively associated with productivity (Groves et al., 1994, 1995; Li, 1997; Li and Wu, 2002; Yusuf et al., 2006).

With a few exceptions, such as Shougang, in the early to mid-1990s demoting managers for poor performance was rare. However, by 2000, it was common in large SOEs in Liaoning (Smyth and Zhai, 2003; Smyth et al., 2004a). In one large SOE, the annual turnover of management in 2002 and 2003 was about 30 per cent, with 10 to 15 per cent of turnover due to poor performance. This high proportion, however, was linked to more general restructuring of the firm at that time associated with the separation of production and service companies, an EDS and the introduction of semi-retirement arrangements for managers (Smyth et al., 2004a). In other SOEs turnover has been much lower. In some SOEs managers are employed on three-year contracts. These contracts can be terminated if the managers do not meet specified performance criteria. However, Hassard et al. (2006) point out that although managers can have their contracts terminated at the end of the three-year period, this does not mean that they will. In the SOE they studied every effort was made to reduce the number of surplus managers by 25 per cent. As part of this process, generous incentives were offered to the managers to take semi-retirement, move into self-employment or take up a comparable position with one of the enterprise's service companies. But in the end, the SOE managed to reduce its surplus managers by only 10 per cent.

## Revitalization of the northeast

In 2003, the central government enacted a policy to revitalize the northeast, the old industrial base. The central government approved 100 projects with an investment of 61 billion RMB for the first group of construction projects (Zhang and Wang, 2003). The support of the central government included: encouraging bankruptcy of some enterprises; improving the social security system; lessening the social burden on enterprises; addressing the bad debt problem; supporting the innovation of key enterprises by providing subsidized interest funds; and supporting the construction of infrastructure such as railways, energy and irrigation (Chen, 2007; Zhang and Wang, 2003). In 2003 SOEs dominated the economy of the three provinces in the northeast. At the end of 2002, the output of industrial SOEs in Liaoning accounted for 62 per cent of the total industrial output, which was 20 per cent higher than the national average. The figure was even higher in Heilongjiang and Jilin, in which SOEs accounted for about 80 per cent of industrial output (Zhang, 2004). There were several problems impeding the performance of those SOEs. Economic development in the northeast was slower than in many other regions. The dominance of SOEs in the economy hindered the development of the non-state sector. Within these SOEs, there were several problems, such as a large number of redundant workers, social welfare burden and a high level of debt to the banks (Liu and Shou, 2005).

The goal of the new policy was to establish a 'modern enterprises system' via ownership reform of SOEs. Up to 2008, over 9,000 SOEs in the northeast had completed ownership reform. The state has withdrawn from almost all the small and medium-sized enterprises. The ownership of large SOEs has been diversified. Many large local SOEs have been merged with central-government-controlled enterprises (Bureau for Revitalization of the Northeast, 2009). For instance, in Liaoning, among the forty local-government-controlled large industrial enterprises, which were planned to undergo shareholding reform in 2007, thirty-six finished shareholding reform. Among those thirty-six, 50 per cent were merged with central-government-controlled enterprises. These local enterprises received over 8 billion RMB from other investors. After the Huajin Group's merger with the China Weaponry Industrial Group, Huajin received enough investment to finance the renovation of its ethylene and petrochemical plants with a capacity of 5.5 million tonnes per annum. Another measure is to attract investors from overseas. For instance, in June 2007, Shenyang Machinery Group transferred 30 per cent of its state shares to the American Jana Fund (Bureau for Revitalization of the Northeast, 2008).

Since the enactment of this policy, investment in fixed assets has been increasing steadily. At the start of the new policy, investment in fixed assets in the northeast was increasing at 20.8 per cent per annum, while the comparable figure for China as a whole was 27.7 per cent. However, in 2006, investment in fixed assets was increasing at 37 per cent for the northeast, compared with 23.8 per cent for China as a whole. The rates of increase in FDI and exports in the northeast have also been higher than the national average since 2003. The gap between gross regional product in the northeast and in other regions has been narrowing since 2003 (Wei, 2008).

# Case studies

The information in this section is based on interviews conducted between June and August 2000 and in November 2007 and May 2008, supplemented with primary and secondary materials on the FPC. Between June and August 2000, at the height of the restructuring, we interviewed senior managers in three subsidiaries of FPC – Fushun Detergent Company (FDC), Fushun Ethylene Company (FEC) and Fushun No. 2 Oil Refinery (FOR) – as well as local government officials. FDC, FEC and FOR are representative of FPC's subsidiaries. FOR is a typical Chinese state-owned refinery that was built in the 1930s. It processes Daqing crude oil and produces a range of fuels and petrochemicals. FDC and FEC were built in the Seventh Five-Year Plan (1986–90) and have relatively modern plants. In November 2007 we interviewed Li Ruoping, the present general manager of FPC, to update our information on the restructuring and discuss his management philosophies. In May 2008 we interviewed a middle-level manager at FPC.

We also provide case studies of Li Ruoping and of his predecessor as general manager of FPC – Liu Qiang.

## Organization case 5.1 Fushun Petroleum Company

### Company background

FPC is located in Fushun, a city of approximately 2.3 million people, situated about 45 kilometres northeast of Shenyang in Liaoning. Fushun was traditionally a coal city and is badly polluted. It also has a state-owned heavy industrial base. In the late 1990s in Fushun the state-owned sector comprised 90 per cent of enterprises in the city and employed in excess of 85 per cent of the city's workforce. FPC was founded in 1982 and became a subsidiary of CNPC in 1998 following the restructuring of CNPC and SINOPEC. On the eve of restructuring, in 1996, FPC ranked 25th among the 500 largest industrial enterprises in China on the basis of pre-tax profits and 60th on the basis of net assets (*ZGSYHGZGSNJ*, 1997: 601–02). FPC consists of eight subsidiaries: Fushun Nos. 1, 2 and 3 Oil Refineries, FDC, FEC, Fushun Acrylic Fibres Company, Fushun Plastics Company and Fushun Oil Storage and Transportation Company.

### Enterprise restructuring in FPC

Prior to restructuring, FPC faced many of the same problems as other large SOEs. The debt–asset ratio in FPC as a whole was 78 per cent, while the debt–asset ratios in

continued

the newly established subsidiaries of FDC and FEC were in excess of 90 per cent. This was much higher than the international oil majors such as Exxon and Shell, in which the debt–asset ratio is about 50 per cent. FPC had a large number of surplus workers. The proportion of surplus workers in Fushun in the late 1990s was higher than in most other parts of China, reflecting the importance of the state sector in the local economy. In the interviews conducted in 2000, one senior local government official told us that, in his view, the surplus labour force in the state sector in Fushun was as high as 70 per cent. Prior to restructuring, FPC was also saddled with a range of 'non-productive' social welfare functions, such as hospitals, schools, cafeterias and restaurants. In addition, FDC and FEC each had their own hotel, which did not charge a room rate, but instead were used to house visiting foreign experts.

Between June and October 1999 the subsidiaries of FPC were separated into production and service companies. When the restructuring process was completed at the end of 1999, the production company of FPC issued H-shares in Hong Kong and N-shares in New York as part of the listing of CNPC. To address the issue of the high debt–asset ratio, several avenues were pursued. First, most of FPC's debt was left with the FPC production company and CNPC used some of the equity raised through the stock market listing to reduce the debt level. Second, the central government waived some of the interest owing on the loans by FDC and FEC and converted some of the FDC and FEC debt into equity under an EDS. Third, the FDC and FEC service companies received tax relief following separation from the production companies.

Prior to restructuring, FPC had about 38,000 employees. Following restructuring, it had 36,000 workers, of whom just 13,000 were employed in the production company, while 23,000 were employed in the service company. Thus, as a result of restructuring, the overall workforce was reduced by just 2000. This figure, though, represents only those workers who cut their ties with the enterprise. It does not include workers who no longer worked at FPC but still retained links to the enterprise, such as workers classified as *li gang* or *xiagang*. The three subsidiaries of FPC that we visited in 2000 had few workers labelled *xiagang*. FDC claimed to have none, in FEC 3 per cent of its workforce were *xiagang* and FOR had about 300 *xiagang* workers. In FDC the label *xiagang* is given to a specific group of workers: 'the poorest-performing workers who are sent for retraining'. The term *li gang* is more commonly employed in FPC. Following the restructuring, FPC had 7,500 workers who were classified as *li gang*. These workers receive 80 per cent of their position wage until they reach retirement age. Because these workers were still officially employed by FPC, they were listed among the 23,000 employees of the service company. Thus, following restructuring, the service company actually had fewer employees than on paper.

As part of the separation of production and service companies, the local government assumed responsibility for a range of social welfare functions, such as funding for an elementary school, middle school and hospital. The cafeterias, restaurants and hotels were divested to the service companies. The objective was to make the service companies as self-sufficient as possible. This objective entailed marketing services to the public wherever possible. An example is the FDC service company, which was given the hotel, previously used exclusively to house visiting foreign experts. The FDC service company commenced charging a room rate and made the hotel available to foreign tourists. However, in the period after restructuring most of the service companies struggled to survive. This reflects the fact that the best assets were left at the production company. Take the FDC hotel, for instance. While it started accepting foreign tourists, it was always going to be difficult for a hotel to break even in Fushun, a city which is not frequented by many tourists. The service companies were unable to market products successfully to other firms and were almost 100 per cent dependent on providing services to the production company.

By 2006–07 the production company was profitable. It had raised large sums of money on the stock market and was benefiting from booming oil prices (*China Petroleum Newspaper*, 2007c). On the other hand, the service company was making losses. In June 2007, the FPC production and service companies were again merged. The merger was replicated in other CNPC subsidiaries in Daqing, Dalian, Jilin, Lanzhou and Liaoyang in the same year. In mid-2007 the merger of the listed and unlisted parts of the Daqing oilfields was also under consideration. These mergers have been met largely with indifference by the employees in the relevant CNPC subsidiaries. For example, one employee who had worked in the FPC production company told us the merger made no difference to him because his income and working conditions remained unchanged. Some middle-level managers in Liaoyang Petrochemical Company expressed disquiet that following the merger there will be less opportunity for promotion because there will be fewer managerial positions (XinhuaNet, 2007). By May 2008, it was apparent that one objective of the mergers in FPC was to streamline managerial positions. This has caused consternation among the managers in the service companies, who are generally less educated and less experienced than their counterparts in the production company.

The merger between the production and service companies of FPC was reported in the press as being for 'the harmonious development of the company' (Fushun News Network, 2007). This description can be interpreted as the profitable production company being harnessed to assist the loss-making service company. Mergers of profitable and loss-making enterprises in China over the last decade have been criticized by many observers. For example, Yusuf and Nabeshima (2006: 37) note that such mergers 'can burden successful firms with unwanted baggage rather than creating larger and more dynamic entities. It is much better to let market forces do their job, and manage development with the help of a sound competition policy.' The merger is a concession that the experiment to separate the production and service companies did not work. However, merging the production and service companies of FPC cannot be viewed as the same as merging profit-making and loss-making companies that have no shared history. The financial position of the service company at the time of the merger in 2007 was path dependent in the sense that it reflected the fact that it had subsumed all of FPC's non-core activities that made the listing, and ultimately the financial success, of the production company possible. Indeed, while FPC was separated into production and service companies, it never stopped being one company in the eyes of CNPC senior management.

While the service company did not become self-sufficient, viewing the experiment as a failure is misleading. The merged FPC of 2007 is a different entity to the company that existed prior to the separation in the late 1990s. In 2006, prior to the merger, the service company had about 18,000 workers and the production company had about

continued

10,000 workers. The workers that *li gang* ('left their post') in the late 1990s have since reached the official retirement age and have largely not been replaced, so the merged firm has approximately 10,000 fewer workers than it had prior to the separation. The debt–asset ratio has been substantially lowered using funds from the stock market listing and the enterprise is no longer responsible for a raft of social welfare responsibilities that have been transferred to the local government.

While CNPC is listed on the stock market, the board of directors and shareholders have little, or no, role in the managerial appointment process at FPC. The general manager of Beijing CNPC appoints the senior management of FPC. The general manager of FPC appoints the senior management in each of its subsidiaries, with some input from the party secretary of FPC. Most candidates are from inside FPC with few outside candidates given consideration. Managers that we interviewed at FPC were adamant that selection was based primarily on performance and that there was no political interference in the selection of managers. Promotion is tied to performance and non-performing managers can be demoted. Demotion is based on performance in an annual written exam. At FPC each middle-level manager contributes five questions to a database. An annual written exam is administered to middle-level managers based on questions randomly drawn from this database. Managers who score the lowest on the test are pinpointed as candidates for demotion the following year. If these managers do not improve their performance in the written exam the following year they will be demoted. However, while it is possible to be demoted for poor performance on the exam, such demotion rarely occurs.

Source: interviews with Mr Li Ruoping, general manager of FPC, in 2007 and 2008.

## Manager case 5.2 Mr Qiang, former general manager, Fushun Petroleum Company

### Background

Liu Qiang was born in 1964 in Faku County, Liaoning Province. He received his bachelor's degree in 1987 from Dalian University of Technology. In 1990 he received his master's degree from the same university. Liu had a rapid rise which illustrates the promotion possibilities for young, well-educated managers who gain practical experience in the state sector in China. From 1990 to 1994 he worked as an operator in the ethylene workshop of the FEC. In 1994, he was promoted to the head of the ethylene workshop. In 1997 he was promoted to become the vice chief manager of No. 3 Refinery of FPC. Later that same year he returned to the FEC as the deputy general manager. In 1998, he was promoted to general manager of the FEC. In 1999, he was promoted to become the deputy general manager of FPC and in 2001 he became general manager of FPC. In 2004, he left FPC and was appointed mayor of the Fushun municipal government. In 2008, he was appointed party secretary of Fushun Communist Party.

## Reasons for FPC's success, in Liu's words

At the Sixteenth Party Congress Liu was interviewed about the changes in FPC.

Reporter: What are the main changes in FPC since the Fifteenth Congress?

Liu Qiang: First, the company changed from a traditional company of various functions to a listed company. During this process, separation of production and service functions and strengthening of key parts of the company were completed. As a result, capital and resources were optimized; the organizational structure and operating procedures were rationalized and the company became more competitive. Second, the perspective of employees changed. In the past, the employees were completely dependent on the company. They 'wait for, depend on, and ask from' the company. Third, the environment of the company changed. There were a series of favourable policies from the headquarters of CNPC, such as reduction of debt, improving the social security system and the separation of redundant employees. The environment is a key factor for the success of SOE reform.

Reporter: What is the main measure to improve core competence?

Liu Qiang: There are five strategies, which are: increasing profitability, improving innovation, increasing talent, increasing investment strategy, and improving company culture. Among these five, the key is the profitability strategy of the company. To be profitable, there were two requirements. One is to improve efficiency, and the other is innovation. The company needs to import some mature technologies for innovation in order to improve existing operating efficiency, improve the quality of the product and lower production cost. At the same time, the company is researching and developing its own techniques, such as how to produce ethylene from heavy oil. This technique is especially relevant for Daqing oil. The technique is to change 'from oil to chemical', 'from heavy (oil) to light (oil)' and 'from gas (products) to solid (products)'.

Source: *China Petroleum Newspaper* (2002).

## Manager case 5.3 Mr Ruoping, current general manager, Fushun Petroleum Company

### Background

Li Ruoping is an example of one of the emerging, relatively young, dynamic leaders of large SOEs in China. Li was born in 1963 and graduated from the Fushun Petroleum Institute in 1985, majoring in engineering. In 2006, he received an EMBA from Northeastern University, where he is currently studying for a PhD on a part-time basis.

continued

Li joined FEC as an engineer in 1987 and, after exhibiting exceptional performance, was invited to join the Communist Party in 1991 (CCP News, 2007). He later became a workshop head and department head in FEC before becoming general manager of FEC in 1999. He was appointed deputy general manager of the production company of FPC in 2001 and general manager and party secretary of the production company of FPC in 2004. When the production and service companies of FPC were merged in 2007, Li was appointed general manager of the merged entity, while the general manager of the service company was appointed party secretary of the new company. He has received several citations for outstanding performance, including 'Model Party Member of Liaoning Province', 'Model Manager of Liaoning Province' and in 2006 'National Outstanding Entrepreneur'. He was a delegate to the Seventeenth Communist Party Congress in October 2007.

## Reasons for success

Li's success as a manager has been based on two factors. First, he has been forward looking in product development and pushing FPC products into international markets. In 2001, while still deputy general manager of FPC, Li suggested that FPC start producing a range of wax products, which are used in construction materials, electronics and rubber products. FPC now exports wax products to over fifty countries and FPC wax products have been patented in several countries, including Germany, Italy, Spain, Russia and the United States. FPC wax exports to the United States are exempt from inspection by the US Drug and Food Administration because of their high quality. In 2004, FPC's production of wax was 460,000 tonnes per annum, accounting for 35 per cent of China's wax exports (*China Petroleum Newspaper*, 2007a). By 2007, FPC's wax exports accounted for 15 per cent of world trade in wax, making FPC the biggest exporter of wax in the world (*People's Daily*, 2007). Since he became general manager, FPC's production of detergent, ethylene, diesel oil and gasoline have also increased. FPC is now the largest producer of detergents in Asia and is the only firm in China that produces diesel oil and gasoline that meet Euro 2 standards for light-duty petrol and light-duty diesel emissions. Each of these products is now exported to the rest of Asia, Europe and the United States.

The second reason for Li's success is that while many large SOEs have been criticized for blind expansion, Li has pursued a more balanced approach. Under Li, the development strategy of FPC has been 'competitiveness first, scale second' (*People's Daily*, 2007). Li has emphasized the benefits of corporate social responsibility, which couples growth with environmental protection. Prior to the Seventeenth Communist Party Congress, his attitude towards social responsibility was featured in a full-length article on page one of the national *People's Daily* in the following terms:

> Li Ruoping's philosophy on social responsibility is that people with skills but no sense of social responsibility are not talented, while companies that earn profits but lack social responsibility are not good companies. On the one hand, a company is responsible for creating wealth; on the other, it has to take responsibility for society as a whole. The ultimate objective of the company is to maximize the

value of the whole society. Establishing a harmonious society is not only the task of the Chinese Community Party and government, but a task for companies as well.

The final sentence of this passage is important because it links Li's conception of corporate social responsibility to the Hu-Wen concept of a harmonious society that stresses societal balance rather than economic growth *per se*. For Li, an important component of corporate social responsibility is promoting the environmental friendliness of FPC products. The article in the *People's Daily* goes on to state:

> Li Ruoping said energy conservation and pollution reduction is a strategic objective of the state. It is also an important part of the company's social responsibility. The leadership and staff of FPC have stressed the importance of environmental protection. Li said the focus of FPC is on ensuring harmony between the economy, energy and the environment.

In an interview in the lead-up to the Seventeenth Communist Party Congress, Li stated: 'economic growth on its own is not real growth; only green growth is real growth' (*China Petroleum Newspaper*, 2007b). Between 2002 and 2007, energy intensity in FPC decreased 8 per cent per annum and discharge of pollutants fell by 50 per cent (*China Petroleum Newspaper*, 2007b). Li's emphasis on environmental protection taps into an emerging environmental awareness among China's leadership. While much has been made of what Economy (2006: 171) calls 'the environmental dark side of China's economic boom', China is now rapidly, although still somewhat haphazardly, developing a system of environmental governance (Mol and Carter, 2006). China's leadership is starting to promote concepts such as green gross domestic product and national environmental model cities (Economy, 2006). Li's vision is not just for FPC, but for Fushun as a whole. He wants to transform Fushun from a coalmining city and old industrial base to a modern petrochemical manufacturer that produces clean energy. FPC is negotiating with the Fushun municipal government to develop a 'petrochemical development zone' which will house seventy projects with total investment of 9.5 billion RMB (Li, 2005). FPC's focus on being environmentally friendly under Li's leadership, particularly in an old coal city such as Fushun where pollution is extreme, has made FPC stand out from other large petrochemical firms. The prominence of FPC under Li in terms of building a 'harmonious society' is reflected in the fact that the firm has been certified as one of the hundred best environmental protection companies in China and has been endorsed as one of the main providers of clean energy for the 2008 Beijing Olympics.

Sources: various, as cited in the text.

# Key challenges

## Developing world-class industrial companies

While firms like FPC have developed internationally competitive products such as detergents and waxes, China lacks world-class industrial companies. Yusuf and Nabeshima (2006: 35) suggest that, with the exception of Haier and possibly Huawei and Lenovo, no Chinese industrial enterprise or enterprise group has the size, management skills and mix of capabilities to operate on a global scale. In the late 1990s, some, albeit heterodox, observers of China's transformation pinned their hopes for China building internationally competitive enterprises on the late industrialization paradigm (Lo, 1997; Nolan, 1996; Nolan and Wang, 1999; Smyth, 2000). These commentators pointed out that state sponsorship of big business groups has support from the experience of advanced capitalist economies in Europe and the United States in the eighteenth and nineteenth centuries, and the successful late industrialization programmes pursued by Japan and South Korea in the 1950s and 1960s.

China, however, is attempting to realize in just a few decades the managerial and organizational changes that occurred in the United States over the course of a century. China has been largely unable to replicate the success of industrial policies in post-World War II Japan and South Korea because the institutional framework of the Chinese state differs from those two counterparts. Sun (2007) presented a detailed study of industrial restructuring in the Chinese steel sector from the late 1980s to the early 2000s and found that the fragmented and uncoordinated Chinese bureaucracy substantially impaired the implementation of industrial policies. One of the most sobering evaluations of the achievements of China's industrial policies on the eve of China's accession to the World Trade Organization in 2001 was presented by Peter Nolan, a long-time supporter of China's approach and the relevance of the late industrialization paradigm to China's transformation. Based on decades of case studies conducted under the auspices of the China Big Business Programme at the Judge Institute of Management at the University of Cambridge, Nolan (2002: 130–31) concluded: 'The micro-level evidence of case studies suggests that, in most key respects, China's industrial policies of the 1980s and 1990s failed . . . The blunt reality is that after two decades of reform, the competitive capability of Chinese firms is still extremely weak in relation to the global giants.'

## Corporate governance and managerial depth

There is much evidence that firm performance is affected by corporate governance. Internationally, the importance of corporate governance has been highlighted in the fallout from scandals such as Enron and HIH. The collapse of Enron suggests that meaningful corporate governance depends on the composition, chairmanship and independence of the board of directors so as to provide oversight on accounting practices, auditing standards and business strategies (Gillan and Martin, 2007; Yusuf and Nabeshima, 2006). Large and medium-sized SOEs in China, including those listed on the stock market, are subject to weak and idiosyncratic governance. Where the parent company is not listed, but the subsidiaries are, the corporate governance relationship is often muddied. Jian and Wang (2005) document that a group-controlled firm in China is more likely to use related transactions to manipulate earnings and tunnel firm value. Chen et al. (2006) find that various corporate governance shortcomings in China are associated with the incidence of fraud. Liu and Lu (2007) find evidence of tunnelling in state-controlled listed firms and conclude that agency conflicts between controlling shareholders and minority investors account for a significant proportion of earnings mismanagement in Chinese listed firms.

The relationship between production and service companies following separation is also muddied by poor corporate governance. As discussed earlier, the evidence from case studies of EDS swaps in the early 2000s suggested these were not effective in improving managerial accountability. However, by 2006, there were over 1,200 SOEs listed on China's two stock markets and the formation of limited liability companies and limited liability shareholding companies was starting to have an effect on managerial accountability, with attempts to strengthen minority shareholder rights (Yusuf et al., 2006). This was starting to extend to the large SOEs in strategic sectors, with subsidiaries of the 159 'central enterprises' under the control of SASAC constituting one-third of the value of China's domestic stock markets (Mattlin, 2007).

Many large and medium-sized SOEs have dynamic leaders who are successful production managers and are achieving good results (Yusuf and Nabeshima, 2006). A few of the large and outward-looking SOEs as well as those that have entered into joint ventures are setting the pace. Companies such as Haier, the Jialing Group, the Meidi Group and the Guomei Group have sought to introduce new management approaches, including matrix management (Hu and Bao, 2003). The problem is at the middle-management level, where those with the professional expertise are lacking. The absence of managerial depth shows up in the structure of large and medium-sized SOEs. While the trend worldwide is towards flatter hierarchies, large firms with national or international operations must have the organizational resources and managerial hierarchies to deal with complex and widely ramified operations (Yusuf and Nabeshima, 2006). Lack of managerial depth is not specific to China. South Korea and other economies that are higher than China on the development ladder have also struggled to find good professional managers (Yusuf and Nabeshima, 2006). Since 2005, one response to the dearth of good professional management in the state sector has been to hire foreign managers in large SOEs (Yusuf et al., 2006).

## Labour redundancies and social unrest

In 2005 SASAC estimated that there were approximately 1.6 million redundant workers to be disposed of in SASAC-supervised large SOEs (SASAC, 2005: 69). Assuming the average cost of a redundancy package is three to four times the annual salary, or in the range of 60,000–80,000 RMB, Imai (2006) estimates that the cost of ongoing labour restructuring will amount to between 90 and 130 billion RMB, equivalent to 10 to 15 per cent of the annual expenditure of the central government. China has to go slow on redundancies because of the potential for social unrest and the embryonic nature of China's social security system. Even in a city such as Shanghai, which has resources at its disposal that are the envy of many other cities, studies suggest that 70 to 80 per cent of firms do not comply with the minimum prescribed social insurance contributions (Maitra et al., 2007; Nyland et al., 2006). The inherent conflict between promoting efficiency and social stability also undermines the ownership reforms. For example, Siqueira et al. (2009) apply a common agency model to demonstrate why enterprise reforms that assign SASAC a greater role in running China's SOEs are likely to fail. In a theoretical framework they show that local principals' incentive payments are likely to clash with those of SASAC as the former promote social stability while the latter bolster SOE efficiency.

Further undermining confidence in the embryonic social security system are scandals such as that which unfolded in Shanghai in the later half of 2006. Leading party and state officials in Shanghai, including Party Secretary Chen Liangyu and the director of the Ministry of Labour and

Social Security, Zhu Junyi, were sacked for allowing the misappropriation of some ten billion RMB from Shanghai's municipal pension and social security funds as capital investment in speculative real estate deals. It is likely that if there were large-scale redundancies in the state sector, the current state of the social security system is such that many workers would have neither unemployment insurance nor adequate pensions and many would lose housing, schooling and medical benefits (Yusuf *et al.*, 2006).

Demonstrations by workers laid-off from the state sector are becoming increasingly common, particularly in the cities of central and northeast China. Aggrieved workers have become much more vocal in reminding the state of its socialist claim to legitimacy and of promises of egalitarianism made during the Maoist past. One famous example is the case of Wang Shanbao, a retrenched fifty-five-year-old worker whose protest in 2001 took the form of drawing sketches of Mao on the pavement outside his factory. These drew daily crowds until the factory managers gave him back his job (Forney, 2003). Hassard *et al.* (2006) go as far as to suggest that a major crisis in urban China has been averted only because the unrest is still largely localized and sporadic in nature and because attempts to organize independent trade unions have been successful for a short period and on a small scale.

## Conclusion

The China of today would be virtually unrecognizable to the leaders who met at the Third Plenum of the Eleventh Central Committee in 1978. The market reforms have had a considerable effect for the better on the lives of millions of ordinary Chinese. Most of China's high growth over the last three decades is attributable to the rapid expansion of the non-state sector. Observers such as Qian (2002) have noted that the state-owned sector is an area where the reforms have yielded relatively meagre returns. The outcomes of attempts to build large SOEs and enterprise groups that can compete in global markets have not been as successful as had been hoped. The process of gradually improving the accountability and efficiency of SOEs through corporate governance reform and streamlining worker numbers has been a slow one. Progress has been impeded by a lack of depth of managerial talent and the need to go slow on redundancies because of the underdeveloped nature of the social security system and fear of social unrest.

China is at a critical juncture in reforming its state-owned sector. The importance of reforms to SOEs is crucial not only because of the traditional importance of the state sector in the former planned economy, but because of the intimate link between enterprise reform, financial reform and social security reform. Informed scholars of China's domestic economic and political interface, such as Fewsmith (2002), have speculated that if the Hu-Wen administration can make substantial progress on reforming SOEs, this will act as a catalyst for finalizing associated financial and social security reforms. Yusuf *et al.* (2006: 5) echo these sentiments, suggesting: 'It would not be an exaggeration to say the future level of growth in China will depend on completing the prolonged transition of the enterprise sector from a planned system to a market-based economy.' China is starting to make progress in improving the standard of management in the state sector. Recent attempts to improve minority shareholder rights in listed companies are starting to have an effect on improving managerial accountability, and recent moves to bring in foreign professional managers will add to managerial depth. With the fourth generation of leaders now at the helm, and continuing commitment to SOE reform confirmed at the Seventeenth Communist Party Congress, it is important that the process that was kick-started by their forebears at the Third Plenum of the Eleventh Central Committee be completed.

# Bibliography

Armitage, C. (2003) 'China's "iron rice bowl" gets the chop', *The Australian* (Sydney), 13 January, 12.

Bureau for Revitalization of the Northeast (2008) 'SOE reform in Liaoning has made significant progress', http://chinaneast.xinhuanet.com/2008–01/31/content_12369477.htm, accessed on 7 March 2009.

—— (2009) 'Revitalization of northeast China' http://chinaeast.xinhuanet.com/2009–02/09/content_15639320.htm, accessed on 7 March 2009.

CCP News (2007) 'Brief introduction to Li Ruoping', News Centre of the Seventeenth Communist Party Congress, October (in Chinese), http://www.cpcnews.cn/GB/105011/105472/6404593.html, accessed on 3 January 2008.

Chen, A. (1995) 'Inertia in reforming China's state-owned enterprises: the case of Chongqing', *World Development*, 26, 3: 479–95.

Chen, G., Firth, M., Gao, D. and Rui, O. (2006) 'Ownership structure, corporate governance and fraud: evidence from China', *Journal of Corporate Finance*, 12, 4: 424–48.

Chen, P. (2007) 'Analysis of the effect of the strategy for the revitalization of the northeast', *Social Science Arena*, January: 56–59 (in Chinese).

Child, J. (1994) *Management in China during the Age of Reform*, Cambridge: Cambridge University Press.

*China Petroleum Newspaper* (2002) 'Bigger and stronger is the first priority of SOEs: interviewing the 16th Chinese Communist Party Congress representative, general manager and party secretary of FSCNPC, Liu Qiang', www.oilnews.com.cn/gb/misc/2002–10/25/content_138138.htm, accessed on 11 May 2009.

—— (2007a) 'China's wax going to the world', 6 August (in Chinese), http://www.cnpc.com.cn/paper/2007/08/06/plate8/010.htm, accessed on 5 January 2008.

—— (2007b) 'Interview with representatives of Seventeenth CCP Congress – interview with Li Ruoping, general manager of Fushun CNPC', 18 September (in Chinese), http://www.cnpc.com.cn/paper/2007/10/18/plate1/002.htm, accessed on 3 January 2008.

—— (2007c) 'What should the petrochemical companies do following the increase in oil prices?', 15 November (in Chinese), http://www.cnpc.com.cn/paper/2007/11/15/plate2/002.htm, accessed on 3 January 2008.

Dong, X. Y. and Xu, L. C. (2008) 'The impact of China's millennium labour restructuring program on firm performance and employee earnings', *Economics of Transition*, 16, 2: 223–45.

—— (2009) 'Labour restructuring in China: toward a functioning labour market', *Journal of Comparative Economics*, 37, 2: 287–305.

Economy, E. (2006) 'Environmental governance: the emerging economic dimension', *Environmental Politics*, 15, 2: 171–89.

Eslake, S. (2006) 'Catch me if you can', *Monash Business Review*, 2, 1: 16–22.

Fewsmith, J. (2002) 'Generational transition in China', *The Washington Quarterly*, 25, 4: 23–45.

Fishman, T. C. (2004) 'The Chinese century', *New York Times*, 4 July: 1.

Forney, M. (2003) 'Worker's wasteland', *Time Magazine Asia*, 13 December, http://www.chinalaborwatch.org/news/031213.htm, accessed on 30 June 2007.

Fushun News Network (2007) 'Fushun CNPC more competitive following restructuring', 3 September (in Chinese), http://Fushun.nen.com.cn/80784422122553344/20070903/1889829.shtmlthe, accessed on 3 January 2008.

Gillan, S. and Martin, J. (2007) 'Corporate governance post-Enron: effective reforms or closing the stable door?', *Journal of Corporate Finance*, 13, 4: 929–58.

Goldstein, A. (2006) 'The political economy of industrial policy in China: the case of aircraft manufacturing', *Journal of Chinese Economic and Business Studies*, 4, 3: 259–73.

Groves, T., Hong, Y., McMillian, J. and Naughton, B. (1994) 'Autonomy and incentives in Chinese state enterprises', *Quarterly Journal of Economics*, 109, 1: 183–209.

—— (1995) 'China's evolving managerial labour market', *Journal of Political Economy*, 103, 4: 873–92.

Hassard, J., Morris, J., Sheehan, J. and Xiao, Y. (2006) 'Downsizing the danwei: Chinese state-enterprise reform and the surplus labour question', *International Journal of Human Resource Management*, 17, 8: 1441–55.

Hovey, M. and Naughton, T. (2007) 'A survey of enterprise reform in China: the way forward', *Economic Systems*, 31, 1: 138–56.

Hu, Z. and Bao, X. (2003) *Classic Management Models for China's Top Enterprises*, Beijing: Central Compilation and Translation Press.

Huang, G. (2001) 'Do a good job on the equity for debt swap', Speech to the Third Session of the Ninth Political Consultancy Bureau of China (in Chinese), http://www.beinet.net.cn/macro-econ/qg313.html, accessed on 22 December 2003.

Imai, K. (2006) 'Explaining the persistence of state-ownership in China', Institute of Developing Economies, JETRO Discussion Paper No. 64.

Jian, M. and Wang, T. (2005) 'Earnings management and tunnelling through related party transactions: evidence from Chinese corporate groups', Working Paper, Chinese University of Hong Kong.

Khanna, T. and Palepu, K. (2007) 'Emerging giants: building world-class companies in emerging markets', Manuscript, Harvard Business School.

Li, D. and Wu, C. (2002) 'The ownership school versus the management school of state-owned enterprise reform: evidence from China', William Davidson Institute Working Paper 435, William Davidson Institute.

Li, R. (2005) 'Develop the local economy based on petrochemical resources', Fushun News Network, 1 September (in Chinese), http://fushun.nen. com.cn/80784422122553344/20050901/1710301.shtml, accessed on 3 January 2008.

Li, W. (1997) 'The impact of economic reform on the performance of Chinese state-owned enterprises, 1980–89', *Journal of Political Economy*, 105, 5: 1080–106.

Liu, J. and Shou, Z. (2005) 'The approach for northeast revitalization with reference to the experience of Germany', *Commercial Research*, 15, 323: 188–89 (in Chinese).

Liu, Q. and Lu, Z. (2007) 'Corporate governance and earnings management in Chinese listed companies: a tunnelling perspective', *Journal of Corporate Finance*, 13, 4: 881–906.

Lo, D. (1997) *Market and Institutional Regulation in Chinese Industrialization 1978–1994*, London: Macmillan.

Maitra, P., Smyth, R., Nielsen, I., Nyland, C. and Zhu, C. (2007) 'Firm compliance with social insurance obligations where there is a weak surveillance and enforcement mechanism: empirical evidence from Shanghai', *Pacific Economic Review*, 12, 5: 577–96.

Mattlin, M. (2007) 'The Chinese government's new approach to ownership and financial control of strategic state-owned enterprises', Bank of Finland Institute for Economies in Transition (BOFIT) Discussion Paper 10/2007.

Mol, A. and Carter, N. (2006) 'China's environmental governance in transition', *Environmental Politics*, 15, 2: 149–70.

Morris, J., Sheehan, J. and Hassard, J. (2001) 'From dependency to defiance: work unit relationships in China's state enterprise reforms', *Journal of Management Studies*, 38, 4: 5–22.

Nolan, P. (1996) 'Large firms and industrial reform in former planned economies: the case of China', *Cambridge Journal of Economics*, 20, 1: 1–29.

—— (2001) *China and the Global Economy: National Champions, Industrial Policy and the Big Business Revolution*, New York: Palgrave.

—— (2002) 'China and the global business revolution', *Cambridge Journal of Economics*, 26, 1: 119–37.

Nolan, P. and Wang, X. (1999) 'Beyond privatization: institutional innovation and growth in China's large state-owned enterprises', *World Development*, 27, 1: 169–200.

Nolan, P. and Yeung, G. (2001) 'Large firms and catch-up in a transitional economy: the case of Shougang Group in China', *Economics of Planning*, 34, 1/2: 159–78.

Norton, P. and Chao, H. (2001) 'Mergers and acquisitions in China', *China Business Review*, 28, 5: 159–78.

Nyland, C., Smyth, R. and Zhu, C. (2006) 'What determines the extent to which employers will comply with their social security obligations? Evidence from Chinese firm level data', *Social Policy and Administration*, 40, 2: 196–214.

*People's Daily* (2007) 'Seventeenth CCP Congress Representative Li Ruoping: actively taking social responsibility', 19 September, 1 (in Chinese).

Qian, Y. (2002) How reform worked in China', CEPR Discussion Paper 3447, Centre for Economic Policy Research, London.

Siqueira, K., Sandler, T. and Cauley, J. (2009) 'Common agency and state-owned enterprise reform', *China Economic Review*, 20, 2: 208–17.

Smyth, R. (2000) 'Should China be promoting large scale enterprises and enterprise groups?', *World Development*, 28, 4: 721–37.

Smyth, R., Deng, X. and Wang, J. (2004a) 'Restructuring state-owned big business in former planned economies: the case of China's shipbuilding industry', *New Zealand Journal of Asian Studies*, 6, 1: 100–29.

Smyth, R., Wang, J. and Deng, X. (2004b) 'Equity-for-debt swaps in Chinese big business: a case study of restructuring in one large state-owned enterprise', *Asia Pacific Business Review*, 10, 3/4: 382–401.

Smyth, R. and Zhai, Q. (2001) 'Reforming China's large-scale state-owned enterprises – the petrochemical sector', *Asia Pacific Journal of Economics and Business*, 5, 2: 82–104.

—— (2003) 'Economic restructuring in China's large and medium-sized state-owned enterprises: evidence from Liaoning', *Journal of Contemporary China*, 12, 34: 173–206.

State Assets Supervision and Administration Commission of the State Council (SASAC) (2005) *China State-Owned Assets Supervision and Administration Yearbook*, Beijing: SASAC.

Steinfeld, E. (2001) 'China's program of debt-equity swaps: government failure or market failure?', Paper presented at the Conference on Financial Sector Reform in China, John F. Kennedy School of Government, Harvard University, 11–13 September.

—— (2004) 'Chinese enterprise development and the challenge of global integration', in Shahid Yusuf, Kaoru Nabeshima and M. Anjum Altaf (eds) *Global Production Networking and Technological Change in East Asia*, New York: Oxford University Press, 61–83.

Sun, P. (2007) 'Is the state-led industrial restructuring effective in transition China? Evidence from the steel sector', *Cambridge Journal of Economics*, 31, 3: 601–24.

Wei, H. (2008) 'Evaluation of the effectiveness of the policy of revitalization of the northeast and some new ideas', *Social Science Journal*, 22: 59–65 (in Chinese).

XinhuaNet (2007) 'Restructuring of Liaoyang CNPC', http://chinaneast. xinhuanet.com/2007–04/11/content_9752138.htm, accessed on 5 January 2008.

Yang, K. (2008) 'State-owned enterprise reform in post-Mao China', *International Journal of Public Administration*, 31, 1: 24–53.

Yusuf, S. and Nabeshima, K. (2006) 'Two decades of reform: the changing organisation dynamics of Chinese industrial firms', World Bank Policy Research Working Paper 3086.

Yusuf, S., Nabeshima, K. and Perkins, D. (2006) *Under New Ownership: Privatizing China's State-Owned Enterprises*, Washington, DC: Stanford University Press and the World Bank.

Zhang, W. (2004) 'Revitalizing the northeast and innovation of SOEs reform', *Macroeconomics Management*, 7: 37–39 (in Chinese).

Zhang, Y. and Wang, X. (2003) 'State Council establishing a bureau for the revitalization of the north-east taking a substantial step', http://unn.people. com.cn?gb/22220/29090/29091/2215224.html, accessed on 7 March 2009.

*Zhongguo shi you hua gong zong gong si nian jian* (*ZGSYHGZGSNJ*) (1997) *China's Petroleum Industry Yearbook*, Beijing: Petrochemical Publishing House (in Chinese).

# 6 The changing face of small and medium-sized enterprise management in China

*Li Xue Cunningham and Chris Rowley*

- Introduction
- Context
- Case studies
- Key challenges
- Conclusion

## Introduction

China's economic development and the importance of its large firms have received an increasing amount of attention in political and popular discourse, the media and academia. Since the 1990s, small and medium-sized enterprises (SMEs) have played an increasingly important role in this economic growth. For instance, according to some estimates, registered numbers of SMEs exceeded 4.3 million in 2007 (Xinhua News Agency, 2007). The same estimates provided the following figures on SMEs. Along with another 37.7 million individuals running their own household business in the country, SMEs in China account for 99.6 per cent of the country's total enterprises. SMEs have become important as a source of employment and as contributors to the economy and structural reform. At the end of 2005, for example, China's SMEs contributed 50.2 per cent of the country's total tax revenue and 60 per cent of its total exports. SMEs in China also make 66 per cent of the country's patent applications and more than 75 per cent of its technological innovations, and they develop over 80 per cent of its new products (Xinhua News Agency, 2007).

However, despite this growth and the fact that SMEs contribute 60 per cent of the country's gross domestic product (GDP) and over 75 per cent of urban job opportunities, they face enormous challenges as China integrates more into the world economy (Zhou and Xie, 2001). Influences, such as globalization, technological innovation and demographic and social change (Yu *et al.*, 2001), as well as the level of technology deployed, innovative ability, financial support and entrepreneurship, can be found in the business environment, and all impact as both external and internal factors. Therefore, how SMEs are managed is critical. Furthermore, whether management is changing in this area is also important.

The remainder of this chapter is structured as follows. First, we provide an overview of SMEs in China by looking at their historical development and examining their current situation in the socio-economic environment. The chapter shows that key political and economic reforms form a backdrop to the development of SMEs in China. It also demonstrates the significant role of SMEs in the national economy. Then, case studies on indigenous SMEs and managers are presented to bring to life the debates and issues. The evidence illustrates that institutions and culture play critical roles in SMEs' development, especially in shaping their entrepreneurship in China. Finally, key challenges facing entrepreneurs in SMEs in China are identified.

## Context

The context in which SMEs are grounded and operate is critical. We provide an overview of this and changes within it in terms of: key characteristics of periods of historical development; World Trade Organization (WTO) membership; labour markets in terms of unemployment, retention of talent and labour-management relations; and social inequality.

## Historical development of China's SMEs

In general, the development of SMEs in China can be divided into three key stages after China turned to state socialism after 1949, when the Communist Party took power.

### Pre-reform period (1949–78)

From 1949 to 1978 China followed the Soviet model of central planning based on the control of inputs and outputs (Anderson *et al.*, 2003). This ideology emphasized collective ownership and identity. It also asserted that the hierarchical control of organization was legitimate. All privately owned enterprises (POEs), including SMEs, were absorbed into the state sector of the economy. Unregulated markets were eliminated so as to limit the power of the 'capitalist entrepreneurial class'. As a result, private entrepreneurship was virtually eradicated and became a political taboo (Guiheux, 2006; Peng, 2004).

During this period, the development of SMEs rose and fell with the turbulent social and economic situation. During the 'Great Leap Forward' (1958–65), for instance, SMEs continued to develop in the first three years, stimulated by the 'people's commune' campaign. Conversely, SMEs subsequently declined and collapsed as the government closed down or merged them in the last three-year period. Finally, from 1966 to 1976, with the Cultural Revolution ongoing, SME numbers grew from around 30,000 to 80,000 (Zhou and Cheng, 2003).

## Reform period (1979–91)

After 1978 a highly centralized, planned economy began shifting towards a new, more market-based socialist economy, as China's policy-makers recognized the inefficiency of traditional methods of economic management, outdated technologies and market distortions. A series of reforms and open-door policies were initiated. As one of the key reform aspects, SMEs were emphasized by the central government as supplemental to the socialist market economy (Dana, 1999). SMEs developed steadily. The number of registered small business owners, such as POEs (more than eight employees) and getihu (literally 'one-person business', but used more widely for those with fewer than eight employees), in urban areas increased from 1 million in 1980 to 1.47 million in 1982 and 2.31 million in 1983. By 1992 there were over 15 million small business owners in industry and commerce (Dana, 1999).

Moreover, to reduce problems involving uncontrollable urbanization, from 1978 rural enterprise development was encouraged. As a result, township and village enterprises (TVEs) emerged, with an average 30 per cent annual growth rate (Zhou and Cheng, 2003). Further, while retaining the overall framework of predominantly public ownership, the government adopted a policy of opening trade and investment links with the rest of the world. Fourteen coastal cities were opened to overseas investment in 1984 (Anderson *et al.*, 2003). Large amounts of foreign direct investment (FDI) were encouraged by government policy. Importantly, FDI not only provided capital and entailed spillovers to local SMEs, but many FDI firms were themselves SMEs. However, despite the re-emergence of private business, entrepreneurship was 'shunned' in the country in the 1980s (Wehrfritz and Seno, 2003) and the role of the entrepreneur was considered suitable only for individuals who were unable to find other jobs (Nair, 1996).

## Post-reform period (1992–98)

With the 1992 renewal of economic reforms, China enjoyed faster economic growth, with an average annual GDP growth rate of nearly 10 per cent, and external trade growing by more than 15 per cent a year (Zhai and Wang, 2002). While China has consistently maintained its preference for public ownership as a means of achieving its version of a socialist market economy, entrepreneurship was increasingly encouraged by the government. As Malik (1997: 185) comments, 'the traditional entrepreneurial spirit sprang up in almost every corner of China'.

In this more encouraging environment, SMEs expanded rapidly in all ownership sectors. They not only helped to expand the scale of the market economy, but contributed to the creation of the system of socialist market economics as a whole. For instance, the role of private non-agricultural enterprises increased quite rapidly in light industry such as manufacturing, service and merchant activities in both urban and rural areas. These sectors had been neglected in China's industrialization strategy, which had focused mainly on the development of heavy industry. Since more than 95 per cent of SMEs are privately owned, this ownership structure also certainly influences the pattern of the country's economic growth.

Additionally, an increasingly significant role for SMEs in social and economic development encouraged some change in the mindset of the government, whose policies have extended support to all sorts of firms, and especially SMEs. For example, Jiang Qiangui, a deputy minister in charge of the State Economic and Trade Commission, asserted that large-scale production is not the only means of profit (Xinhua News Agency, 2002). Liu Mingkang, head of the China Banking Regulatory Committee, stated that SME funding would be a priority as the financial system restructures. Also, a 2003 law on SME promotion affirmed their role in the economy (Xinhua News Agency, 2003). Furthermore, counties and cities gave more attention to the development of SMEs for economic growth. For instance, Beijing hoped to boost SMEs by increasing international cooperation (*People's Daily*, 2002a), while Ji Yunshi, governor of Jiangsu, attributed the province's economic power mainly to SMEs (Xinhua News Agency, 2002).

Table 6.1 summarizes the key reforms that are associated with the major development of SMEs in China. On the one hand, the table indicates that the degree of change in policy has affected SMEs' development profoundly. On the other hand, the historical development of China's SMEs reflects the country's economic evolution. The development of SMEs in China also suggests that the influences on Chinese entrepreneurship from government policies and formal legal institutions have gradually shifted, moving from strict prohibition towards more tolerance, accommodation and encouragement (Peng, 2004).

## SMEs and World Trade Organization (WTO) membership

Since 2002 China has adapted its institutional and legal system to comply with WTO-related undertakings. An important change is that China has been granted the right to act as a 'player of equal footing' in the arena of trade and on the world political stage (Hsiung, 2003). Some commentators foresee large challenges for domestic enterprises, including increased competition, law reform and social effects. Others point out that the threat to domestic companies is in reality reduced since the government will find ways to protect them from foreign competitors. Furthermore, even if the advantages and disadvantages of WTO accession remain contested, its significance should not be understated since the implementation of WTO-related reforms will lead to far-reaching changes in the economy. Consequently, the development of SMEs and the entrepreneurship within them are profoundly affected.

First of all, WTO accession speeded up economic development, but at the same time increased competition within China, both among and between domestic and foreign companies. With SME development based mainly on economic liberalization, local government protection and the sclerotic transportation network, for example, the recent rapid construction of highways, which provide an alternative to state-run railways, has intensified internal competition as the barriers for new entrants into the market are removed (*Foreign Policy in Focus*, 1999).

**Table 6.1** Key economic reform policies and the major stages of SME development

| Year | Policy | SME development |
|------|--------|-----------------|
| 1978 | Open Door Policy; Joint Venture Law; Price Liberalization of Farm Products | A shift from a 'black' economy to a legitimate and formally recorded enterprise. |
| 1980 | Fiscal Autonomy to Local Government; Creation of Special Economic Zones; Private Income Tax | |
| 1981 | Individual Enterprises Encouraged in Urban Centres | **SME is a supplement to** |
| 1982 | Price Liberalization of Industrial Products; Patent and Trademark Laws | **the socialist market economy.** |
| 1983 | SOEs Taxed Instead of Profit Sharing; COEs Encouraged; People's Bank of China Begins to Assume Some Functions of a Central Bank | |
| 1984 | Fourteen Coastal Cities Opened up to Overseas Investment; Director-Responsibility System TVEs Created | |
| 1986 | Labour Contract System Introduced | |
| 1988 | SOE Contract Responsibility System; Regulation on PEs Published; Enterprises and Bankruptcy Laws Passed | |
| 1989 | New Regulations on Mergers; Joint-Stock Companies; Commercialization of Banks | |
| 1990 | Copyright Law | |
| 1991 | Delegation of Direct Foreign Trade Rights to SOEs; Pensions and Housing Reform; Establishment of Shanghai and Shenzhen Stock Markets | |
| 1992 | Deng's Southern Tour; Patent and Trademark Laws Revised; New Operating Mechanism and Autonomous Rights to SOEs | |
| 1993 | Decision of the Third Plenum on Establishing Modern Enterprise System; New Competition Law; New Accounting Standards Introduced | |
| 1994 | Foreign Exchange Reform; Fiscal and Tax Reform; Implementation of Company Law | |
| 1995 | New Commercial Banking Law; People's Bank of China Law; Provisional Regulations Guiding Foreign Investment; Insurance Law | |
| 1997 | Merger/Acquisition in Light Industry Sector so as to Form Large Conglomerates | |
| 1998 | SME Division Forms Part of the State Trade and Economic Commission | |
| 1999 | Constitution Amendments | Formally acknowledge the role of the private sector. |
| 2000 | The All-China Working Management Group for Promoting the Development of SMEs | |

**Table 6.1 (contd)**

| Year | Policy | SME development |
|------|--------|-----------------|
| 2001 | Some Comments on Intensifying Work on Managing Loans for SMEs; Several Opinions on Strengthening the Administration of Credits of SMEs; Establishment of an SME Agency to Institutionalize a Framework of Supports for SMEs | **SME is an important component of market-based socialist economy.** |
| 2003 | SME Promotion Law; Provisional Stipulations of the Standards of SMEs | |

Source: Cunningham and Rowley, 2008.

In addition, WTO membership has helped reverse the decline in FDI since 1999, when chaotic rules and poor infrastructure had made profit-generation difficult. After WTO accession, for instance, foreign investor interest revived. FDI rose by 15.1 per cent in 2001 to US$46.88 billion and in 2002 to over US$52 billion for the first time (*China Statistical Yearbook*, 2001, 2006). Since then FDI has continued to increase at a steady pace. However, the growth of FDI has exacerbated internal competition, social inequality and regional disparities as most companies prefer to invest in the coastal, rather than inland, areas. Partly as a result of WTO membership, hence, China's SMEs are not only facing threats from increasing competition within China but accelerated internal conflicts due to the growing diversity of ownership, new distribution patterns, and restructuring of industries (Zhu and Warner, 2003).

## Labour markets

### *Unemployment*

Figure 6.1 shows that the levels of employment between state owned enterprises (SOEs) and non-SOEs have changed as the reforms have progressed. It shows that the unemployment rate has worsened as SOE reforms have accelerated. According to official data, 26 million SOE employees were laid-off between 1998 and mid-2002 (*People's Daily*, 2002b). The number of unemployed was 14 million in 2002 and the effective rate of urban unemployment was 7 per cent, with total unemployment of 22 million, exclusive of rural surplus labour (Yuan, 2002). Simultaneously, the rate and number of the re-employed

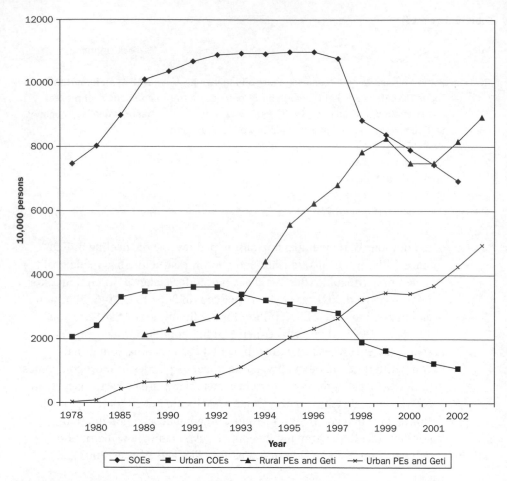

**Figure 6.1** Total numbers of employed persons at year-end by different ownership, 1978–2003

Source: Cunningham and Rowley, 2008.

deteriorated. Official data shows this collapsed from 45 per cent in 1998 to 27 per cent in 1999 and continued to decline to reach 25 per cent by 2000. Hence, both the increasing number of unemployed and the declining number of re-employed have put more pressure on SMEs as they have become the major option to absorb the massive number of laid-off workers from the labour market.

## Retention of talent

By 2005, the population of China had reached 1.3 billion (excluding Hong Kong and Macau), with 70.82 per cent of the workforce in employment. China also has one of the highest labour participation rates in the world, which was 83.3 per cent in 2004 (*Zhongguo Jinji Shibao*, 2006). However, a plentiful labour force does not mean a skilled workforce and may even constrain pressures to up-skill labour (and production). Indeed, some commentators point out that China's large population just helps boost labour-intensive industry at low cost in the initial phase of reform (*People's Daily*, 2003).

In addition, Zhu and Warner (2003) argue that the regulation of the Chinese labour market is insufficient to stipulate demand/supply of labour as it is still in a 'nascent stage'. As a result, there is a structural imbalance in the labour market, with a shortage of skilled professionals, on one side, and an oversupply of unskilled labour, on the other (Warner, 2003). Statistics show that by the end of 2004 the increased working population of 752 million contained only 20.6 per cent with qualifications above college level, equivalent to 'A' level in the UK (*Zhongguo Jingji Shibao*, 2006). Therefore, the unregulated labour market has led to sharper competition for highly qualified staff. Since most SMEs will not offer remuneration packages or promotion hierarchies similar to those available in larger firms because of their restricted size and resource base (Marlow, 2000), the difficulties in recruiting and retaining highly skilled workers have increased.

## Labour–management relations

The tensions among different interest groups are caused not only by social inequality but by the change in labour–management relations. Of course, there is debate as to whether there is something inherently 'different' about industrial relations in non-capitalist societies (see Hyman, 1975) or whether they are the same as in the West (Dunlop, 1958; Fox, 1966, 1974). Since the economic reforms, labour–management relations have metamorphosed from workers being seen as the 'master' ('*zhuren*') of enterprises to the more recent explicit relationship of managers and workers as employees in most firms (Zhu and Warner, 2003). Consequently, as management has increasing power over issues such as recruiting, labour contracts, promotions and so on, tensions with employees have emerged (Zhu and Campbell, 1996).

Large foreign-owned multinational companies (MNCs), such as Wal-Mart, Kodak and Samsung, have resisted attempts from the All-China Federation of Trade Unions (ACFTU) to establish trade unions in their plants. This is despite laws that allow unions at the 'behest' of workers (McGregor, 2005).

In addition, competition and insecurity have become more obvious. A report on Tangxia, Zhejiang Province, shows tensions among party leaders, unions and the independent workers' association and its members (Pan, 2002). Likewise, another study provides evidence of the strong sense of destitution and betrayal experienced by most state workers who used to be the 'labour aristocracy', while official statistics show that worker unrest is becoming more frequent (Mok *et al.*, 2002).

## Social inequality

As the gap between the numbers of unemployed and employed widens, social inequality has increased. Regional disparity has also increased (see Figure 6.2). Economic growth is much more rapid in the coastal areas. During the 1980s and early 1990s some of the most rapid rates of growth were recorded in the southern province of Guangdong in general and in the Pearl River Delta in particular, boosted by an influx of capital, technology and entrepreneurial skill from neighbouring Hong Kong. Since the early 1990s, Guangdong and Fujian have benefited from Taiwanese investment – most private sector analysts estimate that Taiwanese companies have invested more than US$100 billion in China since 1990.

More recently, official attention has been focused on promoting the Yangtze Delta, with Shanghai as the 'Dragon's Head', and western provinces have been left behind. For example, the contribution to the total GDP of Jiangsu Province (9.9 per cent of the total national GDP) was nine times that of Gansu Province (1.1 per cent of the total national GDP) in 2001 (*China Statistical Yearbook*, 2002). Meanwhile, income disparity among individuals has accelerated and was exacerbated after WTO accession. For example, high-income residents (20 per cent of the total of more than 40,000 urban families surveyed) owned 42.5 per cent of total wealth in 2000. The income gap between the top and bottom 20 per cent income populations grew from 4.2 times in 1990 to 6.9 times by 1996 and to 9.6 times in 1998 (Yuan, 2002). Clearly, the rich are getting richer in relation to the poor.

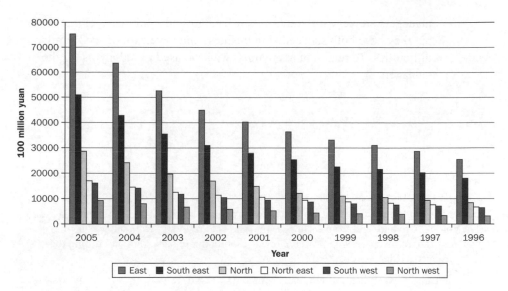

**Figure 6.2** Regional disparity in GDP, 1996–2006

Source: Cunningham and Rowley, 2008.

Regional and income disparity encourages a 'floating population' of economic migrants and the widening of gaps between skilled professionals and unskilled workers. It is reported that migrant workers have occupied almost 60 per cent, 80 per cent and 50 per cent of vacancies in the manufacturing, building and service sectors, respectively (*Zhongguo Jingji Shibao*, 2006). Social inequality has increased among and between rural peasants, migrant workers and urban employees. Consequently, the resentment and conflicts among different interest groups and regions have worsened and become a serious threat to social and political stability in China (Mok *et al.*, 2002).

As can be gleaned from the above points and analysis, SMEs, some of the major economic forces in the economy, are facing enormous pressures, both internal and external, to change. We can now explore these further in case studies of SMEs and their managers.

## Case studies

The following cases of individual owner managers and the development of their companies illustrate the successes and challenges for China's SMEs in a competitive and changing business environment. The two managers are very different in their backgrounds and management styles, but they have both succeeded in business and have experienced similar difficulties. To maintain anonymity, we have used pseudonyms for the managers.

## Organization case 6.1 Oriental Ltd

### Company background

Oriental Ltd (OL) was set up by its owner, Mr Liu, in the early 1990s, with 20,000 RMB (about £2000). The limited start-up fund had come largely from Mr Liu's close relatives. The company rented land from local peasants and set up several workshops. The main business activity is processing preserved fruits, including repackaging and selling the final products to different parts of China.

As the business expanded, OL gradually rented more land from locals. However, problems emerged because of a lack of quality control on products and an ineffective management of rental payment. In 1999, to solve these problems, OL moved its main production line into the Technology and Economic Development Zone, where a better business environment was provided by the province. In the same year OL started a formal recruitment process so as to find better-qualified and/or skilled employees. Ex-managerial staff from SOEs and university graduates have become OL's main sources of recruitment since then.

By 2005 OL had two distribution centres, three factories and 300 salesmen around the country. Besides domestic business, OL also exports its products to the overseas market via state-owned import/export companies. The total sales for 2005 were 2 billion RMB (£200 million), and the total assets were more than 1 billion RMB (£100 million).

Sources: interviews with managers of OL by Cunningham, 2006.

## Organization Case 6.2 NPG Ltd

### Company background

In the early 1990s, NPG Ltd was set up as a joint venture (JV) that produced parts for an automatic door system, while the partner in Taiwan was in charge of marketing and sales. The company rented an office at a very cheap price due to personal connections. The firm's machinery was imported from Germany to ensure quality. However, the business was not going anywhere because of poor market focus and a turbulent political environment. As its owner manager, Ms Xu, explained:

On the one hand, companies who produced household appliances could not afford to use our products due to their high price which stemmed from a high production cost. On the other hand, most large SOEs (i.e. hotels) didn't trust the product which was made by a JV. They preferred to purchase a similar product made in Germany. While the business in the domestic market looked gloomy, the sales in the overseas market were also badly hit, especially in the US, due to the student demonstration in Tiananmen Square, 1989.

In 1994 NPG shifted the focus of its business. It became a sole agency for a clothing brand from Taiwan. It also cooperated with a military service department to build a six-floor office building in the downtown area. In return, NPG got a freehold tenure for the top two floors of the building. Beginning with one brand, NPG started to expand its agency business to multi-brands in multi-regions.

In 2003, through a connection with local government, a repossessed industrial plant of about ten acres in the Technology and Economic Development Zone was bought at a very favourable price (two years after NPG bought the land, its value had doubled). In 2005 NPG set up its own clothing company with its own brand.

In 2006, the company had more than 300 employees, owned several factories, and ran more than forty retail shops in the region. On average, NPG's total sales per year are around 4 billion RMB (£400 million). The next step for NPG is to enter overseas markets (e.g. Australia). In the meantime, it is resuming production of the automatic door system. This time, the system will be sold to large Chinese shipping companies as a product that has been approved by the military.

Source: interviews with managers of NPG Ltd by Cunningham, 2006.

## Manager case 6.3 Mr Liu, owner manager, Oriental Ltd

Mr Liu came from a peasant family. He started his business career as a pedlar in the city when he was sixteen years old. In 1995, instead of working as a small street trader, he set up his own company, Oriental Ltd.

Mr Liu is keen on modern management concepts and practices. He has enrolled on an MBA course at the local university, attends business seminars regularly, and invites university professors to be external directors on his company's board. The company has also set up a human resource (HR) department, and the HR manager is highly involved with decision-making processes. Mr Liu described the essence of his company's strategy as:

> How to consolidate internal and external resources effectively rather than grow bigger. To achieve this goal, I believe a robust company structure is the key, since a good structure can provide support in forming a cohesive organizational culture, maximizing internal and external resources, and then gaining competitive

continued

advantages from both products and marketing. In addition, managing talented employees is a core concept throughout the business operations. Overall, my strategy to achieve business success is to have an accurate strategic plan, an effective team and a well-run system.

Mr Liu expressed his appreciation of China's economic reforms, admitting:

I feel very lucky in today's environment. Economic reforms are very helpful in supporting the business. Frankly speaking, I would not have today's success without reforms. If we were still in a planned economy, there would be no chance for me to have my own company. Nowadays, the government provides a platform for business to grow. As an example, I bought land (approx 4,000 square metres) to build a factory with little tax to pay, since the purpose of land usage in this location is to build a factory rather than accommodate houses.

Despite facing increasing competition in the domestic market after WTO accession, Mr Liu remains optimistic. He does not feel threatened by the situation, though there are some foreign competitors who are trying to enter into the market. Instead, 'there are many opportunities', he said. Because preserved fruit is a traditional product, Mr Liu feels that the difference in product market strategy results in a lack of direct competition between foreign companies and local firms. Saying this, however, he feels pressure from government institutions, such as the state bank, tax office and other financial departments. For instance, Mr. Liu complained about bank loans which had been rescheduled as the state-owned bank had shortened the loan period and tightened the inspection procedures.

Looking at the impact of Chinese culture on business operations, Mr. Liu sees the phenomenon of *guanxi* as a long-standing issue which can not be ignored. As he said:

It is difficult to change people's mindsets, traditional culture, and a value system that has been formed after thousands of years' development. Compared to Westerners, who care more about a clear standard and regulations, we are more concerned about interrelationships. Personal connection is the most important element in Chinese people's lives. My many business connections are developed based on a kinship, clan or region.

To form a better company structure, Mr. Liu is gradually going to withdraw from the company. He claimed: 'I am in a transition, namely, shifting myself from an owner to a professional manager, and ultimately, an investor.' In 2006, he resigned and appointed his brother-in-law as the general manager, though Mr Liu is still the biggest shareholder of OL.

Source: interview with Mr Liu, owner manager of OL, by Cunningham, 2006.

## Manager case 6.4 Ms Xu, owner manager, NPG Ltd

Ms Xu was an academic who worked for the state's medical research department after being a university lecturer. In the early 1990s her uncle from Taiwan showed some interest in business on the mainland and proposed her as the director for a company there. After taking a long time to consider, Ms Xu resigned from the research department and started the business as a self-employee. She recalled:

> It was very hard to make a decision at that time. I had a decent job with a nice working environment and a fairly good income. It also was my profession. To leave a steady, likeable job and start something totally unknown was out of my character. I still feel shocked by my courage when I think of it now. It was an adventure for me.

Ms Xu agreed that the economic reforms provided great opportunities for SMEs to grow. As she commented:

> We have benefited a lot from the reforms. The reforms bring energy into the business by activating the market, improving people's living standards and stimulating purchasing power. The overall economic situation has been improved. Indeed, the investment environment in the domestic market is much more proactive than before.

While emphasizing the importance of the reforms on the development of SMEs in China, Ms Xu argued that the major barriers, such as cultural boundaries, had prevented the entry of foreign companies into the Chinese market, and had therefore substantially reduced the impact of WTO accession. Even though there was increasing competition for finding and retaining highly skilled employees after WTO accession, Ms Xu stated that the impact of accession on the labour market was insignificant to her company. She claimed:

> There are ample human resources in the labour market. First, there are few difficulties in obtaining a large number of cheap workers, since government economic reforms created a mass of laid-off SOE workers in the market. Second, many university graduates who were born in the 1980s were available and looking for a job as well. For instance, there were over a hundred graduates who applied for jobs with our company in last year's recruitment conference. Indeed, the supply is greater than the demand. Facing the difficulties in finding talented personnel, we also began to train our own staff by sending them for further education, inviting specialists in for seminars, or creating forums for the exchange of ideas between professionals in the industry.

Ms Xu described *guanxi* in the business operation by stating that: '*Guanxi* is a device which acts as a bargaining chip. In today's highly competitive market environment, nothing works if you don't have the ability to perform. But if you have the aptitude and the right connections, you can gain a better deal for sure.' She continued to interpret the

continued

nature of *guanxi* in the market by noting that: 'In the market economy, *guanxi* is a phenomenon resulting from unfair competition and an inadequate legal system. *Guanxi* is an exchange of interests among connected parties.'

There is a growth of direct communication between management and employees, such as team briefings every Monday morning and various meetings between senior managers and employees. However, a hierarchical organizational structure and a low level of employee involvement are evident. For example, the information passed to middle managers and employees was selective and mostly based on business needs. Ms Xu admitted that middle managers obtained only information that was related to their departmental operation, and employees were merely informed when the information was performance-related and/or motivation-oriented. A trade union does not exist and the HR department is the communicator between the owner manager and her employees. One of the line managers in the company argued for the absence of a trade union:

> I don't think that it is necessary to have a trade union in our company. A trade union provides an opportunity for the employees to express their negative feelings. This will result in negative effects on the company and create problems in the job. In addition, a trade union does not have real influence on business matters since it does not have decision-making power.

> Source: interview with Ms Xu, owner manager of NPG Ltd, by Cunningham, 2006.

## Key challenges

The above discussion and analysis have shown that SMEs in China face a set of powerful, key challenges. These are influenced by: the institutional environment; national culture; and labour–management relations.

## Institutional environment

It is evident that state regulations and policies encourage the development of China's SMEs and their entrepreneurship. For example, a new logic for entrepreneurship was provided by Deng Xiaoping's famous statement: 'To be rich is to be glorious'. Following the 1978 reforms, new laws were enacted by the government to protect private property and intellectual property rights. To gain legitimacy within international institutions, such as the WTO, many laws were abolished or amended in order to respect private entrepreneurship and ownership of private property. Therefore, the formation of new institutions and governance structure are likely to promote entrepreneurship and support the growth of SMEs.

The case studies reinforce our argument concerning challenges to SMEs and their entrepreneurs by showing that institutional environment in China has a strong influence on the decision-making process in SMEs, especially relating to their organizational structure and the focus of their business practices. Although Mr Liu and Ms Xu came from different social backgrounds, the reforms and institutions have played critical roles during both of their companies' business expansion. For instance, land purchase at a very favourable rate was a key method to increase the wealth of each company. A good relationship with educational institutions always helped in generating new ideas for future development. And strong government support was a determinant in the business success.

While the reforms provided great opportunities for SMEs to grow, the turbulent political, economic and legal environment also created barriers and put pressure on firms' development. Following the 1989 Tiananmen events, for instance, the actions of the government's conservative faction severely impacted private entrepreneurs. It is estimated that PEs declined by 50 per cent in that year (Ling, 1998). The case studies also illustrate that entrepreneurs in SMEs have faced challenges not just from economic policy reform but from sweeping legal changes which ensure that domestic regulation of foreign economic relations conforms to WTO standards (Hsiung, 2003). By the end of 2000, legislation had been completed in seven areas, including customs, product quality, patents, contracts, foreign investment and so on. Accordingly, SMEs now face pressure from both the state and from international bodies dealing with trade regulations and labour standards. As Yeung (2002) points out, WTO accession tilted the playing field against SMEs through bureaucratic red tape and the enforcement of new government policies. Hence, entrepreneurs in China's SMEs have had to adjust their business plans to cope with the situation.

In short, evidence has shown that economic reforms resulted in dramatic changes in organizational structures, and led to SMEs in China becoming more market-oriented and profit-driven. Although the impacts were not straightforward, it is clear that WTO accession increased competition in the domestic market by lifting restrictions on foreign companies and putting pressure on domestic enterprises to follow international rules and regulations. As SMEs are highly sensitive to changing tendencies and environments (Siu, 2000), the volatile socio-economic situation in China creates more unpredictable elements in their day-to-day survival. Therefore, in line with Siu and Glover's (2001) discussion of the barriers to effective managerial practices in enterprises in China, our chapter and cases imply that the political, economic and legal changes in the Chinese domestic market may hinder accurate forecasting for SMEs, and hence increase their market risk in business operations.

Thus, this study suggests that the institutional environment has a strong effect on the development of SMEs and entrepreneurship. Consequently, to survive in such an institutional environment is one of key challenges for SMEs in China.

## National culture

Chinese cultural traditions have long been underpinned by four significant Confucian values that have great influence on people's mindsets and social behaviour (Bond, 1991; Child, 1994). First, 'harmony': keeping good relationships with reciprocal obligations and duties between members of the same clan. Second, 'hierarchy': respect for seniority and age, which means that older people and those of higher social rank can and should receive more respect and favours. Third, 'collectivism': thinking and behaving within accepted social norms and avoiding hurting others within the same kinship or same social environment. Fourth, 'family': the primary unit of identity and loyalty and the primary source of vertical loyalty and duty.

While these key values all have significant effects in social and working life in China, two major expressions of them have been identified by various authors (Child and Warner, 2003; Easterby-Smith *et al.*, 1995). One is *mianzi* (face), which is of particular importance as a critical element in harmony. The other is *guanxi*, which denotes relationships or particular ties among individuals. In Chinese society, 'you cannot clap with a single hand', as Han Fei-tzu aptly puts it. One must therefore expend considerable effort to maintain and extend one's social bank account, thereby nurturing the primary unit of identity and loyalty (Bond, 1991). Essentially, *guanxi*, as one of key characteristics of Chinese culture, reinforces the social bond that makes the Chinese system function smoothly (Child and Warner, 2003).

Our cases have confirmed that *guanxi* is important in today's China. Both managers argued that it is an important cultural factor that is difficult to change since it has become part of social behaviour. Moreover, Mr Liu pointed out that the influence of *guanxi* is now even stronger than it was several years ago (before WTO accession) because of the pressures from the highly competitive market and increasing unemployment. Ms Xu also implied that, to a certain extent, *guanxi* forms part of the social resource of China and has its own market value. She claimed that a positive *guanxi* could generate profit for the company by strengthening the cooperation and communication in the market, improving a firm's efficiency, and reducing its expenses. Consequently, *guanxi* is depicted by both managers as 'a kind of productivity', 'a resource' or 'a means'.

However, both companies also faced problems created by *guanxi*. Described as a double-edged sword, *guanxi* introduces a tricky situation into business operations. For instance, the HR manager at OL claimed that: 'Too much *guanxi* in the company results in unnecessary problems and difficulties in management. For example, on the one hand, destructive behaviour may be encouraged if the management ignores a problem. Conversely, a useful connection may be damaged by acting upon a problem with an employee hired by *guanxi*.' To avoid the problems, therefore, OL limited *guanxi* to a group of workers who were usually the least important in terms of business performance, such as part-time employees. Likewise, NPG started to shift its focus from recruiting new employees from external labour sources to improving the competence of their existing workforce. By doing this, both companies tried to minimize the effects of *guanxi* to the lowest organizational levels. In other words, where entrepreneurship in the West is about identifying profitable opportunities, in China, as Krug (2004) argues, the ability to form an alliance (*guanxi*) with those who control financial, physical or human resources is critical for success.

The evidence from our cases also reveals that 'respect for seniority', which remains a strong influence on people's mindsets, impacted effective communication within the companies. For instance, employees expressed concern about presenting ideas that were different from those of their managers since a contradictory idea might be taken badly or viewed as criticism by senior staff. On the other hand, when discussing the lack of feedback from his workers, a line manager from OL stated,'It is not a common practice in the workplace for workers to do such a thing. The workers are not used to the idea that they could come and talk to me freely about their job. They prefer to take an order and do what you say. They feel uncomfortable having a chat with you after work.'

As strong socio-cultural forces from the external environment, therefore, cultural factors, such as great concern for relationships, harmony and preservation of 'face', still influence management practices in SMEs in

China. In addition, our cases indicate that the impact of cultural factors on SMEs' development is yet more complicated and subtle. For Boisot and Liang (1992: 72), 'the Chinese enterprise's economic scope is narrower than a Western one, but its social scope is much wider'. Hence, another challenge for SMEs in China is to find a way to nurture cultural factors so that traditional culture provides support rather than becoming an obstacle to SMEs' future development.

## Labour–management relations

Our cases illustrate that a trade union presence was not encouraged in SMEs for both legitimate and practical reasons. For instance, employees from both companies expressed a preference for consulting directly with each other or through the HR department, rather than through a trade union. Line managers and HR practitioners also mentioned that there was no legal regulation that obliged owner managers to set up a trade union in their company. As the HR manager from OL pointed out: 'A trade union would have no real impact on the organization since the company is too small. Based on my own experience [previously worked as an HR manager in both SOEs and FIEs], in reality, a trade union may have some influence (around 10 per cent) in some larger organizations, especially in SOEs and FIEs.'

Second, our cases illustrate that employees' benefits in SMEs were minimal. Neither of the companies provided a full range of social welfare (i.e. health, pension, unemployment and minimum living standard insurance) for their employees. Besides showing that the companies overlooked legislative requirements even when they were applicable, the evidence showed that housing, training and free computer use were accessible only to a small group of employees in the companies, such as senior managers and key staff. Although neither OL nor NPG dismisses its employees, this is partly due to the negative consequences that may result from such dismissals, such as having to pay a large amount of compensation or damaged company reputation and brand image.

Overall, our cases showed that power in the workplace in SMEs was unbalanced, tilting strongly towards employers, and unitary in perspective (Fox, 1966). Therefore, soothing the relations between labour and management has become a key challenge for SMEs in China.

# Conclusion

This chapter provides an outline of the changing face of SMEs and their management in China. The historical development and current situation of SMEs in a socio-economic environment have been examined and discussed. The importance of SMEs is confirmed by the shifting role of non-SOEs in the economy, and the changing mindset of the government. Our study suggests that the performance of SMEs and the changing pattern of Chinese entrepreneurship are determined not only by environmental factors in the market economy but by institutional factors. It is evident that the development of Chinese SMEs and the entrepreneurship within them are strongly associated with key economic reforms. It is also clear that Chinese entrepreneurship is actively encouraged because there has been a rapid shift in formal institutions that deal with it. While the government plays an important role in SMEs' development, myriad factors linked to China's integration into the world economy are pushing through fundamental changes in institutions related to Chinese entrepreneurship.

In summary, the changing face of SMEs in China shows that SMEs and their management are vital to the nation's economy and the development of Chinese entrepreneurship. Yet, the increasing competition after WTO entry has created new challenges for Chinese SMEs. As one of the world's most entrepreneur-friendly countries (*America*, 2007), overcoming those challenges while promoting and facilitating entrepreneurial thinking and practice has become vital to Chinese SMEs' future development.

# Bibliography

*America* (2007) 'The next Bill Gates', 196, 2: 4.

Anderson, A. R., Li, J. H., Harrison, R. T. and Robson, P. J. A. (2003) 'The increasing role of small business in the Chinese economy', *Journal of Small Business Management*, 41, 3: 310–16.

Bond, M. H. (1991) *Beyond the Chinese Face – Insights from Psychology*, Oxford: Oxford University Press.

Boisot, M. and Liang, X. G. (1992) 'The nature of managerial work in the Chinese enterprise reforms: a study of six directors', *Organisation Studies*, 13, 2: 161–84.

Child, J. (1994) *Chinese Management during the Age of Reform*, Cambridge: Cambridge University Press.

Child, J. and Warner, M. (2003) 'Culture and management in China', in
    M. Warner (ed.) *Culture and Management in Asia*, London: RoutledgeCurzon,
    24–47.
*China Statistical Yearbook* (2001, 2002, 2006), Beijing: China Statistics Press.
Cunningham, Li. and Rowley, C. (2008) 'The development of Chinese SMEs and
    HRM', *Asia Pacific Journal of Human Resources*, 46, 3: 353–79.
Dana, L. P. (1999) 'Small business as a supplement in the People's Republic of
    China (PRC)', *Journal of Small Business Management*, July: 76–80.
Dunlop, J. (1958) *Industrial Relations Systems*, New York: Holt.
Easterby-Smith, M., Malina, D. and Lu, Y. (1995) 'How culture sensitive is
    HRM? A comparative analysis of practice in Chinese and UK companies',
    *International Journal of Human Resource Management*, 6, 1: 31–59.
*Foreign Policy in Focus* (1999) 'China in the WTO: the debate', December,
    http://foreignpolicy-infocus.org, accessed on 4 May 2008.
Fox, A. (1966) 'Industrial sociology and industrial relations', Royal Commission
    Research Paper No. 3, London: HMSO.
—— (1974) *Beyond Contract: Work, Power and Trust Relations*, London: Faber
    & Faber.
Guiheux, G. (2006) 'The political "participation" of entrepreneurs: challenge or
    opportunity for the Chinese Communist Party', *Social Research*, 73, 1:
    219–46.
Hsiung, J. C. (2003) 'The aftermath of China's accession to the World Trade
    Organisation', *Independent Review*, 8, 1: 1086–107.
Hyman, R. (1975) *Industrial Relations: A Marxist Introduction*, London:
    Macmillan.
Krug, B. (2004) *China's Rational Entrepreneurs: The Development of the New
    Private Business Sector*, London: RoutledgeCurzon.
Ling, Z. (1998) *ChenFu: 1989–1997 Zhongguo Jingji Gaige Beiwanglu* [*Ups and
    Downs: Memorandum of China's Economic Reform during 1989–1997*],
    Shanghai: Tongfang Chuban Zhongxin.
Malik, R. (1997) *Chinese Entrepreneurs in the Economic Development of China*,
    Westport, CT: Praegar.
Marlow, S. (2000) 'Investigating the use of emergent strategic human resource
    management activity in the small firm', *Journal of Small Business and
    Enterprise Development*, 7, 2: 135–48.
McGregor, R. (2005) 'Multinationals resist introduction of Chinese unions',
    *Financial Times*, 5 January, 1.
Mok, K., Wong, L. and Lee, G. (2002) 'The challenge of global capitalism:
    unemployment and state workers' reactions and responses in post-reform
    China', *International Journal of Human Resource Management*, 13, 3:
    399–415.
Nair, S. R. (1996) 'Doing business in China: it's far from easy', *USA Today*, 124,
    2608: 27–29.
Pan, P. P. (2002) 'When workers organize, China's party-run unions resist',
    *Washington Post*, 15 October.

Peng, Y. (2004) 'Kinship networks and entrepreneurs in China's transitional economy', *American Journal of Sociology*, 109, 5: 1045–74.

*People's Daily* (2002a) 'Beijing seeks international cooperation for SME development', http://www.peopledaily.com.cn, accessed on 5 June 2008.

—— (2002b) 'The situation of labour and social security presented by the leaders from the Ministry of Labour and Social Security and the ACFTU', http:// www.peopledaily.com.cn, accessed on 8 June 2008.

—— (2003) 'Higher priority to be given to human resource', http://www. peopledaily.com.cn, accessed on 8 June 2008.

Siu, W. (2000) 'Marketing philosophies and company performance of Chinese small firms in Hong Kong', *Journal of Marketing Theory and Practice*, Winter: 25–37.

Siu, N. and Glover, L. (2001) 'Barriers to effective managerial practices in China', *Asia Pacific Business Review*, 7, 3: 57–74.

Warner, M. (2003) 'China's HRM revisited: a step-wise path to convergence?', *Asia Pacific Business Review*, 9, 4: 15–31.

Wehrfritz, G. and Seno. A. A. (2003) 'Chugging along: no one saw China as one of the big "engines" that could drive the world out of a slump, until now', *Newsweek*, 42, 23 June.

Wong, L., Mok. K. and Lee, G. (2002) 'The challenges of global capitalism: unemployment and state workers' reactions and responses in post-reform China', *International Journal of Human Resource Management*, 13, 3: 399–415.

Wright, P., Szeto, W. F. and Cheng, L. T. W. (2002) '"Guanxi" and professional conduct in China: a management development perspective', *International Journal of Human Resource Management*, 13, 1: 157–82.

Xinhua News Agency (2002) 'SMEs vital for sustained growth of China's economy', http://www.xinhuanet.com, accessed on 8 June 2008.

—— (2003) 'Four Laws, two judicial interpretations put into force', http://www. xinhuanet.com, accessed on 10 July 2008.

—— (2007) 'China's registered SMEs surpass 4.3 million', http://www. xinhuanet.com, accessed on 2 June 2008.

Yeung, G. (2002) 'WTO accession, the changing competitiveness of foreign-financed firms and regional development in Guangdong of southern China', *Regional Studies*, 36: 627–42

Yu, J. G., Wang, Y. P. and Song, L. (2001) 'Zhongguo xiaoqiye fazhan zhanlue yanjiu [A strategic study on the development of small enterprises in China]', *Management World*, 2: 157–66.

Yuan, Z. (2002) 'Disidai mianlin yanzhong shihui tiaozhan [The fourth generation faces serious social challenges]', *Open Magazine*, December, 192: 46–49.

Zhai, F. and Wang, Z. (2002) 'WTO accession, rural labour migration and urban unemployment in China', *Urban Studies*, 39, 12: 2199–217.

Zhou, S. L. and Xie, Z. Y. (2001) 'Join WTO and the development of small and medium-sized enterprises in China', *Zhongguo Gongye Jingji*, 12: 8–14 (in Chinese).

*Zhongguo Jingji Shibao* (2006) 'DiaoChaBaoGao: woguo laodongli shichang fengchen mingxian, zongti suzhi dixia', http://www.sme.gov.cn, accessed on 21 May 2008.

Zhou, S. D. and Cheng, D. M. (2003) *A Study on Competitive Capability of Small and Medium-Sized Chinese Enterprises*, Nanjing: Nanjing University Press (in Chinese).

Zhu, Y. and Campbell, I. (1996) 'Economic reform and the challenge of transforming labour regulation in China', *Labour and Industry*, 7, 1: 29–49.

Zhu, Y. and Warner, M. (2003) 'Human resource management "with Chinese characteristics": a comparative study of the People's Republic of China and Taiwan', *Asia Pacific Business Review*, 9, 2: 21–42.

# 7 The changing face of performance management in China

*Irene Hon-fun Poon, Jean Qi Wei and Chris Rowley*

- Introduction
- Context
- Case studies
- Key challenges
- Conclusion

## Introduction

The Chinese economy has undergone substantial reform since the 1980s as a policy of gradual reform towards a market economy has gathered momentum. Economic reforms and new labour legislation have brought change to Chinese management and its practices, such as the introduction of labour contracts, the endorsement of performance rewards and contributory social insurance (Ng and Warner, 1998). These changes have also promoted fair competition and more open performance evaluation to break status demarcation. In combination with China's accession to the World Trade Organization (WTO) and the focus on 'informatization' strategy, two important consequences of this are the introduction of greater market mechanisms in human resource management (HRM) practices and commensurate changes in performance management (PM).

Previous literature has shown that performance appraisal (PA) practices in China were based more on seniority, political orientation and moral integrity than on performance, competence and business profitability (Cooke, 2008; Von Glinow and Teagarden, 1998). Chow (1994) found that Chinese managers perceived PA as a necessary tool for the 'proper' management of personnel. Zhu and Dowling's (2002) study argued that many traditional HRM practices in China had changed and there was clear evidence that a more complex and hybrid management model was emerging as a result of increasing levels of marketization and enterprise autonomy. How to identify, develop and evaluate intellectual capital, and how to motivate and reward workers to maximize their productivity can be challenges for many companies, especially knowledge-intensive firms. Developing a strategic performance system is hence important for companies to improve performance, allocate rewards, plan goals and control work.

Notwithstanding these changes, HRM practices in China, including PA practices, are different from practices in the West, even though they are, in many cases, adaptations of those Western practices (Deng *et al.*, 2003). As Saha (1993) argued, environment, national culture and organizational characteristics shape a country's HRM practices . In particular, the Chinese institutional environment, cultural values and type of firm ownership have influenced the adoption of Western HRM practices. So, if changes in the PM system (PMS) have indeed occurred, which elements of the system have changed (*change content*)? The difficulties in executing PA are widely reported in the literature. Given the fact that knowledge-intensive organizations are characterized by possessing a large number of highly skilled employees, it could be expected that PA of intangible intellectual skills would be even more difficult in them. So what factors have facilitated or hindered the implementation of new PM (*change context*)?

This chapter first reviews changes in the PMS that have taken place, or are currently occurring, in China. Knowledge-intensive industries are used as an example to illustrate the content and the context of change in the PMS at the industry level. Which key elements of PM have changed and which institutional and cultural factors have affected those changes are discussed. The chapter then provides four case studies to highlight the characteristics of PMS and change issues in various knowledge-intensive firms. The first two cases examine the context of change from an organizational perspective and the later two cases investigate the implementation of PM from a managerial perspective. These cases usefully provide detail and 'real life' examples and give 'voice' to issues, development and experiences in the area. It is concluded that while changes in the PMS have been observed in different types of firm ownership, the content of change is different. Organizational inertia, employee resistance and the role of HR clearly affect the implementation of PMS change.

# Context

PA is a widely researched HRM practice. Early research examined technical measurement issues and problems, such as the frequency of the evaluation process (Landy *et al.*, 1978), the format (Dipboye and de Pontriand, 1981) and the relationship between appraisal and compensation (Wanguri, 1995). More recent research has focused on social and emotional factors in PA. For example, Cooke (2008) divided the factors into behaviour measurement and outcome measurement. Moreover, there is tension in appraisals. Rowley (2003) explains that there is tension between the extent to which evaluation issues (such as pay, promotion and so on) are discussed and examined at the same time as development issues (such as career development, objectives and so on), and tension between methods, systems and procedures of PA.

Yet, the concept of PA has changed over the years. PA has usually been equated with annual appraisals which measure the entire year's effort of an employee, often in numerical terms (Rao, 2008). More recently the concept has been expanded to PM, a broader term that encompasses many elements and aspects of a system, for instance planning, development, improvements, recognition and so on. Many people (e.g. Armstrong and Baron, 1998) regard PM as a strategic and integrated approach which can increase the effectiveness of organizations by improving the performance of people and by developing the capabilities of teams and individual contributors. PM allows the company to retain and reward high performers and to offer guidance and improvement to poor performers (Smith and Rupp, 2003). PMS, Performance Development System and Performance Improvement Programme are some of the latest names for this concept.

# Content of change

## *Elements of PM*

While the functions of PM have diversified, the content of PM has also changed to fit with different functions. Ilgen *et al.* (1993) conclude from their extensive review of the literature that the four important elements of PM are: purposes of evaluation, characteristics of ratees, characteristics of raters, and evaluation methods. Chu (2002) extends the framework and includes six elements: purposes, ratees, criteria of judgements, methods,

**Table 7.1** Changes in the content of PM before and after 1978

| Key areas of PA | Before 1978 | 1978 to 1990s |
| --- | --- | --- |
| Target group | Workers and cadres | Workers and cadres |
| Frequency of evaluation | Once a year | Once or twice a year |
| Criteria of judgement | Heavily reliant on political loyalty and seniority | Good morals, adequate competence, positive working attitude |
| Evaluation methods | Superior rating subordinate | Management by objectives, internal subcontracting |
| Appraisal process | Self-evaluation and department assessment | Self-evaluation, peer-group opinions and department assessment |
| Emphasis of measurement | Political ideology | Individual and team performance objectives |
| Linkage to development | No linkage | Limited linkage |
| Linkage to rewards | No linkage | Line of sight too long |
| Function of PM | Monitor attendance and skill test | Evaluate performance (i.e. between individuals) |

timing, and process. This chapter consolidates previous studies and investigates several key elements of PMS, including target group, frequency of evaluation, criteria of judgement, evaluation methods, appraisal process, emphasis of measurement, linkage to development, linkage to rewards, and function of PM. Table 7.1 shows the change in content of PM in China before and after 1978 up to the 1990s.

## Function of PM

PM as a system performs many functions. It helps managers make administrative decisions, especially regarding pay and promotions, and meet developmental objectives, such as coaching staff and assessing training and development needs (Brumback, 1988). Cleveland *et al.* (1989) provide a comprehensive list of PM functions:

1 between individuals (e.g. salary administration, promotion, retention/termination, recognition of individual performance, lay-offs, identifying poor performance);
2 within individuals (e.g. identifying individual training needs, performance feedback, determining transfers and assignment, identifying individual strengths and weaknesses;
3 system maintenance (e.g. personnel planning, determining organizational training needs, evaluating goal achievement, evaluating personnel systems, reinforcing authority structure, identifying organizational development needs); and
4 documentation (e.g. criteria for validation research, documenting personnel decisions, meeting legal requirements).

Drawing from the literature review, a wide range of other functions of a PMS has been suggested. These functions include improving performance, validating personnel selection, facilitating supervisory feedback, providing a platform for organizational diagnosis, and assessing development needs (Jacobs *et al.*, 1980; Taylor and O'Driscoll, 1993). Recent studies also suggest that PM is a management tool to assess employees' efficiency in the workplace.

The change in PM function from an annual appraisal exercise to performance improvements through ongoing activities is also proposed in China. Zhu and Dowling (1998) noted that before 1976 the main functions of PA in China were administration and monitoring attendance. Since the 1990s, the new PMS has been more widely and systematically adopted by some Chinese organizations. Many Western management practices were introduced, including management by objectives, balanced scorecard, key performance indicator (KPI) and so forth.

# Context of change

## Institutional and cultural level

The PMS, as an important part of the organizational management system, is affected by the national and institutional context within which the organization operates. Stonich (1984) argues that PM in an organization should be in tune with its structure and institutional environment. Many researchers (e.g. Fletcher and Perry, 2001; Hofstede and Bond, 1988) also question the universality of Western performance feedback across national boundaries. The effectiveness of incentive systems with concomitant PM processes is likely to vary because of institutional heritages and cultural value differences (Hofstede, 1980).

Previous studies (Warner, 1993; Zhu *et al.*, 2005) show that a comprehensive, systematic PMS is difficult to implement in a collectivist society where it is hard to single out an individual who is accountable for results. Thus, China has a far weaker tradition of evaluating performance (Chow, 2004). Chinese culture places value on harmony and face; and great differentiation is uncomfortable and undesirable. Giving feedback in performance review sessions and free expression of views are very difficult in such high power-distance cultures. Work in collectivist societies does not emphasize individual achievement but social outcomes, for example maintaining harmony within in-group relationships (Mendonca and Kanungo, 1996). Thus, cultural factors may moderate the PMS.

### Managerial level

Furthermore, although changes in PM tools, forms and systems can be introduced, managers may not internalize the basic assumptions and guiding principles (Rowley and Benson, 2002). The extent to which new PM practices are implemented may be blended with existing values held by Chinese managers. Organizational inertia and resistance from managers deeply rooted in the historical heritages of Chinese companies can act as a brake on the full transference and absorption of the changes (Ding *et al.*, 2000; Warner, 1999).

## Knowledge-intensive industry in China

### Industry background

The trend towards a more knowledge-based economy has brought many changes in Chinese society in recent years. China has placed more emphasis on reforming and modernizing its information and communication technology industries than most developing countries. The Chinese government under President Hu Jintao and Premier Wen Jiabao devoted massive resources to implement the strategy of 'informatization' (Zhao, 2008). This means there is wide application of IT, development of talent to support the economy and promotion of innovation. The idea of the knowledge economy places the fundamental of HRM on a different footing (Soliman and Spooner, 2000; Storey and Quintas, 2001). HRM systems need to be geared towards creating and promoting a learning environment. Among the most important challenges to be considered are how to motivate and maintain key knowledge workers. This also puts the PMS at the forefront of the focus of knowledge-intensive companies.

Knowledge-intensive industries in China have achieved rapid growth, not only in terms of productivity, but in the number of people employed. Many knowledge-intensive companies have emerged from traditional, small-scale business operations to become large-scale, more enterprising organizations. The success of these companies relies on managing and developing knowledge workers. In the face of ever-increasing numbers of such personnel, a more comprehensive HRM policy is needed to address issues arising from these changes in business operations and management systems, both of which are becoming increasingly complicated.

In addition, knowledge-intensive organizations are often characterized by:

1  having intellectual capital as the most important asset (with physical assets of secondary importance);
2  gathering and applying new information and knowledge as essential for the success of the organization; and
3  producing mass customized products and services with close relationships with customers, suppliers and strategic partners (Edvinsson and Malone, 1997).

These characteristics imply that these organizations will require large amounts of human capital investment in sales and research and development (R&D). Employees, even at lower levels in such organizations, are required to be qualified and skilful because of the nature of the work involved. As intellectual capital is the key competitive advantage in knowledge-intensive companies, an accurate and realistic PMS is crucial to measure intellectual capital and motivate skilful knowledge workers.

## Type of firm ownership

Due to the nature of the Chinese transitional economy, various types of organizational arrangement have emerged, all with different threats and supports for PM practices. Indeed, change in the PMS varies by type of organization. The strategic orientation of the parent company can affect the adaptation of HRM systems in the subsidiaries. For example, state-owned enterprises (SOEs) have long been characterized by the traditional personnel administration system. Some studies show that even though China has been transforming into a market economy, many HRM practices, including PM, still carry the traditional legacy. Privately owned enterprises (POEs) have made significant changes in HRM policies, learning from Western examples, and have linked practices to the enterprises' strategic context (Law *et al.*, 2003; Zhu *et al.*, 2005). Multinational corporations (MNCs) have the advantage of direct connections with their home countries and thus have greater opportunities to diffuse HRM practices from the Western world (Shen and Edwards, 2004).

Owing to the fact that SOEs, POEs and MNEs operate differently in China, and hence may have different PMSs, it is worthwhile to compare the characteristics of PM and issues in the implementation of PMSs among various types of firm ownership. The next section presents cases from different firm ownership types to illustrate the content and context of change in the PMS and to give 'voice' to the changing face of PM in China.

## Case studies

A report by the China Salary Survey Database (2007) showed that, among the top ten highest-paying industries in China, the top three were knowledge-intensive: banking and finance, IT and high-tech. These highest-paying knowledge-intensive industries were probably the ones that required the best-trained and most highly educated employees and invested heavily in human resource development (HRD). Noticeable changes have been observed in the structure of the industries: for example, the roles of employees have changed from simple and controlled work to complicated knowledge and application of modern technology (Qing, 2001). These changes have contributed to the introduction of a series of transformations in HRM policies and practices. Thus, the knowledge-intensive industries represent an interesting and useful industry context for assessing change in PMSs in China.

In order to illustrate the content and context of change, four cases from banking, financial services, investment and pharmaceutical industries are presented in this chapter. Data are extracted from companies' websites, industry reports and the authors' long-term research and work experience in this area. Information was collected between 2005 and 2008 from many interviews with top managers, owners and representatives from

**Table 7.2** Background of case companies

| Background | Bank of China | Bank of America | Zhan Investments | Estra |
|---|---|---|---|---|
| Industry | Banking | Financial services | Investment | Pharmaceutical |
| Ownership | SOE, publicly listed in Hong Kong and Shanghai | MNC, publicly listed in New York and Tokyo | POE | MNC |
| Firm size (employees) | 200,000 | 1,300 in China | 1,500 | 500 in Shanghai |
| Year of establishment | 1912 | Founded in 1904, but started in China in 1991 | 1989 | 1993 |

Sources: authors' interviews and company websites.

HR departments. The use of case studies can encourage examination of multiple points of view and allow various voices to be heard. The first two cases examine the context of change in PM from an organizational perspective and the latter two cases investigate the implementation of PM from a managerial viewpoint. Table 7.2 summarizes the backgrounds of the case companies.

## Organization case 7.1 Bank of China

### Company background

Founded in 1912, BOC is one the oldest banks in China and one of the 'Big Four' state-owned banks (SOBs). Once 100 per cent owned by the central government, it was transformed into a public listed company in 2006, when it was listed on both the Hong Kong Stock Exchange and the Shanghai Stock Exchange. BOC is the perhaps the most internationalized of the Big Four SOBs, with over 600 branches in 28 countries, including Australia, Brazil, France, Japan, South Korea, Singapore, South Africa, UK, US, etc. Foreign investors, like RBS, UBS and ADB, were brought in as strategic partners to strengthen its strategy. Since then, several changes have been observed in BOC's HRM practices, in particular rewards and PM.

A high staff turnover rate in the banking industry, plus fierce competition from foreign banks after China's accession to the WTO, implies that attraction and retention of people are particularly important. Therefore, after BOC's public listings, the board of directors brought in many new ideas which triggered major changes in the bank.

continued

## PMS characteristics

BOC used to have a traditional PA method, similar to many SOBs. Managers usually set the goals for their subordinates rather than mutually discussing targets with them. At year-end there was self-evaluation as well as appraisal by direct supervisors and department heads. However, appraisal results were rarely communicated to employees.

BOC introduced a new PMS, which carried similar features to those in the large foreign banks operating in China. Its PMS included an objective-setting meeting, a mid-year review and a year-end evaluation. Evaluation was not only on individual performance, but also on competency (e.g. interpersonal skills, decision-making, etc.). A competency model was established to link performance evaluation results to rewards. It was believed that linking pay with the results of performance evaluation could improve outcome expectancies for employees, which in turn improved employees' motivation and organizational effectiveness.

## Issues in change in PM

Nevertheless, a few years after implementing the new PMS, several issues emerged. Although at the surface level new PA forms and evaluation methods were used, at the deeper level supervisors became confused as to why the bank had adopted the new scheme and employees had no commitment to the PMS. For instance, according to BOC's PM policy, supervisors were required to hold mid-term review meetings with their employees during which they were asked to discuss mid-year progress. However, most supervisors, in practice, did not follow the guidelines and ignored these meetings. The problem was that policies were formulated at the top management level in isolation and then cascaded down to each bank branch in a bid to attain a uniformity of objectives. Employees could not approach their HR department directly and line managers were not encouraged to provide feedback in the implementation process. A gap between policy formulation and practice implementation was apparent.

Furthermore, the new PMS has not established its position in BOC's corporate culture in comparison to Chinese culture in general. Giving feedback in performance review sessions and free expression of views were still not common practices in BOC. Supervisors feared that employees might feel upset and were threatened by negative feedback and weaknesses. A settlement supervisor explained that giving negative feedback 'caused individuals to lose face' and 'hurt the harmonious work relationship'.

Many modifications in the PM forms, processes and mechanisms were introduced thereafter. The HR department had spent a lot of time and effort pushing forward the new scheme, with little success. In many cases, the evaluation was not conducted on a systematic basis or the development had not received employees' support. This reduced the accuracy and significance of the new PMS.

Sources: www.bankofchinahk.com; personal interviews with senior managers and HR managers at BOC.

## Organization case 7.2 Bank of America

### Company background

BOA was the largest bank by assets and the second-largest commercial bank by deposits and market capitalization in the US in 2007. Its clients included 98 per cent of the *Fortune* 500 companies in the US and 79 per cent of the global *Fortune* 500 companies, which span Europe and Asia. It was among the first global foreign banks to enter the Chinese market in 1991. It currently operates four branches in Shanghai, Guangzhou, Beijing and Nanjing. In 2005, BOA acquired a 9 per cent stake in China Construction Bank (CCB), the second-largest bank in China, one of the Big Four SOBs. This stake represented the company's largest venture into China's banking sector. Under the agreement, BOA could access CCB's 14,000 branches nationwide and hence could reposition itself to take advantage of the opening of China's banking sector. Kenneth Lewis, CEO of BOA, described this as allowing the company to 'tap into economic growth to consider an investment in China'. This position is particularly crucial in the post-2008 global financial crisis as financial companies explore new businesses and attempt to secure new funds.

At BOA, HRM policies and practices are driven from the global headquarters. The Global HRM team plays an integral role in aligning HRM strategies to business strategies and cascades corporate policies to the regional HRM departments. These regional HRM teams partner with the business executives to ensure consistent execution of HRM policies across the region. The Country HRM team then provides local expertise in the labour market, and manages and delivers local recruiting, payroll and compliance.

### PMS characteristics

In terms of PM, BOA chose an ethnocentric approach and its PMS was inherited from its US head office. The assessment process included the use of competency-based interviews to measure key aptitudes, attributes and values that an individual must demonstrate to be successful in the job. Performance evaluation for senior executives also involved the use of the 360-degree feedback approach.

The advantage of having a global approach in performance evaluation was that it created, in BOA's terms, a 'cross-platform partnership'. As it was put: 'It's the unique combination of resources and talents throughout our global company that sets Bank of America apart. We partner within and across lines of business . . . integration is part of every business plan.'

### Issues in change in PM

Standardized PM forms and mechanisms were practised across regions and in overseas subsidiaries without much local adaptation. Customization of the PM scheme in China

continued

was not observed because modification required approval first from Regional HR and then from Global HR. A member of the Regional HR team believed that 'our business scale in China is too small to justify having local system'.

The implementation of standardized performance measures suggested that the US head office was concerned with consistent HRM policies across its overseas operations, and that it was interested in having the ability to compare employees' performance across countries. Nevertheless, transferring global practice without any adaptation to the local market led to at least two problems. First, a Western PM scheme was difficult to implement in the Chinese context. Line managers attributed the problem to the fact that its PM scheme was not well documented and supervisors were not well trained. Second, the performance review was done but, it was argued, PM was 'not seriously carried out in China' because the supervisors viewed the PM scheme as 'irrelevant'. An HR administration manager made an even more serious criticism:

> There is no official performance evaluation meeting. Each department has its own practice. It is not sure whether the department heads have actually conducted the appraisal. When we [HR] request written documentation of performance evaluation, the departments will give one to us. Otherwise, they will not submit the documentation . . . We can only trust that the departments have done the evaluation. This is the way of doing business in China.

Sources: www.bankofamerica.com; personal interviews with managers at BOA.

In addition to the overview of the organizational practices presented in the above two cases, we provide two case studies of individual managers to add detail and allow 'voice' to come through in this area of management.

## Manager case 7.3 Mr Tang (pseudonym), deputy managing director, Zhan Investments Holding Co. Ltd

### Background

As deputy managing director (DMD), Mr Xingyu Tang has led business development in Zhan since 2004. After obtaining his PhD from King's College, London, in the 1980s, Xingyu returned to China and chose to start his career in this industry. He initially joined a small joint venture (JV) held by Zhan Investments Holding and the local government. Due to his knowledge and skills, he soon become the general manager of that JV.

Zhan Investments Holding was founded in 1989, originally as a clothing manufacturing firm. It was then developed into a capital investment holding company and it is now one of China's top-tier domestic enterprises. Its five key business units are Zhan Science and Technology Group, Cerun Venture Investments Group, Zhan Group, Zhan International Cooperation Development and Zhan Science and Technology Venture Park Development. With Zhan's expansion into an investment holding company, Xingyu earned promotion to DMD of the holding company.

## PMS characteristics

The role of DMD required Xingyu to ensure that different JVs worked well and contributed to the success of the holding company. Consequently, Zhan Investments introduced a 'Total Budget Control' model. It managed its multiple JVs via an annual budget control system, which included budget setting and performance evaluation. A PMS was designed that was based on this model. As described by Xingyu, the main objective of its PMS was to 'measure financial objectives based on budget control requirements'.

The details of the PMS were as follows. The performance of executives was measured by several key financial indicators, such as sales revenue, total profit, stock and cash flow. Performance of non-executives was measured by individual job descriptions. Evaluations were purely result-driven and mostly based on financial data. While the whole PMS was simple to administer and easy to understand and measure, Xingyu, together with many other top executives, expressed concern over it.

## Issues in change in PM

First of all, performance objectives were solely set by the board of directors. Managers had no input into the objectives nor any involvement in the process. Even though Xingyu was a DMD, he believed that there could be unexpected events that were beyond management control and could affect the attainment of the rigid performance objectives.

Second, there was no formal HRM department in Zhan. The administration department performed HRM functions. However, the administration department was fully occupied with dealing with public affairs, recruitment, organizational structure and corporate culture. It therefore had little time to roll out the new PMS properly or seriously consider the career development of employees.

Finally, since performance was purely evaluated on the 'hard' figures, the 'soft' aspects (such as leadership, teamwork and customer relationship) were largely ignored. Xingyu felt that the new PMS could not give a fair and comprehensive evaluation of employees.

Sources: personal interviews with owner and manager of Zhan Investments Holding Co. Ltd. Pseudonyms have been used.

## Manager case 7.4 Ms Shen (pseudonym), marketing manager, Estra

### Background

Ms Peihua Shen has recently been transferred from the sales department to the marketing department of Estra. She is now in charge of a team of eight marketing professionals and is responsible for devising marketing strategy, maintaining customer relationships, and training, cost control and performance evaluation of her team. Coming from a medical physician background in Shanghai No. 2 Hospital, Peihua joined Estra's Shanghai office in 2002. She was not exposed to any PMS in her previous job in the hospital.

Estra is one of the world's leading pharmaceutical companies. It produces a broad range of medicines in several important areas of healthcare. It employs over 66,000 people worldwide, with 58 per cent of its workforce in Europe, 27 per cent in the Americas and 15 per cent in Asia, Africa and Australasia. In China, Estra pharmaceutical Co. Ltd (China) was established in 1993 and now has 12,000 employees. Its Chinese subsidiary is the largest Estra investment in Asia.

### PMS characteristics

At Estra, HRM policies and practices are designed by the head office and then transferred to local subsidiaries. For example, its PMS was designed to link up with corporate '4P' business objectives:

- Performance: to be sales leader in the industry.
- Product: to drive sales through share gain with core and new-launch brands.
- People: to build and strengthen talent base through recruitment, retention, PM and development.
- Productivity: to maximize productivity and business integrity while investing for growth.

These business objectives, together with PM, were cascaded to countries, departments and individual line managers. Line managers needed to achieve goals and implement strategy. Their performance was measured by some KPI in the areas of market share, department expenses control and staff turnover rate, as well as by several other behaviour indicators, such as leadership skills. In theory, the PMS developed by the head office had a clear linkage between performance, rewards and development.

### Issues in change in PM

While the PM scheme was well designed and developed, there were a number of issues when it was implemented in Estra (China). First of all, line managers were not involved in the rewards decisions. Pay decisions were always a surprise to the employees. Peihua commented that she gave performance ratings to her team, but the final decision about rewards was made by the top management, who did not have direct contact with team members. As she stated: 'Sometimes, there is no pay difference between the person who has 3.0 rating [average performance] and the one with 3.9 rating [excellent performance].' So there was no direct correlation between performance and rewards.

Furthermore, the local office did not follow through career development plans that were proposed by the head office. Individual development plans were drafted after the PA, but there was no proper follow-up to them. Training programmes were more related to present job duties rather than future career development. According to Peihua:

> While middle management does have training opportunities each year, those opportunities are short-term training courses or one–two-day international conferences . . . Our top management emphasizes coaching rather than knowledge acquisition through formal training and development.

Last but not least, the implementation of the PMS was unsuccessful because the HRM department was not functioning properly as it did not have a strategic role. HR staff performed only a supportive role and did not act as the agents between top management and employees or the bridge between the head office and China's subsidiary. Peihua attributed this to the fact that HR staff were not exposed to change in the PMS:

> The average age of our HR staff is about twenty-seven. They are too young and not experienced enough to implement firm policies. They cannot perform the change agent role in the PM system. They have not held a single meeting with me to explain the change in the PMS. Generally, I feel there is a lack of communication between the line managers and the HR department.

> Sources: personal interviews with a manager of Estra.
> Pseudonyms have been used.

## Key challenges

## Content of change

### Change in PM elements

PM, as a modern Western HRM concept and a new technique, has been embraced by many Chinese companies. In our cases, it was observed that there were changes in all key elements of the PMS (see Table 7.3). For example, the criteria of judgement changed from political loyalty and work attitude to performance results, skills and competency. Ratees were expanded to include people from different feedback sources (e.g. peer

**Table 7.3** Comparison of key elements of PMS

| Key elements | Bank of China | Bank of America | Zhan Investments | Estra |
| --- | --- | --- | --- | --- |
| 1. Target groups | All employees | All employees, both headquarters and overseas | Executives and non-executives of the holding company | All employees, both headquarters and overseas |
| 2. Frequency of evaluation | Once a year; mid-year review largely ignored | Once a year and mid-year review | Once a year | Twice a year |
| 3. Criteria of judgements | Both quantitative and qualitative | Both quantitative and qualitative | 100 per cent by results and based on hard figures | 60 per cent quantitative and 40 per cent qualitative measures |
| 4. Evaluation methods | Results and competency-based measurements | Results and behavioural-based measurements | Results measurement | Results, skills and behavioural-based measurements |
| 5. Appraisal process | Self-evaluation and supervisor assessment | 360-degree feedback (self, manager, subordinates and peer) | Self-evaluation and supervisor assessment | Self-evaluation, supervisor assessment and customer evaluation |

| | | | | |
|---|---|---|---|---|
| **6. Emphasis of measurement** | Balanced scorecard approach, includes financial, operational, customer and learning measures | Both financial objectives and individual competency assessment | Executives: financial figures Non-executives: individual job descriptions | Individual performance objectives, functional related knowledge, skills and leadership (e.g. customer focus, teamwork, learning/adaptability, leadership/people management) |
| **7. Linkage to development** | No plan | Link to personal development plan | No plan | Link to personal development plan |
| **8. Linkage to rewards** | Link to variable pay only | Strong link to total pay | Link to variable pay only | Some link to total pay |
| **9. Function** | Salary administration, recognition (between individuals), performance feedback (within individuals) | Promotion (between individuals), performance feedback (within individuals), organizational needs (system maintenance), legal requirement (documentation) | Salary administration, recognition (between individuals), performance feedback (within individuals) | Promotion (between individuals), performance feedback (within individuals), training needs (system maintenance) |

groups, subordinates and external clients). Both 'hard' quantitative financial objectives and 'soft' qualitative competence and skills were considered in evaluations. The results of evaluation were, to various degrees, linked to rewards and personal development.

However, not all changes were as smooth as envisaged and planned. It was found that some PMS focused more on results and short-term achievements than long-term learning and development. The connection between PM and cognitive learning/career development plans was somewhat missing. Banks, financial institutions and pharmaceutical companies are knowledge-intensive organizations. They require a large human capital investment. It is therefore essential for knowledge-intensive companies and their top management to induce changes in those PM elements that encourage knowledge workers to update product knowledge, improve long-term skills and enhance competencies.

### Change in PM function

As in our cases, the purposes of PM served as identifying strengths and weaknesses, setting appropriate pay levels, and evaluating subordinates' goal achievements. These purposes corresponded to PMS prevalent in the West. In SOEs, PM functioned as a salary administration tool and feedback source, or between individuals and within individuals function in the terms of Cleveland *et al.* (1989). Documenting performance and developing a plan were viewed as the least important elements in SOEs and POEs. PM in MNCs has a high impact on promotion (between individuals), performance feedback (within individuals), and identifying organizational and individual needs (system maintenance) and legal compliance (documentation). It seemed that SOEs, POEs and MNCs somehow used PM differently; and if change in PMS continues, they might not converge towards one another.

## Context of change

### Institutional forces

Why has change in PM occurred in China? One explanation is that a range of institutional forces has pressurized companies to gain legitimacy for their behaviour. Importing 'best practice', competition and cooperation, and opening the market created additional forces for change. China's accession to the WTO, reforms in the economy and the post-2008 global financial crisis have all brought rapid change and restructuring. Some institutions were replaced by new institutions and norms. As environments changed, companies changed to realign themselves with the new conditions (see the contingency approach suggested by, among others, Greer and Ireland, 1992; Lawrence and Lorsch, 1967).

## Cultural barriers

However, making changes in PMS or adopting 'best' PM practice did not automatically guarantee effective transfer and adoption. Culture can be a barrier to change. It is not isolated and unchangeable but constantly changing, being modified and transforming. Chinese culture is built on a long Confucian tradition of familism and authoritarianism, creating norms of dependence and acceptance of hierarchy (Redding, 1990). These societal values are in conflict with the development of individual responsibility and initiative (Child, 1991), which are central ingredients of Western PM practice. Therefore, this social heritage may restrict the introduction of performance-based pay at the expense of hierarchical position. The roles of 'face' and harmony are also significant aspects of social and organizational life in China. The manager who criticizes a subordinate, whether in private or in the presence of others, can cause that subordinate to 'lose face'. This can complicate performance feedback between managers and subordinates and upset group harmony (see Rowley and Bae, 2003). So, for new elements of performance feedback to be implemented in the Chinese context, behavioural changes among managers and employees are essential. HRM approaches and ideas tend to fit better with some cultures when developed and tested in culturally compatible settings (Rowley et al., 2010).

## Firm ownership

While the function and elements of PM have changed, different types of organization have used PM differently. Although PM practices in POEs and SOEs are now more formalized than before, their practices are still primitive compared to those used in MNCs. Our cases show that firm ownership can be an institutional factor affecting PM implementation.

For example, the pluralistic management style in POEs, owners' objectives and their belief in PM can all influence process, measurement and rewards. On the other hand, country-of-origin, dominance effects and pressures on international integration (Edwards and Ferner, 2002) can affect MNCs' ethnocentric strategy in the adaptation of PM to local situations (as in Organization case 7.2 and Manager case 7.4). The SOE (Organization case 7.1) made significant changes to its PMS, though the process was not easy. Some three years after implementation of the new system, there were still many modifications to the forms and mechanisms.

## Challenges in PM change in China

### Inertia and resistance

It was found that organizational inertia, deeply rooted in the institutional heritage of companies, can act as a brake on the full absorption of HRM changes (Ding *et al.*, 2000). Rules, standard operating procedures and patterns of decision-making were all emphasized and inhibited divergent changes. Organizations remained committed to retaining past, proven competencies, because doing so was more efficient than trying to develop new ones (see Organization case 7.2). In knowledge-intensive industries, being innovative to create and promote a learning environment and motivate and maintain knowledge workers are the keys to success. Organizational inertia and resistance to change in turn stifle knowledge companies' ability to alter current strategies.

### Manager ownership of PM

Resistance of line managers in the change process could hinder change in PM content. For example, line managers resisted change because they thought that the new PMS required them to do more work, such as in discussing objectives with employees and filling-in more evaluation forms than before (see Organization case 7.1). As a result, the new PM scheme never became popular and it was not internalized. Furthermore, the involvement of management in the implementation of PM could affect the internalization process. In Manager cases 7.3 and 7.4, we see that the line managers had little participation in goal-setting and performance evaluation, except for passively allocating predetermined objectives. Since line managers did not bear the responsibility in the process, they had little incentive to implement the change. As they were not required either to be accountable for the attainment of objectives or to monitor the progress, they did not have much dedication to the new PMS, but held a partial, pragmatic commitment to the change. The transfer process was mostly at a pre-institutionalization stage (Tolbert and Zucker, 1996) and at the surface level (Kostova, 1999), where few managers understood and adopted the new PM scheme. Corresponding change in HRM philosophies at a deeper level was relatively limited (Rowley and Benson, 2002).

## Strategic role of HRM

HRM can play a critical role during the change process, affecting the pace of change and institutionalizing change at a deeper level (Chang and Chi, 2007). During the change process, the HRM department can work to create a culture for change, bridging the gap between different levels, and add value to a business by building organizational capability. Whether HRM performs a strategic role in providing guidance to line managers and communicating PMS can affect the effectiveness of change.

The idea of the knowledge economy places great importance on HRM. Nevertheless, the HRM department has been generally underdeveloped and most HRM staff have emphasized the specialized functional aspects of their work — compensation, benefits, recruitment, training, etc. HRM practices have exhibited reactive and highly operational-oriented characteristics. The level of HRM sophistication varies across SOEs, POEs and MNCs. When the company does not have a proper HRM department (as in Manager cases 7.3 and 7.4), the relationship between the line managers and HRM can be problematic. Consequently, the implementation of change in PM can be hampered.

# Conclusion

This chapter provides an understanding of change in PM in China. Key elements and functions of PM were examined in various types of firm. In general, internal and external forces have led to changes in PM, but these also feel the force of resistance from contextual variables.

Many PMS changes have been sweeping through China's knowledge-intensive industries. It is difficult to estimate when these changes will stop. Change in the content of the PMS was observed in all types of firm ownership, but the context of change was different. No matter whether the changes were about the criteria of judgements, evaluation methods or appraisal process, companies faced delays and challenges. It seemed that the pace of reforming the old PA system in China was uneven; and the process was far from easy. This chapter has illustrated the evolutionary nature of change in PM in China.

While new elements and function in the PMS have been introduced, full adoption of a performance-based culture in China is still far from widespread. Shift in the content of PM practices could not be treated as discrete activities, nor could practices be considered in isolation from the context in which change took place. The move towards fostering a performance-based culture required support from many other areas, such as having a strategic HRM role in PM and involvement of line managers in the process. The lack of consistent change at other HRM principle levels suggested that some idiosyncratic cultural and institutional heritages remained crucial constraints on HRM change. One of the future challenges for HRM researchers is to access the complex interaction of culture, institutions and societal norms and to clarify the change in different contexts. Future studies need to be directed to a deeper level of the HRM system for a better understanding of the means and degree of change.

Practices associated with the new PMS have been transferred, to various extents, to companies in China. Yet, many practices have not yet been fully internalized in policy choices or system architecture (Rowley and Benson, 2002). The complexity of the transitional Chinese economy can involve the field of change forces operating at different system areas. As long as the facilitators and barriers of HRM changes continue to be present, future changes could occur and new practices could be expected in China. To have a more clear view, research on change in PM needs to be studied using a comparative approach across different types of firm, at different time periods and for different PM elements. Future studies can also deepen the links between PM and Chinese culture at both national and organizational levels (Wei and Rowley, 2009). In summary, this chapter has shown the changing face of PM in China to be complex and ongoing.

# Bibliography

Armstrong, M. and Baron, A. (1998) 'Out of the tick box', *People Management*, 4, 15: 38–41.

Brumback, G. B. (1988) 'Some ideas, issues and predictions about performance management', *Public Personnel Management*, 17, 4: 387–403.

Chang, H. T. and Chi, N. W. (2007) 'Human resource managers' role consistency and HR performance indicators: the moderating effect of interpersonal trust in Taiwan', *International Journal of Human Resource Management*, 18, 4: 665–83.

Child, J. (1991) 'A foreign perspective on the management of people in China', *International Journal of Human Resource Management*, 2, 1: 93–107.

China Salary Survey Database (2007) *The Present State of Salary in China*, http://www.xincou114.com, accessed on 1 July 2009.

Chow, H. S. (2004) 'The impact of institutional context of human resource management in three Chinese societies', *Employee Relations*, 26, 6: 626–42.

Chow, I. (1994) 'An opinion survey of performance appraisal practices in Hong Kong and the People's Republic of China', *Asia Pacific Journal of Human Resources*, 32, 3: 67–79.

Chu, C. M. (2002) 'The essence and effects of performance appraisal systems: adopting the expectation/reality discrepancy model', *Taiwan: NTU Management Review*, 9, 1: 113–52 (in Chinese).

Cleveland, J. N., Tziner, A. and Murphy, K. R. (1989) 'Does conscientiousness moderate the relationship between attitudes and beliefs regarding performance appraisal and rating behaviour?', *International Journal of Selection and Assessment*, 10, 3: 218–24.

Cooke, F. L. (2008) 'Performance management systems in China', in A. Varma and P. Budhwar (eds) *Performance Management Systems around the Globe*, London: Routledge, 193–209.

Deng, J. S., Menguc, B. and Benson, J. (2003) 'The impact of human resource management on export performance of Chinese manufacturing enterprises', *Thunderbird International Business Review*, 45, 4: 409–29.

Ding, D. Z., Goodall, K. and Warner, M. (2000) 'The end of the "iron rice-bowl": whither Chinese human resource management?', *International Journal of Human Resource Management*, 11, 2: 217–36.

Dipboye, R. L. and de Pontbriand, R. (1981) 'Correlates of employee reactions to performance appraisals and appraisal systems', *Journal of Applied Psychology*, 66, 2: 248–51.

Edvinsson, L. and Malone, M. S. (1997) *Intellectual Capital: Realizing Your Company's True Value by Finding its Hidden Brainpower*, New York: Harper Business.

Edwards, T. and Ferner, A. (2002) 'The renewed "American challenge": a review of employment practice in US multinationals', *Industrial Relations Journal*, 33, 2: 94–111.

Fletcher, C. and Perry, E. L. (2001) 'Performance appraisal and feedback: a consideration of national culture and a review of contemporary research and future trends', in N. Anderson, D. S. Ones, H. K. Sinangil and C. Viswesvaran (eds) *Handbook of Industrial, Work and Organizational Psychology*, Thousand Oaks, CA: Sage Publications, 1, 1: 127–44.

Greer, C. and Ireland, T. (1992) 'Organizational and financial correlates of a "contrarian" human resource investment strategy', *Academy of Management Journal*, 35, 5: 956–84.

Hofstede, G. (1980) 'Motivation, leadership, and organization: do American theories apply abroad?', *Organizational Dynamics*, 9, 1: 42–63.

Hofstede, G. and Bond, M. (1988) 'The Confucius connection: from cultural roots to economic growth', *Organization Dynamics*, 16, 4: 5–21.

Huo, Y. P., Huang, H. J. and Napier, N. K. (2002) 'Divergence or convergence: a cross-national comparison of personnel selection practices', *Human Resource Management*, 41, 1: 31–44.

Ilgen, D. R., Barnes-Farrell, J. L. and McKellin, D. B. (1993) 'Performance appraisal process research in the 1980s: what has it contributed to appraisals in use?', *Organizational Behaviour and Human Decision Processes*, 54, 1: 321–68.

Jacobs, R., Karifry, D. and Zedeck, S. (1980) 'Expectations of behaviourally anchored rating scales', *Personnel Psychology*, 33, 3: 595–640.

Kostova, T. (1999) 'Transnational transfer of strategic organizational practices: a contextual perspective', *Academy of Management Review*, 24, 2: 403–28.

Landy, F. J., Bames, J. L. and Murphy, K. R. (1978) 'Correlates of perceived fairness and accuracy of performance evaluation', *Journal of Applied Psychology*, 63, 6: 751–54.

Law, K. S., Tse, D. K. and Zhou, N. (2003) 'Does human resource management matter in a transitional economy? China as an example', *Journal of International Business Studies*, 34, 3: 255–65.

Lawrence, P. R. and Lorsch, N. (1967) *Organization and Environment*, Boston, MA: Harvard University Press.

Mendonca, M. and Kanungo, R. (1996) 'Impact of culture on performance management in developing countries', *International Journal of Manpower*, 17, 4/5: 65–72.

Ng, S. H. and Warner, M. (1998) *China's Trade Union and Management*, London: Macmillan.

Qing, W. (2001) 'The challenges facing China's financial services industry', in P. Nolan (ed.) *China and the Global Business Revolution*, London: Palgrave, 813–37.

Rao, T. V. (2008) 'Lessons from experience: a new look at performance management systems', *Journal of Decision Makers*, 33, 3: 1–15.

Redding, G. (1990) *The Spirit of Chinese Capitalism*, Berlin: Walter de Gruyter.

Rowley, C. (2003) *The Management of People: HRM in Context*, London: Spiro.

Rowley, C. and Bae, J. (2003) 'Culture and management in South Korea', in M. Warner (ed.) *Culture and Management in Asia*, London: Curzon, 187–209.

Rowley, C. and Benson, J. (2002) 'Convergence and divergence in Asian HRM?', *California Management Review*, 44, 2: 90–109.

Rowley, C., Poon, H. F., Zhu, Y. and Warner, M. (2010) 'Organizations – approaches to IHRM', in A. W. Harzing and A. Pinnington (eds) *International Human Resources Management*, London: Sage Publications.

Saha, S. (1993) 'Managing human resource: China vs. the West', *Canadian Journal of Administrative Sciences*, 10, 2: 167–77.

Shen, J. and Edwards, V. (2004) 'Recruitment and selection in Chinese MNEs', *International Journal of Human Resource Management*, 15, 4/5: 814–35.

Smith, A. and Rupp, W. (2003) 'Knowledge workers: exploring the link among performance rating, pay and motivational aspects', *Journal of Knowledge Management*, 7, 1: 107–24.

Soliman, F. and Spooner, K. (2000) 'Strategies for implementing knowledge management: role of human resource management', *Journal of Knowledge Management*, 4, 4: 337–45.

Stonich, P. J. (1984) 'The performance measurement and reward systems: critical to strategic management', *Organizational Dynamics*, 12, 1: 45–57.

Storey, J. and Quintas, P. (2001) 'Knowledge management and HRM', in J. Storey (ed.) *HRM: A Critical Context*, London: Thomson Learning.

Taylor, P. and O'Driscoll, M. (1993) 'Functions and implementation of performance appraisal systems in New Zealand organizations', *Asia Pacific Journal of Human Resources*, 31, 1: 20–32.

Tolbert, P. and Zucker, L. (1996) 'The institutionalisation of institutional theory', in S. Clegg, C. Hardy and W. Nord (eds) *Handbook of Organization Studies*, Thousand Oaks, CA: Sage Publications, 175–90.

Von Glinow, M. A. and Teagarden, M. B. (1988) 'The transfer of human resource management technology in Sino-US cooperative ventures: problems and solutions', *Human Resource Management*, 27, 2: 201–29.

Wanguri, D. M. (1995) 'A review, an integration, and a critique of cross-disciplinary research on performance appraisals, evaluations, and feedback: 1980–90', *Journal of Business Communication*, 32, 3: 267–93.

Warner, M. (1993) 'Human resource management "with Chinese characteristics"', *International Journal of Human Resource Management*, 4, 1: 45–65.

—— (1999) 'Human resources and management in China's "hi-tech" revolution: a study of selected computer hardware, software and related firms in the PRC', *International Journal of Human Resource Management*, 10, 1: 1–20.

Wei, Q. and Rowley, C. (2009) 'Changing patterns of rewards in Asia: a literature review', *Asia Pacific Business Review*, 15, 4: 489–506.

Zhao, S. (2008) 'Application of human capital theory in China in the context of the knowledge economy', *International Journal of Human Resource Management*, 19, 5: 802–17.

Zhu, C. J., Cooper, B., De Cieri, H. and Dowling, P. J. (2005) 'A problematic transition to a strategic role: human resource management in industrial enterprises in China', *International Journal of Human Resource Management*, 16, 4: 513–31.

Zhu, C. J. and Dowling, P. J. (1998) 'Performance appraisal in China', in J. Selmer (ed.) *International Management in China*, London: Routledge, 115–36.

—— (2002) 'Staffing practices in transition: some empirical evidence from China', *International Journal of Human Resource Management*, 13, 4: 569–79.

# 8 The changing face of mergers and acquisitions management in China

## Kun Huang and Fang Lee Cooke

- Introduction
- Context
- Case studies
- Key challenges
- Conclusion

## Introduction

Mergers and acquisitions (M&As) has been a major strategy deployed by firms to continue to grow, access resources, strengthen their market positions and exploit new market opportunities (Buono, 2003; Ghauri and Buckley, 2003; Harrison, 2002). It was reported (Cartwright and Schoenberg, 2006) that in 2004, some 30,000 acquisitions were completed globally, equivalent to one transition every eighteen minutes. The total value of these acquisitions reached US$1,900 billion, which exceeded the gross domestic product (GDP) of several large countries. Unlike Western economies, which have been through several waves of M&As since the early twentieth century, M&A activities started to emerge in China only in the mid-1980s and have gained popularity only since the mid-1990s. However, much of the M&A activities took place between Chinese firms. Cross-border M&A deals remain a relatively small proportion and insufficiently understood (Cooke, 2008a). This is in spite of the fact that China is one of the largest foreign direct investment (FDI) recipient countries in the world. What is known is that cross-border M&As in China mainly take place in the form of acquisitions and that acquisition activities in the twenty-first century are shifting away from traditional industries towards new, high-tech and high-value-added industries (Wang *et al.*, 2004).

Meanwhile, the information technology (IT) industry, a relatively new industry but designated as a strategic industry by the Chinese government, has been expanding rapidly (Cooke, 2008a; Lu, 2000; Roseman, 2005). The explosive growth of China's electronics and IT industry is necessarily a result of its catching up with the technology through technological adaptation and innovation in the last decade or so (e.g. Fan, 2006; Lu, 2000). It is believed that China's telecom-equipment market is one of the most competitive in the world and that 'innovation capability and self-developed technologies have been the key to their catching-up with the multinational corporations (MNCs) and to determine who the domestic industrial leaders are' (Fan, 2006: 362). In some areas, Chinese firms are now among the world's technology leaders. The most successful of them is perhaps Huawei, which has established itself as a strong global competitor through heavy investment in the development of the third-generation (3G) mobile communication systems and the global system for mobile communications (Cooke, 2008a). Its global expansion since the early 2000s has been achieved through low cost, high quality, speedy customer service and strategic alliances with leading international telecom operators in the host countries (Cooke, 2008b). As Kambil and Lee (2004: 1) observed:

> Everyone recognizes China as a low-cost manufacturer and a huge potential market. But most do not realize China is emerging as a key player in shaping technology standards – standards that could define the nature of global competition in the technology, media and telecommunications sector for years to come. From operating systems and software applications to storage media, wireless communications and satellite positioning, Chinese Government agencies and companies are looking to break the hold of developed economies on standards and working to shape new technology standards for economic advantage.

China is one of the world's largest cellular mobile markets with an output of 548 million mobile phones in 2007 (Xinhua News Agency, 2008). About three-quarters of the mobile phones produced were for export (*China Daily*, 2007). By the end of 2006, the country had a total of 461 million mobile phone subscribers and 137 million Internet users, a sharp increase from 145 million and 33.7 million, respectively, in 2001 (*China Statistical Yearbook 2007*). With the explosive growth of mobile phone and Internet subscribers in the last decade, the Chinese information communication technology (ICT) market has been a lucrative as well as a competitive arena for many Chinese and foreign firms.

This chapter first provides an overview of the brief history of M&As in China, with a focus on foreign investors' acquisition activities there. It then provides two company case studies and two manager case studies that summarize the acquisitions of private Chinese firms by foreign-owned MNCs in the IT and telecom industry. These case study examples reveal the motives and processes of the acquisitions, the bargaining power held by the two parties, the challenges of post-acquisition integration and the new business dynamics that emerged during the post-acquisition integration. The chapter then outlines some of the key challenges facing cross-border acquisitions in China. These include: regulative confusion, limited availability of professional services to facilitate M&As, competence deficiency of Chinese management in handling cross-border M&As, and interventions from local government. The chapter concludes that post-acquisition integration and development is often an emerging process rather than an execution of a predefined plan and that a value-added business strategy and high commitment model of HRM are crucial factors for successful acquisitions.

## Context

While the words 'mergers' and 'acquisitions' are often used inter-changeably in academic literature and in the business world (Ghauri and Buckley, 2003), they can be distinguished in terms of the various degrees to which the target's ownership and assets are transferred before and after M&As. In a merger, the new entity combined by two originally separate corporations is often owned by the shareholders from two merged parties. By contrast, the acquired firm in an acquisition may lose its ownership and is most likely to become a subsidiary or business unit of the acquirer (Ghauri and Buckley, 2003; Sudarsanam, 1995, 2003). Consequently, acquisitions seem to bring greater challenges than mergers (Child et al., 2001; Hubbard, 1999). This is in part because the former tend to trigger more radical organizational change that may lead to stronger, and what are often perceived as negative, impacts on the workforce, such as redundancy, relocation, cultural change and loss of organizational identity. It must be noted that, in reality, the number of genuine mergers is very small – usually, although the deal is initially presented as two equal partners combining, in the end one party tends to dominate the other (Ghauri and Buckley, 2003).

## Cross-border acquisitions in China

M&A activities have grown rapidly in the last two decades in China, with a 20 per cent increase annually in recent years (*China Business*, 2005). It was reported that the M&A deal volumes (excluding outbound transactions) grew by 18 per cent to over 1,700 transactions and 25 per cent by value to over US$80 billion between 2006 and 2007 (Third Annual Mergers and Acquisition Proceedings, 2008). In 2006, inbound acquisitions of Chinese companies by foreign firms were reported to be in the vicinity of US$20 billion, accounting for nearly one-third of the total foreign investment in China (*People's Daily Online*, 2007). It is believed that a growing number of global MNCs are buying a stake of Chinese firms as part of their strategic development in China (Wang *et al.*, 2004; Cooke, 2008a). Market access, expansion of domestic customer base and distribution network, and acquisition of low-cost capacity have been the major driving forces for foreign firms' acquisition of Chinese businesses across all sectors (Jin *et al.*, 2003; *People's Daily Online*, 2007).

Acquisitions, rather than mergers, have been the main form of Sino-foreign alliances (Cooke, 2008a). In line with the overall pattern of FDI in China, the majority of cross-border acquisitions have been taking place in the manufacturing sector, though expanding into other sectors in recent years. Manufacturing has been characterized by relatively high capital investment and technological content. The sector also has the comparative advantage of cheap labour costs. Foreign-invested firms are now well established in this sector, with garments, footwear, toys, drinks, automobiles, petrochemicals and engineering the most popular industries for investment. For example, by the late 1990s, ten of the fifty largest and strongest Chinese tyre factories were acquired by MNCs (Chen, 1999). China's pharmaceutical industry and the medical market is another entry point for MNCs through M&As. By the late 1990s, over 45 per cent of the key Chinese pharmaceutical companies had been acquired by MNCs (Chen, 1999).

In addition, China's accession to the WTO and the subsequent opening up of its retail industry to FDI have persuaded the majority of the world's leading retail giants to set up operations in China. More recently, M&A focus has been turning to the finance and banking, telecommunication, energy and insurance industries. M&A is now an important channel for Chinese enterprises to expand, consolidate and compete in the international market (Cooke, 2008a). According to stock market statistics, by early 2003, over 400 foreign banks had either entered or were preparing to enter China's banking sector following the opening up of the industry. More than half of them were already operating in China (Wang, 2003).

The relatively brief history of acquisitions of Chinese firms by foreign investors can be divided into two periods. The first was between the mid-1980s and the mid-1990s; the second from the mid-1990s to the present. During the first period, foreign firms were not allowed to form wholly owned enterprises in China. Instead, they had to form joint ventures with Chinese firms, particularly state-owned enterprises (SOEs). The first period was therefore characterized by the acquisition of SOEs, often as a forced marriage by the Chinese government in an attempt to revitalize ailing SOEs by injecting capital investment, enhancing technological capacity and improving managerial ability. This policy of investment allowed the government a tight control of the operation of foreign firms in China (Björkman and Lu, 2001; Cooke, 2008a; Nolan, 2004; Pomfret, 1991).

Following the abandonment of this policy in the mid-1990s, the second period of acquisitions took off in different directions in terms of the variety of ownership forms and business sectors. In the 1990s, foreign firms mainly acquired smaller SOEs that might be average performers. In the twenty-first century, though, their acquisition activities in China have become more strategic. As the Chinese government has opened up its industries to FDI, foreign firms have started to target larger, profit-making Chinese firms that are key players in their respective industries, instead of acquiring individual enterprises on an *ad hoc* basis. The motivation is to become the key player in the industry and change the dynamics of the competition. For example, in the 1990s, foreign MNCs acquired and gradually dominated the drinks, cosmetics, detergents and film-making industries. This century, MNCs have been expanding into China's rubber, pharmaceutical, and household electrical appliance industries. In the 1980s, MNCs entered the Chinese market with capital and technology assets. In the 1990s, they entered with their own brand-name products that replaced Chinese brands, or they acquired the Chinese brands and then replaced them with their own (Cooke, 2008a). By the end of 2006, there were a total of 274,863 foreign-funded enterprises registered in China – 187,458 in the manufacturing industry, 15,786 in wholesale and retail trades, 14,438 in real estate, and 7,045 in the information transmission, computer services and software industry (*China Statistical Yearbook 2007*).

## Acquisitions in the Chinese IT and telecom industry

The IT industry is a young and showcase high-tech industry for the Chinese government. According to its Tenth Five-Year Plan (Ministry of Information Industry, 2001), the information industry is 'a pillar industry in the national economy', 'a strategic industry fundamental to national security' and 'a driving force for innovation and growth in other industries' (Cooke, 2008a). With the rapid technological breakthroughs of IT in recent years, the business of the IT and telecommunication industries is increasingly intertwined.

The Chinese telecom operators, built on the legacy of the state-planned economy, were monopolized by the Ministry of Post and Telecom prior to the late 1990s (see Roseman, 2005 for a detailed review of the industry). They are considered to be lagging behind their Western counterparts in terms of technology innovation capability, financial and human capital and managerial competence (China Mergers and Acquisitions Research Centre, 2003). By contrast, the telecom equipment suppliers and software companies have grown up in a more market-driven and open environment. Leading IT firms, such as Lenovo (previously known as Legend), Huawei and ZTE, have continued to grow rapidly in the last decade and have become global operations. They are known for their innovative ability, high product quality and customer services. However, the majority of telecom manufacturers and software companies are still operating on relatively small scales, with little finance resource, no core competence in research and development (R&D) and few patented products. They have low efficiency and low profit margins (Tong, 2004; Zhou, 2004). Fierce competition also weakens their competitiveness and long-term development capabilities. In order to address this problem, the government has adopted a number of strategies and measures since the mid-1990s. One of them is to encourage the acquisition of less profitable companies by better performers.

Acquisitions in the Chinese IT and telecom industry started in the mid-1990s after the government issued a policy document to accelerate the advancement of science and technology in 1995, and as the stock market gradually matured. In the stock market, acquisitions in the IT industry increased from 6.1 per cent in 1997 to 38 per cent in 1998 and continued to grow at over 30 per cent annually until 2000 (China Mergers and Acquisitions Research Centre, 2003). However, acquisitions in this period were rather opportunistic in nature, typically with one company acquiring another at a low price and then making a profit by selling it (China Mergers and Acquisitions Research Centre, 2003).

Acquisitions among domestic Chinese companies are driven by a number of motives. First, acquisitions in IT companies accounted for a large proportion of the latest wave of M&As in the Western market, characterized by the IT giants joining forces to lower operating costs, obtain more customers and meet changing customer demands (Qian and Liu, 2000). Chinese firms are also driven by this trend and opt for a strong–strong alliance as an effective way to strengthen their market position. For example, Yongyou Software acquired Anyi in 2002 to form the largest software firm in China, while Shengzhou Digital combined with the Great Wall in 2003 to compete with Legend (now Lenovo). Second, companies have been unable to keep pace with the speed of change in IT, which has become too fast and too expensive (Liu and Qian, 2000). Third, the more profitable companies with good finances tend to acquire firms which are often at the start-up stage and of small scale. These start-up firms possess distinctive technology, market channel or human resources but lack the financial or other resources to develop further. Fourth, M&As of IT and telecom firms are the result of the Chinese government's intervention as part of its strategic intent to restructure and develop the industry (Cooke, 2008a).

The Chinese IT industry has been an attractive area for MNCs due to the upsurge of China's economy and the great market potential for IT products and services. By the end of 2003, 90 per cent of the top 100 IT MNCs had entered the Chinese market, competing among themselves and with Chinese firms (CTTL, 2004). Local firms with special market channels and customer bases tend to be the most favourable targets for multinational acquirers. As the government views the IT industry as strategically significant, it plays an important role in determining the direction and pace of the industry's development. Close links with special market channels, for example government agencies, will be crucial for companies to formulate the right strategy for product development and marketing.

Prior to China's accession to the WTO, MNCs attempted to monopolize the development of the IT industry and control the product market by providing high-value products and services (Wang and Liu, 2002). Their expansion was somewhat restricted to the higher end of the product market in part because of the Chinese government's protectionist policy in order to encourage the growth of domestic firms (Cooke, 2008a). As the IT industry is maturing and the Chinese government has been under increasing pressure to lift its protectionist policy, MNCs have been expanding into the lower end of the product market and into the inland markets since the mid-2000s (MII, 2006). This expansion has also been facilitated by the reduced cost of R&D as ever more MNCs move their R&D centres to China or set up new ones. This expansion has a knock-on effect on local Chinese firms. For example, it was reported that the profit level of local IT companies declined to 2.5 per cent in 2005, the lowest level since 2000 (MII, 2006). Moreover, high-performing local firms with high-quality IT professionals have become targets for MNC acquisition (*Beijing Morning*, 2002). The deepening penetration of foreign firms in the IT industry has intensified competition and fuelled a series of acquisitions.

In the next section, two company case studies and two manager case studies will be presented to illustrate the motives of the acquisition of two Chinese IT firms by foreign firms, the post-acquisition alignment of their business strategies and the impact on their managers.

## Case studies

The first company case is the acquisition of a Chinese privately owned firm (pseudonym: Oriental Power) by a US-owned multinational electric group (pseudonym: US Magic). Oriental Power is a telecom and data network power supplier. The second company case involves the acquisition of a privately owned Chinese mobile value-added service provider (pseudonym: Quick Rabbit) by a large US-owned transnational online media company (pseudonym: Asian Dragon). While the first case provides an example of the acquisition activities carried out by telecom enterprises in their conventional areas, the second reveals the emerging business dynamics across the telecom and Internet businesses.

### Organization case 8.1 Oriental Power and US Magic

#### Company backgrounds

Oriental Power was a subsidiary of a leading telecommunication equipment supplier corporation in China. It was initially created in 1992 as a power division and became a subsidiary in 1996 to facilitate cooperation with other telecom equipment suppliers which had often been the competitors of the parent company. Oriental Power provides the power conversion solutions that ensure the stable and reliable operation of telecom equipment. Recognizing that the firm was lagging far behind foreign competitors in technological innovation in many business areas, the corporation decided to focus its resources on a number of core products in order to achieve comparative technology advantages and breakthroughs. 'Being focused' and 'customer orientation' were at the heart of the firm's business strategy. This has led to the rapid growth of its market share as well as enhanced capabilities in technological development of Oriental Power. By 2000, Oriental Power possessed 30 per cent of the market share in the telecom power business and 40 per cent in electronic monitor systems. It was ranked top in the Chinese market. In 2001, Oriental Power had 1,500 employees and a total sales revenue of 2.8 billion yuan.

Since Oriental Power was originated from one department of the parent company and remained strongly dependent after becoming a subsidiary, it had no autonomy in strategy, finance or management decisions despite the presence of HR and finance offices. It was indeed operated as a fully dependent division, similar to other functional departments such as research & development, finance and sales. All the recruitment and promotion activities were conducted by the HR department of the parent company.

Compared with Oriental Power, US Magic has a much longer corporate history. Founded in the early twentieth century, it is one of the largest global groups providing electric, energy system solutions and infrastructure for the telecommunication industry worldwide, with sales revenue of US$15 billion in 2001. China has been one of the major destinations of the company's global expansion. Following its entry into the country in 1979, US Magic has set up 28 wholly owned subsidiaries and joint ventures (JVs) in 13 cities, employing some 12,000 employees by 2001. The sales revenue in China had increased from US$56 million in 1991 to US$425 million in 2001. This was closely related to the company's continuous investment in the country through JVs and acquisitions as well as its global business strategy that focuses on advanced technology and new products.

## Motives for the acquisition

There are a number of motives for US Magic to acquire Oriental Power. First, despite its increasing expansion in China, US Magic was lagging behind local companies such as Oriental Power itself in terms of market share and the presence of brands in the network power business. This called for the further restructuring and coordination of network power businesses in China to facilitate the firm's global integration and competition. The acquisition of Oriental Power would therefore assist US Magic to obtain 30 per cent of the market share of China's network power business, immediately securing a leading position in the Chinese market and in the Asia-Pacific region as a whole. Second, in response to the proliferation of information and communication technology, US Magic intended to create a single, globally integrated network power division to achieve global leadership in this important segment. Third, the provision of a wide range of product lines by Oriental Power would expand and consolidate US Magic's product portfolio. In addition, the forty-plus technology patents and over 1,000 well-trained R&D engineers employed by Oriental Power would increase US Magic's core competences in technology innovation and development, especially in meeting local customers'

continued

demands. Fourth, the solid sales channel and customer relationships established by Oriental Power would be highly valuable for US Magic.

For the parent corporation of Oriental Power, focusing on its core competence – telecom equipment networks – and international expansion were the motives for selling the subsidiary. In addition, selling the subsidiary would help the corporation to reduce financial pressure following the bursting of the IT bubble in the late 1990s. The divestment of Oriental Power would also benefit the development of Oriental Power through the generation of a larger pool of customers beyond its existing portfolio, as part of US Magic.

The deal was negotiated between the top management teams of the two corporations with the involvement of strategic, legal and management consultants from early 2001. Due to the centralized decision-making style, the top management of Oriental Power was not included in these negotiations. After one and a half years of negotiation and planning, the deal was made: US$750 million in cash for 100 per cent equity of Oriental Power. It was announced in October 2001. The acquisition was not only the largest investment US Magic had ever made in China since its entry in 1979, but at the time was the largest ever acquisition in China by a foreign company. Following the acquisition, the destination sales of US Magic rose from US$700 million in 2002 to more than US$1 billion in 2004. More than one-third of those sales were achieved by taking advantage of the national distribution network brought by Oriental Power.

Despite the fact that the negotiation was undertaken at the top level and in a highly confidential manner, 'rumours' had circulated across various departments within Oriental Power. As all the staff were recruited or appointed by the parent company, they had strong identification with the corporation and took great pride in being employees of a highly prestigious Chinese IT firm. They had never expected to be sold by the parent company. Part of their financial reward came in the form of stock options and their annual bonus had been invested in stock options allocated to them by the firm in order to enjoy long-term profit-sharing. This close bonding with the company – initially designed by the corporation to nurture employee commitment – was undermined by the acquisition. As a result, most employees felt a sense of betrayal by the firm. Many started to look for jobs elsewhere or found ways to transfer back to the parent company. Of course, US Magic recognized the importance of retaining key personnel such as R&D engineers and sales staff in order to benefit fully from the acquisition. Consequently, it asked the former parent company to ensure that key employees remain with Oriental Power for at least three years after the acquisition. Those who were not allowed to transfer back to the former parent company initiated an unprecedented collective-bargaining scheme to cash in their company shares at a price that was acceptable to them.

## Post-acquisition strategy and structure

The post-acquisition integration and strategic development went through three major stages. The first was to create synergy in sales. As was anticipated, the acquisition of Oriental Power has helped US Magic expand its product market and customer base in

China. It also enabled Oriental Power's original network power products to be exported to the international market through the global sales branches of US Magic. The second stage began a year after the acquisition. During this stage the manufacturing centres of US Magic in Europe and Australia were transferred to Oriental Power's manufacturing base. However, while cost reduction and access to the Chinese market were the primary motives for US Magic's acquisition of Oriental Power, US Magic soon realized that the research capabilities of Oriental Power were also valuable. This triggered the third stage of the integration and business development, which had not been anticipated – the relocation of US Magic's R&D centres for network power from Europe to combine with that of Oriental Power in China. The combined R&D centre benefited US Magic's global customers through much lower costs. In 2005, Oriental Power became the sole and integrated centre for developing, manufacturing, marketing and maintaining network power products for US Magic's global business.

The acquisition of Oriental Power was apparently associated with building global leadership for US Magic. For this strategic purpose, Oriental Power's business strategy was very much influenced by the strategic orientation of US Magic. Soon after the acquisition, Oriental Power's original 'focus' strategy was replaced by one that emphasizes quality enhancement, efficiency and steady growth. However, this strategy became clear only with the increased importance of Oriental Power to the global service of US Magic, particularly after the integration of the R&D centre, which has boosted Oriental Power's position significantly.

The emergent strategy change was accompanied by the structural change of Oriental Power within US Magic. For the first two years after the acquisition, Oriental Power was regarded as valuable only for its low-cost manufacturing basis and distribution channels. The chief executive officer (CEO) appointed by the Asia-Pacific regional headquarters mainly had contacts with the regional office on production and sales issues. Except for the CEO and the chief finance officer (CFO), the management of Oriental Power had limited contact with the staff of other subsidiaries. Oriental Power was simply required to produce low-cost products and sell whatever it was asked to sell, even though the product lines had been expanded. The integration of the R&D centre increased the interaction between Oriental Power and the headquarters and other subsidiaries. Work planning, especially strategic product innovation projects, need to be reported and discussed with the headquarters. As a division providing product design at global level, management effectiveness of Oriental Power received more attention from the parent company. Standardized programmes, such as enterprise resources planning (ERP), were introduced to improve management efficiency and effectiveness. The application of these programmes also increased the interaction between Oriental Power and other divisions of US Magic, including international transfer of staff.

According to the managers interviewed, the most important elements of the management process include: action orientation, commitment to planning, and a strong system of control and follow-up. At the end of each year, based on the strategic road map and the annual and mid-term business objectives identified at the corporate planning conference, each division and unit is required to develop its own work plans that guide the activities at the operational level. All plans are reviewed quarterly throughout the year and the performance of units and employees is evaluated against the predetermined targets stated

continued

in the plans. Monthly meetings are held among regional presidents to report progress in relation to their plans and tackle problems. US Magic believes that this is the simplest way to control all divisions and ensure the achievement of the overall business strategy, as was observed by the managing director of Oriental Power:

> We spent 60 per cent of our time every year on the plan. What we all do needs to be aligned with our corporate plan and our divisional objectives. We cannot change it discretionarily. If we change it, we will be asked why it needs to changed. Is it because we did not make a good plan in the first place? If so, we would be asked to make a better plan the next year. But we cannot change this year's plan. Otherwise, the plan will mean nothing if everyone makes it at the beginning and then changes it frequently or easily.

> Sources: interviews with managers and employees of the company in 2005–06.

The US Magic–Oriental Power acquisition has obviously been a successful one that has exceeded its original objectives. The success of post-acquisition integration and business development can be attributed to two major factors. One is that the growing strategic importance of Oriental Power in the global operation means that the transferred employees no longer resent being 'dumped' by their previous employer. This psychological adaptation is aided by the good compensation package offered to those who were affected by the transfer and the ensuing HR policies adopted by US Magic to retain, attract and motivate talent. While substantial financial reward through the company's stock option scheme was the main feature of the HR policy to motivate employees prior to the acquisition, the HR policy adopted by US Magic is a far more developed one that emphasizes heavy investment in training and development, systematic performance management, and encouragement of two-way communication.

The other factor is that the change of ownership has not led to any reduction of power or control within Oriental Power. This is because it never had any power or control in the first place, having been a subsidiary of another parent company. Therefore, the strong control now exerted on Oriental Power by US Magic to ensure global integration is not a departure from the previous management style. If US Magic were not a prestigious global firm, and if Oriental Power were being used simply as a cheap production site and marketing platform in China (as US Magic had originally planned), the integration process might have met with much stronger employee resistance, resulting in a reduced level of success. The emergence of new strategic development which has exceeded the original acquisition motives of US Magic also suggests that post-acquisition integration and development is often an evolving process, rather than the execution of a predefined plan.

## Organization case 8.2 Quick Rabbit and Asian Dragon

### Company backgrounds

Asian Dragon was first established as a Sino-foreign JV specializing in the development of computer software in 1993. Unlike many Sino-foreign JVs at the time, which were formed between state-owned enterprises (SOEs) and foreign partners, Asian Dragon was founded by a Chinese privately owned firm and a US-owned enterprise. In 1996, driven by the boom in Internet technology, Asian Dragon launched its initial online network, providing online news and information and communication services as well as marketing its software. Meanwhile, its Chinese version of the Windows operating system possessed 80 per cent of the market share, which led to a 250 per cent growth rate for the company in 1998. Asian Dragon was acquired by a US-owned Internet company in 1999, which sought to expand in China, and became the largest Chinese-language Internet portal with wholly foreign-invested ownership.

The implications of this acquisition for the company were far more than a simple ownership change and an increase in size. The foreign parent company imposed numerous requirements on the management team which removed the company's paternalistic management style and transformed it into an international company coordinating businesses in different countries in a more market-oriented way. All management and employees from the JV who had kinship relationships with the top management were dismissed shortly after the acquisition. Senior positions were filled immediately by staff appointed by the foreign parent company. All decision-making and business processes originally controlled by the founder of the JV were replaced by more transparent and formalized organizational flows and procedures to ensure the interests of shareholders. In 1999, Asian Dragon further expanded into the Hong Kong market. This strengthened its market-leading position with provisions of Internet software, news, information, online communications and e-commerce services for Chinese online users.

Quick Rabbit was registered as a privately owned IT company in early 2001 by one IT technician and two bankers with their personal savings. Of the three founders of the company, two are experienced in telecom and Internet business and the other has a close customer relationship with the state-owned China Mobile, the country's largest telecom operator, which monopolizes the mobile communication market. The founders, especially the two bankers, initially wanted to follow in the footsteps of many other Internet companies by listing Quick Rabbit on the stock market to make a high financial return rapidly. They selected mobile value-added service – Short Message Service (SMS) – as their major business. SMS was a rather new concept at the time but was

continued

expected to have great potential due to the vast and expanding number of mobile phone users in China. In addition, this new area of business initially attracted little attention from large companies. This meant competition was less fierce and the running costs much lower than in the Internet portal business.

However, the IT bubble burst a few months after the company was established, and this disrupted the plan to list Quick Rabbit on the stock exchange. Instead, the founders were forced to direct their focus on to product development and market expansion. In the meantime, telecom operators such as China Mobile were seeking new opportunities and service provisions in the mobile data application area as growth in conventional mobile voice usage had started to decline. Quick Rabbit therefore attracted a fourth shareholder, who had a close customer relationship with China Mobile as well as rich experience in building sales and distribution channels, to exploit this new opportunity.

Nevertheless, by the end of 2001, the company fell into financial hardship as the products it developed were not mature enough to be marketed. A fifth partner, a wealthy local man, was brought in to rescue the company from its financial crisis and to facilitate product development. In 2002, two new products were launched and applied by China Mobile. They were immediate successes and the company started to enjoy an unanticipated boom, becoming one of the top three service providers in the domestic market. The sales network also expanded from one to six provinces in just six months. By the end of 2002, the company was employing 160 people. This rapid boom can be attributed to the company's early entry into an undeveloped market as a fast mover, to its solid nationwide sales network, and to its speed in updating products. As summarized by a manager of Quick Rabbit: 'Our strategy was "fast, new and change". That was the key to our success.' The implementation of this strategy was closely related to Quick Rabbit's HR practices, which were highly performance driven.

## Motives for Asian Dragon's acquisition of Quick Rabbit

Asian Dragon had been seeking new business opportunities to reduce its reliance on advertising revenue, which was considered by the company to be insufficient to secure its market-leader position long term. Having witnessed the boom of SMS in a short period of time, Asian Dragon made significant investment in developing and marketing mobile value-added products after 2002 in an attempt to increase non-advertising revenue. However, Asian Dragon made little progress in this area and was seriously lagging behind service providers like Quick Rabbit. This reflected Asian Dragon's comparative disadvantage in its technology and sales channels. Therefore, Asian Dragon's first motive for the acquisition was to add two million fee-paying subscribers to its customer base, bringing in US$20 million revenue that was already achieved by Quick Rabbit in 2002. However, the second and more important motive was that the technology and sales channels Quick Rabbit built up would fill Asian Dragon's gaps in the development of wireless products and a nationwide sales force. This would benefit the company immediately and would facilitate the transformation of Asian Dragon from a conventional online portal provider to an online media company with increasing competences in wireless and mobile data business.

For Quick Rabbit, the boom of SMS generated great wealth for its shareholders but at the same time attracted many competitors after 2002. The intensive competition due to the involvement of larger competitors had rapidly increased the costs of marketing and selling new products. The short life cycles of SMS products also put much pressure on the company to increase investment in product development and brand promotion if it wished to maintain its leading position. All of these changes required more financial and market resources for the company to move forward. Asian Dragon's strong platform and online resources would be valuable for Quick Rabbit to develop a wider range of competitive products and reduce the cost of brand promotion. In fact, under the pressure of mobile subscribers' increasing complaints, China Mobile issued a series of regulations to specify more stringent requirements for the scale, scope and quality of service provisions of service providers.

## Post-acquisition strategy and structural change

The acquisition took place relatively smoothly in early 2003. 'Buying' the top management's commitment to stay with the company and continue the operation and expansion of SMS was the top priority in the pre-acquisition negotiations. Handsome compensation packages and full autonomy were granted to the acquired top management team. Based on this commitment from Asian Dragon, the top management team of Quick Rabbit signed their contracts and promised to stay with the company for at least one year after the acquisition to ensure a smooth transition.

It was agreed between the two parties that in order to maintain the flexibility and revenue creation of Quick Rabbit, during the first year after the acquisition, Quick Rabbit would operate as an independent subsidiary in parallel with Asian Dragon's original mobile value-added service unit under the mobile division. The former focused on the expansion of SMS, targeting non-Internet users, while the latter served Internet subscribers. The heads of both units reported to the general manager (GM) of the mobile division, who was actually the vice-president of Asian Dragon but was acting as the GM temporarily to oversee the integration of Quick Rabbit with Asian Dragon. While the GM was consulted on strategic and operational issues, the regional office of Asian Dragon provided administrative and personnel support. Aside from that, though, there was little intervention from the headquarters and the regional office in how the subsidiary is managed. The finance department was the only department that was centralized in order to meet the strict financial requirements of the US stock exchange.

The top management team had much greater freedom in financial and personnel decision-making than other business units of Asian Dragon. When conflicts occurred, Quick Rabbit was usually given flexibility as long as it was beneficial to the business. For example, a 'fast track' was open to Quick Rabbit in gaining approval for financial and administrative procedures. This autonomy proved highly useful to win trust from the acquired staff and provide a stable environment for them to carry out business development in both products and markets.

continued

In addition to securing the top management team's commitment, Asian Dragon made significant concessions in order to retain key engineers and professional staff from Quick Rabbit. HR managers sought employees' views prior to the acquisition. And the reward packages of the acquired employees – who had higher salaries than Asian Dragon staff – were ring-fenced.

By the end of 2003, Quick Rabbit had generated three times the sales revenue it had managed the previous year, which accounted for 60 per cent of the total revenue in wireless fee-based services of Asian Dragon. As business expansion continued and both parties became more familiar with each other's management style, the key technicians of Quick Rabbit were transferred to Asian Dragon's headquarters in another city in China. Once they were working with their counterparts in the headquarters they were able to create a new and more powerful platform for product development that both business units in the wireless division could share. The joint project team for product development facilitated the interaction between Quick Rabbit and the headquarters. Job rotations also took place between employees of Quick Rabbit and those from other business units.

In the meantime, three founders of Quick Rabbit resigned from their positions to start their own business. As one of them remarked: 'being entrepreneurs rather than professional managers employed by others is our personal goal'. In order to reduce the negative impact of their departure on the employees, another founder, who was in charge of sales and marketing, was promoted to GM of the wireless division, in charge of both units covering Internet and non-Internet SMS businesses. A special stock option package was allocated to him to ensure he would stay with the company. In early 2004, as a key member of the integration team, the new GM was involved in the integration with another service provider company purchased by Asian Dragon. After that integration, the wireless division became the company's largest division, contributing 60 per cent of the total annual revenue of Asian Dragon, with Quick Rabbit still the dominant component in terms of both number of employees and sales revenue. An innovation strategy and customer-oriented culture was the common ground to bring together a number of business units and acquired companies.

Compared with Asian Dragon, Quick Rabbit had a more advanced performance management system that was centred on performance-related rewards. Within one year of the acquisition, Asian Dragon had adapted Quick Rabbit's system and rolled it out across the whole corporation. As the HR director of Asian Dragon remarked:

> We had been trying to introduce performance management based on a consultant's project, but it was not successful. We found what Quick Rabbit did was effective and helpful for performance improvement. Both criteria and processes of this performance management method were closely linked with employees' work and organizational objectives. We learned a lot from Quick Rabbit, but the most from its performance management.

In 2005, the majority of managers and employees of Quick Rabbit were relocated from their base in southeast China to another city in the north, where the headquarters is based. They were given similar housing and relocation allowances to those offered to the key technicians who had been transferred two years earlier. With this mass relocation, Quick Rabbit was eventually transformed from an independent subsidiary to an integral and major part of Asian Dragon.

Sources: interviews with managers and employees of the company in 2005–06.

The acquisition of Quick Rabbit by Asian Dragon was the first and largest horizontal deal in the mobile value-added business area of the Chinese market. It reflects the fact that the boundaries between the telecom, media and computer businesses have become increasingly blurred. Indeed, this kind of business integration is now crucial for firms in the ICT industry to survive and remain competitive. The news of the deal immediately triggered a sharp rise in the share price of Asian Dragon on the NASDAQ stock exchange. Acquiring one of the best service providers fundamentally strengthened Asian Dragon's market leader position in the mobile value-added business in China and facilitated its successful transformation from an online portal relying on online advertising towards a media and wireless service provider with greater profitability. In fact, the company itself was formed and grew through a succession of acquisitions.

Compared with the first case, the pre-acquisition negotiation between the two firms in this second case was more smooth. As the acquired firm appeared to have held significant bargaining power, it was given a high level of autonomy in the initial period after the acquisition to carry on with business as usual. However, as business expanded and revenue continued to rise, the acquired firm (Quick Rabbit) became fully integrated with its acquiring firm and successfully played the role for which it had been acquired. Undoubtedly, the promotion of one of the founders of Quick Rabbit has been crucial in facilitating post-acquisition integration. Another key factor in the success of the acquisition was that the two companies seemed to share a common culture that emphasized risk-taking, innovation and customer orientation, although the acquirer had more formalized procedures and processes. Below are two manager case studies of acquisitions that took place in the IT/telecom industry (Manager cases 8.3 and 8.4). These two cases reveal similar business opportunities and management challenges to those revealed in the two company cases, reported in Organization cases 8.1 and 8.2.

## Manager case 8.3 Ms Lee, human resources director, Paradise and Online Star

### Company backgrounds

Driven by the popularity of Internet businesses that had created considerable wealth for venture capitalists and their founders since the mid-1990s, Online Star was originated in 1996 in the US by an overseas Chinese student funded by a number of American venture capital companies. In 1998, Online Star developed its online directory and the first search engine for the Chinese market. Based on this technology infrastructure, in the following three years the company carried out a number of horizontal acquisition activities to create the largest Internet portal with expanded product range and service provisions. But this diversification strategy did not go well. In 2002, Online Star decided to refocus on its online media business as its core business. In the meantime, the top management recognized that a systematic HR system would be crucial for the firm's further development. Ms Grace Lee was therefore brought in as the HR director to develop an HR system. In 2003, Online Star employed 1,300 staff and achieved US$80 million sales revenue.

Paradise was initially set up by Dr Zhang and his friends as an Internet portal in 1999, specializing in providing online news, real estate and job information. In 2003, Paradise was ranked as one of the most influential online real estate communities in a market survey reported by *China News*. Over thirty employees worked for Paradise and brought in 20 million yuan sales revenue.

### Motive for the acquisition

Online Star's acquisition of Paradise was announced in November 2003 after six months of negotiation between the two parties. There were a number of reasons for the acquisition. First, while the real estate sector had become one of the largest Internet advertisers in response to the rapid growth of the real estate industry in the course of China's urbanization, Online Star's real estate content was unable to attract many customers in this area. Purchasing Paradise, one of best online real estate communities, would permit Online Star to increase its advertising revenue by complementing and extending its product lines. Second, the expertise Paradise had accumulated in real estate advertising and its established brand would enhance Online Star's competitiveness in the long run by applying Paradise's successful business model to other products and areas. Third, the acquisition of Paradise would allow Online Star to meet the demands of different groups of users. In the meantime, Online Star would be able to access Paradise's committed staff, who were as influential as its brand in the Internet business. For Paradise, the acquisition would enable it to expand from being a single-city business to a national business through the network platform established by Online Star, which Paradise was unable to achieve on its own due to resource constraints.

## Post-acquisition integration

Retention of the key Paradise personnel, particularly its founding president, was considered essential for the success of the integration. As Ms Lee observed: 'Paradise is a good team with strong cohesion and everyone recognizes the team leader. So we definitely needed to retain him if we wanted to retain the whole team. If he would not stay, the rest would leave as well.' As a result, in addition to providing share options to seven key managers, the integration team led by Ms Lee granted Dr Zhang's requests of maintaining the Paradise logo, keeping the team as a whole, continuing to lead the team and giving them the autonomy to run the business. In addition, Dr Zhang was given full power to integrate Online Star's existing real estate unit into Paradise's team. Six months after the acquisition, he was promoted to the vice-president of Online Star and became a member of the chief executive committee, reporting directly to the CEO. This decision was justified by Ms Lee: 'The financial means, such as stock options, were essential for the retention . . . but they were not the key . . . The complete integration of the hearts and minds of top management and key managers needs other mechanisms, such as giving them a platform and autonomy to work, etc.'

Source: interview with Ms Grace Lee, Online Star Co. Ltd, in 2006.

## Manager case 8.4 Mr Chen, founder, Matador and RichTech

### Company backgrounds

Registered in 1994 as a privately owned company, Matador was founded by Mr David Chen, an IT technologist who held a number of wire phone patents and a sales expert who had been serving a local Chinese telecom company for a number of years and had a solid business relationship with China Telecom. From 1997, in response to China Telecom's analogue network being gradually replaced by digital communication, Matador started developing a mobile billing software system (BSS) in an attempt to maintain high profit margins. The shrinkage in monopolized profits as a result of competition from MNCs in BSS and the increase in technological complexity impelled Matador to enhance its management effectiveness through corporatization and marketization. A new CEO was brought in from a leading MNC to achieve this transformation. The subsequent improvement in business operations and quality management in software solutions enabled Matador to win five BSS contracts from China Mobile in 2000 and 2001. This placed the company in the top position among the providers of BSS software in terms of market share. By the end of 2001, the company had achieved US$15 million sales revenue and employed around 200 staff.

One of the first Internet companies in Texas, USA, RichTech was launched by a number of overseas Chinese in 1993. The founders decided to introduce Internet technology into

continued

the Chinese market and focused on providing backbone infrastructure and system integration planning, design and implementation for Internet service suppliers. This early entry into the Chinese market, where the Internet business grew rapidly, and its new technology enabled RichTech to achieve more than 60 per cent market share in the system integration area by 1998. Meanwhile, in response to the demand for an Internet Protocol (IP) billing system from network operators, RichTech started to develop IP billing software.

After being listed on the NASDAQ stock exchange in 2000, RichTech increased its investment in software development. This was because the great market potential in software became apparent and the demand for hardware system integration from telecom operators continued to decrease. By the end of 2001, RichTech employed 1,000 staff in its American and Chinese offices and had achieved US$44 million revenue, the majority of which came from its system integration and data software business.

## Motives for the acquisition

The news of RichTech's acquisition of Matador was announced in early 2002 after nearly three years of discussion between the two parties. The first motive for the acquisition was that RichTech intended to access Matador's remarkable competence in software solutions development for mobile business. This would help RichTech to achieve a strategic transformation from Internet architect to software supplier of telecom operating systems. Second, Matador's market share and its solid customer base would elevate RichTech's market power considerably. Third, Matador's professional technicians and their experience in developing high-quality software solutions would be essential for RichTech to meet the emerging needs of telecom operators through the improvement of productivity, efficiency and customer services during national expansion. The cost of software development would also be reduced through the deployment of Matador's R&D capabilities. For Matador, the intensifying competition from MNCs and the increasing varieties of customer needs necessitated continual investment in marketing, sales and product development, which exacerbated the company's financial constraints. Being part of RichTech would provide the necessary resources to ensure continuous business success.

## Post-acquisition integration

Due to the significant market position of Matador, David Chen and another founder were granted operational autonomy and freedom in decision-making at the subsidiary level. The HR director and organizational development manager of RichTech also promised the acquired employees training and development opportunities, better welfare and a new reward system after the integration. However, after early 2002, China Telecom operators reduced investment in infrastructure and the procurement of related software as a result of the industry's restructuring. This impacted heavily on the growth of telecom software and service providers such as RichTech. Cost cutting and redundancies therefore had to be carried out in RichTech soon after the acquisition. The chaos arising from such a change drove the top management team to consider diversifying into other industries and areas to reduce the risk of relying on a single industry. In the process of diversification in 2003 and early 2004, Matador enjoyed a high degree of flexibility and autonomy in business operation and HRM with little involvement from headquarters.

However, the diversification strategy did not deliver the anticipated results for RichTech. The company decided to refocus on the telecom software area in mid-2004, so Matador became the most significant part of RichTech's business in China. David Chen and another founder of Matador were promoted to the top level of the OSS division, which was created through integrating RichTech–Matador with two other small divisions in BSS-related business. In line with the new strategy, there is now much more communication between the HR department and the RichTech–Matador division. More systematic training programmes are provided to encourage learning and development of management. Performance management focuses not only on performance improvement but on individuals' personal development. David Chen observed:

> The integration by RichTech was not static but rather dynamic . . . we used to have a high level of autonomy . . . Now we are required to compete with competitors based on innovation strategy that was identified by the top guy . . . Training schemes like 'Mini-MBA' and career development paths are all provided for us.

> Source: interview with Mr David Chen, Matador, in 2006.

## Key challenges

Foreign investors face a number of challenges in the acquisition of businesses in China, particularly those owned by the state (Cooke, 2008a; Luo 2000a and 2000b). A first challenge is the absence of an effective and independent asset evaluation and legal system to facilitate cross-border M&As. While this may be less of a problem for MNCs already operating in the country due to prior familiarity or for large MNCs which can tap into their global pool of expertise to overcome this deficiency, small foreign businesses wishing to expand their operations in China for the first time may find it difficult to find their way around.

A second challenge involves the opportunistic behaviour of Chinese managers in acquisition activities. It has been noted that some senior managers of Chinese firms use M&As as opportunities to advance their own interests instead of those of the enterprise. These include financial benefits (e.g. salary, bonuses and stocks) and non-financial benefits such as power to control, personal prestige and reputation. The absence of an independent asset evaluation system provides an opportunity for senior managers to use their positions to reduce the company asset value for acquisition to bargain for their new positions and terms and conditions in the new organization (Cai and Shen, 2002). This may have a negative impact on post-acquisition integration and business development.

A third challenge relates to intervention from local government. In the acquisition of SOEs, local government tends to have a close involvement in the decision-making and negotiation process. It not only takes on an agency, monitoring and harmonization role in the absence of independent legal and financial advice services, but has vested financial interest in the enterprises. The province-based revenue and taxation system presents further hurdles for MNCs already operating in China that wish to acquire businesses in other provinces (Cooke, 2008a). To some extent, the four cases reported in this chapter were less affected by these problems due to their familiarity with the Chinese system prior to the acquisition as they were already operating in the country. In addition, the acquisitions took place between private firms, thus attracting less bureaucratic involvement from local government.

A fourth challenge concerns the regulatory restrictions on the types of industry and ways foreign investors can acquire Chinese businesses, as mentioned earlier. The Chinese government imposes restrictions on foreign investments in key Chinese industries, such as banking and real estate, in order to maintain control of the economy (in the former case) and prevent overheating of growth (in the latter case). It is worth noting that these restrictions are selective. For sectors in which the government intends to stimulate growth, foreign investments are sought. For others, which are deemed non-strategic, such as the retail sector, foreign investors have flooded in.

Cross-border acquisition of Chinese firms went through a period of confusion and conflict due to the absence of a clear set of legal and administrative policy guidelines (Luo 2000a and 2000b). It was only in the early 2000s that the Chinese government started to issue regulations to provide guidance on M&As involving foreign funds. Even so, some of them proved to be out-of-date very quickly and were replaced by new ones to reflect rapid changes in the economic landscape of the country. For example, in 2003, the Chinese government promulgated M&A regulations which set out a framework for foreign investors' acquisition of all types of domestic enterprises and the restructuring of such enterprises upon acquisition. On 8 September 2006, a new set of Regulations on the Acquisition of Domestic Enterprises by Foreign Investors (hereafter, the 2006 Regulations) took effect. Under the 2006 Regulations, 'the approval of foreign M&A activities is handled under the foreign investment regime, which calls for most transactions to be processed and approved at the local level'. Since most local governments are keen to attract foreign investment, approval for transactions is easily achieved. 'However, this local autonomy can lead to situations where acquisitions are permitted to occur in areas that are not consistent with central government policy' (OECD, 2006: 1). Indeed, tensions between the central government and the regional/local governments have been widely noted (e.g. Cooke, 2008a; Eun and Lee, 2002; Krug and Hendrischke, 2007). The local governments' ability to resist, albeit often in a covert manner, the central government's policy has been a major stumbling block to a coordinated economic development at the macro level. While foreign businesses can take advantage of local government's desire to attract FDI on the one hand, they can be a victim in this power struggle on the other.

Nevertheless, the 2006 Regulations represent a further opening up for cross-border M&As in line with standard international practice and increased corporate transparency and fairness in the M&A process. They also impose a new screening requirement on cross-border M&A transactions if these involve a 'major industry', may have 'an impact on national economic security' and may result in 'the transfer of famous trademarks or traditional Chinese brands' to foreign investors. What these terms mean precisely is left to the interpretation of the government agencies charged with the implementation of the regulations (OECD, 2006).

The 2006 Regulations also reveal the Chinese government's increasing concern about opening up its industries to foreign investors. This concern becomes even more evident in its new policy towards cross-border M&As, as explained in the Eleventh Five-Year Plan (2006–10) published by the National Development and Reform Commission on 9 November 2006. 'The plan sets forth a clear industrial policy prioritizing geographical areas, industrial sectors, levels of technology, environmental protection and efficient use of natural resources' (OECD, 2006: 2). It also emphasizes quality instead of quantity in FDI and the need for critical industries to remain in Chinese ownership (OECD, 2006). On 1 August 2008, the Anti-Monopoly Law became effective. This requires foreign investors seeking to launch large acquisition deals in China to gain approval from the Chinese regulators. The new law superseded similar terms in the 2006 Regulations to provide a clear guideline, in principle, for investors. It also brings further constraints in the types of business foreign investors can acquire in China and how the acquisitions should be handled.

The relatively frequent changes of regulations in addition to the ever-emerging administrative policies at various levels of government in China reflect a trial-and-error approach to regulating the fast-growing economy and a somewhat chaotic juristic environment that is characteristic of emerging economies. This requires foreign investors to keep up to date with the changes and navigate through them.

## Conclusion

This chapter has documented the brief history of M&A as an emerging but increasingly popular business strategy in the Chinese economy. It has provided two in-depth company case studies and two manager case studies on the cross-border acquisition of privately owned firms in the IT and telecom industry. These case studies show that post-acquisition integration and development is often an emerging process rather than the execution of a predefined plan. A value-added business strategy and a high-commitment model of HRM to retain key staff are crucial factors for successful acquisitions. At least this proves to be the case in the fast-growing and highly competitive IT and telecom industry, in which human resources and rapid innovation play vital roles in business success.

Although acquisition has been a major business strategy for firms to grow and survive in the dynamic ICT market worldwide and in China, this is an area that has so far received little attention in academic studies in the Chinese context. This chapter therefore contributes to our understanding of the dynamic development of the IT and telecom industry, the roles foreign and Chinese businesses have played, and the way competitions have evolved and new products developed. However, foreign investors face a number of regulatory and management challenges in acquiring Chinese firms, in addition to barriers to access certain types of industry and business due to national protectionism.

## Bibliography

*Beijing Morning* (2002) 'The policy of foreign investment mergers will be issued at the end of the year – telecom will be the focus', 29 December, p. 2.
Björkman, I. and Lu, Y. (2001) 'Institutionalisation and bargaining power explanations of human resource management in international joint ventures:

the case of Chinese–Western joint ventures', *Organization Studies*, 22: 491–512.

Buono, A. (2003) 'SEAM-less post merger integration strategies: a cause for concern', *Journal of Organizational Change Management*, 16, 1: 90–98.

Cai, L. and Shen, Y. H. (2002) 'An analysis of entrepreneurs' behaviour in the low performance of SOE mergers and acquisitions', *Journal of Zhejiang University*, 1: 137–43.

Cartwright, S. and Schoenberg, R. (2006) 'Thirty years of mergers and acquisitions research: recent advances and future opportunities', *British Journal of Management*, 17, 1: S1–S5.

Chen, C. (1999) 'A study of the mergers and acquisitions of state-owned enterprises by MNCs', *Industrial Technology and Economy*, 6: 34–35.

Child, J., Faulkner, D. and Pitkethly, R. (2001) *The Management of International Acquisitions*, Oxford: Oxford University Press.

*China Business* (2005) *The Review of the Acquisitions in China*, 7th March, p. 3.

*China Daily* (2007), http://www.chinadaily.com.cn/china/2007–02/04/content_800710.htm, accessed on 21 February 2009.

China Mergers and Acquisitions Research Centre (2003) *The Review of Chinese Mergers*, Beijing: Tsing Hua University Press.

*China Statistical Yearbook 2007*, Beijing. China Statistics Publishing House.

Cooke, F. L. (2008a) *Competition, Strategy and Management in China*, Basingstoke: Palgrave Macmillan.

—— (2008b), 'Globalisation and the role of its HR strategy: case study of a leading Chinese telecom corporation – Huawei', Paper presented at the Globalization of Chinese Enterprises: Transformational Politics, Business Strategies, and Future Paths Conference, Harvard University, 9–10 October.

CTTL (2004) 'Foreign investment and competition in the IT Industry', 12 May, http://www.cttl.com.cn, accessed on 27 November 2007.

Eun, J. and Lee, K. (2002) 'Is an industrial policy possible in China? The case of the automotive industry', *Journal of International and Area Studies*, 9, 2: 1–21.

Fan, P. (2006) 'Catching up through developing innovation capability: evidence from China's telecom-equipment industry', *Technovation*, 26: 359–68.

Ghauri, E. N. and Buckley, P. J. (2003) 'International mergers and acquisitions: past, present and future', in C. Cooper and A. Gregory (eds) *Advances in Mergers and Acquisitions* (2nd edition), Greenwich, CT: JAI/Elsevier Press.

Harrison, J. (2002) 'Probing a target in a tough M&A market', *Mergers and Acquisitions*, 37, 1: 7–12.

Hubbard, N. (1999) *Acquisition Strategy and Implementation*, Basingstoke: Macmillan.

Jin, C. X., Qi, P. R. and Li, W. J. (2003) 'An analysis of the issues in MNCs' acquisition of state-owned enterprises', *Modern Economy Research*, 1: 32–37.

Kambil, A. and Lee, P. (2004) 'United Kingdom: changing China – will China's technology standards reshape your industry?', Deloitte, http://www.mondaq.com, accessed on 15 March 2005.

Krug, B. and Hendrischke, H. (eds) (2007) *China in the 21st Century: Economic and Business Behaviour*, London: Edward Elgar.

Liu, Z. R. and Qian, M. (2000) 'Restructuring and transformation: the global telecom merger is waving towards the new century', *Vista and Decision of Electronic Development*, 3: 20–23.

Lu, Q. (2000) *China's Leap into the Information Age: Innovation and Organization in the Computer Industry*, Oxford: Oxford University Press.

Luo, Y. (2000a) *How to Enter China: Choices and Lessons*, Ann Arbor: University of Michigan Press.

—— (2000b) *Partnering with Chinese Firms: Lessons for International Managers*, Aldershot: Ashgate.

MII (2006) 'Implementing large enterprise strategies for the new challenge', 9 September, http://www.mii.com.cn, accessed on 27 November 2007.

Ministry of Information Industry (2001) *The Tenth Five-Year Plan (2001–5)*, http://www.trp.hku.hk/infofile/2002/10–5-yr-plan.pdf, accessed on 13 May 2005.

Nolan, P. (2004) *Transforming China: Globalisation, Transition and Development*, London: Anthem Press.

OECD (2006) 'Recent developments in China's policies towards cross-border mergers and acquisitions (M&A)', Supplement to the *2006 Investment Policy Review of China*, http://www.oecd.org/dataoecd/1/26/37808943.pdf, accessed on 20 February 2009.

*People's Daily Online* (2007) 'Foreign firms turn to M&As for expansion', 27 April, http://english.peopledaily.com.cn/200704/27/ eng2007042_370339.html, accessed on 21 February 2009.

Pomfret, R. (1991) *Investing in China: Ten Years of the Open Door Policy*, Ames: Iowa State University Press.

Qian, M. and Liu, Z. R. (2000) The Chinese IT Industry Development, 4 June, http//:www.cttl.com.cn, accessed on 25 August 2006.

Roseman, D. (2005) 'The WTO and telecommunications services in China: three years on', *Info: The Journal of Policy, Regulation and Strategy for Telecommunications, Information and Media*, 7, 2: 25–48.

Sudarsanam, P. (1995) *The Essence of Mergers and Acquisitions*, London: Prentice-Hall.

—— (2003) *Creating Value from Mergers and Acquisitions: The Challenges, an Integrated and International Perspective*, London: Prentice-Hall.

Third Annual Mergers and Acquisition Proceedings Shanghai (2008), http://www.tvca.org.tw/download/970917.pdf, accessed on 20 February 2009.

Tong, Y. H. (2004) 'Enterprises are the foundation of developing the ICT industry', http//:www.cttl.com.cn, 9 July, accessed on 25 August 2006.

Wang, J. and Liu, X. (2002) 'An analysis of the constraining factors for MNCs' acquisition of state-owned enterprises', *Modern Economic Research*, 8: 51–53.

Wang, R. Z. (2003) 'An analysis of MNCs' acquisition of listed companies in China', *Listed Companies*: 2–6.

Wang, W., Zhang, J. J. and Li, B. (eds) (2004) *China Mergers and Acquisitions Yearbook*, Beijing: Posts and Telecom Press.

Xinhua News Agency (2008) 'China sees mobile phone production growth slow', 30 April, http://www.china.org.cn/business/2008–04/30/content_15039699. htm, accessed on 21 February 2009.

Zhou, B. Y. (2004) 'Develop large companies, build up a powerful country', http//:www.cttl.com.cn, 9 July, accessed on 25 August 2006.

# 9 The changing face of management in Hong Kong

*Ng Sek Hong and Olivia Ip*

- Introduction
- Context
- Case studies
- Key challenges
- Conclusion

## Introduction

Management in Hong Kong owes its current features and pattern largely to the cultural and normative heritages of both Chinese and British custom and practice. Hong Kong's pluralistic and permissive culture is a classic hybrid of Eastern and Western influences. This normative heterogeneity has made Hong Kong and management of its enterprises almost unique and distinct from other young industrial societies in East Asia. Besides, business and organizational changes have been commonplace in both commerce and industry, giving Hong Kong management a high reputation for market sensitivity and flexibility. It has hence earned a reputation as one of the world's few bastions of 'free-wheeling capitalism'. Thus, most Hong Kong enterprises, which are largely small or medium-sized, have been responsive and adaptive to market forces in the external business environment. The way that Hong Kong enterprises have promptly adjusted their business natures to exploit emerging opportunities in the market demonstrates not only their alertness and flexibility but the supremacy of market forces in Hong Kong's private sector decision-making. Enterprises and their management have remained independent, not relying upon state sponsorship to enhance their competitive ability, in spite of globalization and the surge of business competition emanating from that process.

A classic illustration of Hong Kong business flexibility is the mass relocation of Hong Kong factories across the border after China opened up and started liberalizing the investment environment for foreign and overseas capital in the mid- and late 1980s. These moves were spontaneous and private business decisions owed little to government support or prompting. Yet, in the process, these industrial enterprises concertedly reorganized their production lines. In an almost homogeneous pattern, industrial establishments based in Hong Kong were reconstituted into a geographically dispersed network structure. Typically, the Hong Kong operation was scaled down and consolidated into a service and managerial core acting as the head office, distribution centre and warehouse. In parallel, physical production and associated processing activities were hived off and housed in the mainland. The workshops largely drew on local supplies of inexpensive labour and land. These restructuring activities of Hong Kong industrial capital gave rise to a new division of labour and economic partnership between Hong Kong and the mainland and attested to the resilience of its managerial leadership.

In this chapter, we attempt to trace the evolution of management and management practices in Hong Kong in the era of globalization and Hong Kong's reversion to the Peoples' Republic of China in 1997, when it became a Special Administrative Region (SAR). First, we review the historical and theoretical context of the developments in the topic area. Then we turn to a brief discussion of the present challenges faced by Hong Kong businesses and their responses, drawing on data from two local case studies.

## Context

Signs of modernity are evident in Hong Kong, which has grown to become a city-port known for its cosmopolitan nature and cultural pluralism. Its process of modernization and economic growth has generated more affluent patterns of consumption. And this shift towards a consumption-oriented mass culture has stimulated pluralistic growth in the retail business sector. Other important examples of modernity, besides lifestyle, have also affected Hong Kong's economy and society. These include, for instance, the expanded penetration and role of the world's financial markets, the communications revolution, the spread of information technology (IT), and the increasingly strategic roles of the export and re-export sectors and service production. Equally important has been the creeping growth of individualism, a drift towards emphasizing the autonomy of the self, and the accompanying prerogative of freedom of choice over one's life planning, lifestyle and pursuits in career progression.

The above features, as portrayed by the sociologist Giddens (1988), constitute the syndrome of age of modernity/post-modernity. This syndrome is also engulfed by the globalization process, which affects the whole world. 'Globalization, in sum, is a complex range of processes, driven by a mixture of political and economic influences. It is changing everyday life, particularly in the developed countries, at the same time as it is creating new transnational systems and forces', which have also uplifted newer societies, such as Hong Kong. Globalization has therefore been heralded as the central and generic imperative 'transforming the institutions of the societies in which we live' (Giddens, 1988: 33).

Convergence among modern societies often accompanies globalization and helps explain many of the changing practices and institutions governing business and socio-economic life in Hong Kong. Examples are the development of a complex system of financial institutions trading in the growing capital market, policed by a maturing regime of regulating norms extensively modelled upon those of the world's leading financial centres, such as New York and London.[1] Both private business and public sectors are also emulating the examples and practices set by their foreign counterparts. Management in leading corporate businesses, like Cathay Pacific Airways and the electricity power supply companies, are benchmarking their corporate performance and employment practices against those in analogous industries in industrially advanced economies. Even the Hong Kong SAR government, in its zeal to reform the civil service wholesale, is benchmarking itself proactively against many lean public sector bureaucracies in the West. These developments attest, therefore, to a conspicuous propensity for Hong Kong to converge with other industrial societies amid globalization.

Foremost, the globalization of trade, capital investment and associated economic activities has presented businesses operating in Hong Kong with a new dimension of competition, uncertainty and opportunity. Benchmarking, a popular concept in the field of management, denotes attempts to refer to or borrow ideas from the standard practices of leading enterprises. Hong Kong businesses are already benchmarking themselves against industrially advanced economies and elsewhere and evolving practices to emulate them. It is also steadily converging with developed industrial or post-industrial societies (Ng and Lethbridge, 2000: 15).

Yet Hong Kong has attained its current position not only through the world's convergence movement, but because of experiences that are unique to its history. What it has achieved to date is inexplicable without considering its dual processes of recommercialization and deindustrialization. These are specific to Hong Kong and stem from the drama of its reintegration with China, and China's move towards market socialism.

The unique Hong Kong story of economic advance and management growth also raises two issues relevant to developing economies as they move into the realm of modernity under globalization. The first pertains to the role of the state in sponsoring such industrial and economic development. The level of state intervention in fashioning the development process is, however, patently low key in the Hong Kong situation, in spite of public policy shifts which reveal the 'government's anxiety to enhance and sustain Hong Kong's competitive advantage'. These policy shifts became 'highly audible after the inception of the SAR' (Lethbridge *et al.*, 2000: 228–29). The SAR administration's approach, although indicating greater willingness to act proactively in key areas of economic planning, still contrasts sharply with the heavy state involvement characteristic of its East Asian counterparts like Singapore, Taiwan and South Korea. Hong Kong, as one of the world's key bastions of 'free-wheeling' capitalism, attests to the efficacy, as well as the disarray, of relying upon the market mechanism and private sector initiative as the principal adjudicator of its business and economic development. Managerial decisions have been relatively free from the constraint of the official 'visible hands'.

The second issue involves the alleged excellence of Asian values, as popularized by the thesis of the spirit of Chinese capitalism, which has purportedly contributed to the East Asian legend of hastened economic growth. It also involves the postulation that these East Asian societies are able to catch up with the industrially advanced nations as late-developing economies. This ability to succeed is sustained on the basis of two strategic advantages these economies apparently enjoy: the hospitable nature of East Asia's native cultures and values in nurturing business and economic success; and the ability of the late-developing East Asian societies to emulate advanced practices and technology of the West by borrowing discriminately from benchmark examples of the earlier developers. However, doubts have also been cast upon the normative efficacy of the reputed Asian approach to enterprise and management. Hong Kong's last British governor, Christopher Patten, epitomizes this scepticism about the Asian myth in his book *East and West* (Patten, 1998: 149–50 and 163–64):

> The case put for the invented concept of Asian values is so intellectually shallow . . . The Asian-values proponents believe that . . . Asians benefit from a different culture with deep roots in Confucianism . . . [Yet, the] discovery of Confucius as the reason for Asians' economic success would have puzzled some of his most faithful followers as well as earlier European philosophers and historians . . . As Weber argued, it was Confucianism which was responsible for Asia's economic torpor, because it lacked the animating work ethic of Protestantism.

Lending support to this critical perspective was the abrupt collapse of the young East Asian economies in the 1997 financial upheavals, followed by the prolonged agony of region-wide recession, which suggests the fragile basis of the East Asian phenomena of prosperity and modernity.

## The cultural hiatus and managerial success: a myth?
## And empirical evidence

Several studies conducted on Hong Kong businesses and their management during the 1980s and early 1990s are worth noting at the macro level to illustrate how the contextual variable of culture has affected managerial characteristics and performance in this territory.

One important development has been the shift away from reliance upon a casual cheap labour pool of semi-skilled and unskilled workers, as a result of 'decasualization' coinciding with Hong Kong's industrial development during the 1970s and 1980s.[2] A 1976 sample survey of 900 employees, designed to replicate the profile of the general workforce, indicated there was a sizeable fraction of casual workers in the labour force, with as many as 23 per cent of the respondents identified as long-term casual workers (*cheung-saan-kung*) and 16 per cent as temporary casual workers (*saan-kung*). The proportion of workers in regular permanent employment status (*cheung-kung*) was limited to about 60 per cent (Turner *et al.*, 1991: 26–27).[3] There were strong vestiges of Chinese traditional custom and practices in the management of the local workforce, reminiscent of the paternalistic organization of Chinese family business.

From the 1980s onwards, however, many of the corporate bureaucratic employers in Hong Kong started importing and emulating the more enlightened arrangements of Western-style personnel management.

Many firms began to convert their piece-rate and daily-rate compensated casual workers into staff status by placing them on a monthly payroll. Decasualization was also a rational strategy for labour retention, as labour shortage grew steadily around this period of sustained growth and prosperity. People management in Hong Kong became more sophisticated as it was more conscious of and explicit about the logic of enhanced labour force morale and commitment for work and business performance. Such a shift towards permanent employment as the predominant form of hiring, assisted partly by the government's propagation of continuity of employment in the Employment Ordinance, was, however, later arrested by a new wave of recasualization when flexi hiring grew popular in the early 1990s. This recent pattern again emulates Western post-industrial trends of atypical employment.

In a series of small-scale studies sponsored by the Asian Productivity Organization (APO) between the latter half of the 1960s and the early 1980s, the researchers were able to identify cultural traits associated with the so-called Chinese character of both employer and employee in contributing towards the flexibility and adaptability of small and medium-sized enterprises (SMEs).[4] A 1986 study of the impact of computerization on the workplace elucidated the informality with which Hong Kong enterprises introduced numerical and electronic-based technology into their organizations (Kao et al., 1989: 125, 134, 138 and 142–43; Levin and Ng, 1995: 131–41). Most Chinese-owned enterprises appeared to prefer a low-key approach to the management of innovations and change, opting for ad hoc adjustments which lacked a coherent strategy for restructuring. Informality and loosely structured procedures were widely believed to lie at the core of Hong Kong industry's versatility, having a structural looseness along with a resilience to adapt and adjust promptly to changing perimeters in the market and environment.

These attitudes have been cherished and upheld as an endemic advantage of this Oriental city economy, which prides itself on its ability to excel as an exemplary model of 'free market and enterprise'. It has become a world legend of recent economic success, inspiring Western businesses through the virtues of bureaucratic leanness and deregulation. These admired features are widely labelled as the SAR's 'legal permissiveness' and 'institutional openness'. Such inherent adaptability has been heralded as a key Hong Kong strategic advantage in global competition, having allowed a wide latitude of free market adjustments and business flexibility for both capital and labour. The pervasive image of Hong Kong management in its post-war economic development is hence hallmarked by 'the relative fluidity and elastic structure of business and employing units in the economy' when conducting and reshaping their activities (Cheung *et al.*, 2000: 180).

In research published in 1997 that summarized and reviewed a series of APO-sponsored studies on workplace culture and productivity, some local findings elucidating adjustments in managerial approach leading to the introduction of changes and innovations were yielded from a small sample of case studies conducted on service businesses (Ng *et al.*, 1997a). The subject enterprises included a trading conglomerate, a Chinese family-based bank and a travel agency. The creeping pressures of labour shortage and inflated demand hastened the pace of economic and price growth in the early 1990s, and emasculated paternalistic workplace labour practices. The latter phenomenon is exemplified in the case of a standard-bearing Chinese family bank, which began to assimilate an incentive bonus scheme and other aspects of a high-performance management system (HPMS) into its standardized personnel policy, designed originally to provide an employee with job security and income stability. But this example aside, these cases basically reiterated the Chinese preference for unspecified trust as the nexus of managing change and workplace labour relations amid these changes. The authors emphasized, as a core feature of their report, the instrumentality of these values for cementing a 'psychological contract':

> An obvious factor in this connection is the element of 'trust' as mutual between labour and management. In a sense, it epitomizes the implicit 'psychological contract' at work perhaps best exemplified by the welfare 'paternalism' of Japanese and Chinese enterprises and managerial ethos . . . The psychological contract is hence a moral embodiment of that diffused bond of trust and affective commitment between the parties to an employment relationship. In the instance of our case studies, signs of such a cementing an 'implicit' contract are traceable from the 'corporate mission' inculcated by the trading conglomerate, the enterprise and work culture cherished by the travel agency, and the paternalistic style of benevolent management pursued by the bank.
>
> (Ng *et al.*, 1997a: 81–82)

The authors hinted, in their discussions, at a euphoria attached by popular management writings to the legendary efficacy of Asian values, which pivots around Confucian ethics in a way that is similar to the relationship between Western capitalism and Protestantism. Such imagery helps to give a perspective to Hong Kong's success. As a new industrial society with an Asian cultural heritage, Hong Kong has successfully conserved 'vestiges of the Confucian tradition in its value systems which still affect important industrial and work values of the employer and the employed' (Ng *et al.*, 1997a: 82). The continued practice of a Confucian approach towards the etiquette of people governance has yielded a local preference for managerial paternalism, co-operation, mutual trust, harmony and aversion to open conflict. Hence the thesis emerges that the Hong Kong approach towards people management and enterprise governance diverges materially from 'the "adversarial" model of western industrial relations', and 'favors instead labour–management collaboration and helps explain the relative quiescence of the workplace in accepting technological and productivity innovations initiated by management at the workplace' (Ng *et al.*, 1997a: 82–83).

Asian branding can be problematic, and the authors express serious doubt about the 'transferability' of the Hong Kong prescription to those Asian economies lacking a similar history of colonial pluralism. They argue that Hong Kong businesses 'appear to have owed much of the structural and manpower flexibilities they enjoy' also to a 'widely documented "parochial" character of this territory – that is, its respect for the "natural logic" of the market and "free enterprise" and, by implication, its tradition of "institutional permissiveness" to private sector activities and voluntary practices' (Ng *et al.*, 1997a: 83). Of hallmark significance are the absence in Hong Kong of any legal provisions for a minimum wage and any statutory controls on standard work hours (except for young persons employed in factory work), as well as the weakness of union representation and the practices of collective bargaining and joint consultation in the private sector.

The supposed uniqueness of Hong Kong's advances into industrialism and post-industrialism has given rise to scepticism about its usefulness as a model for other Asian new economies. In an essay arguing against Hong Kong as a model for emulation, the authors pointed to the irony that Hong Kong's achievements 'are probably the results of accident, not design'. They suggest that the Hong Kong success legend attests more to a 'market or culturist approach' than to the widely acclaimed law of global convergence, as Hong Kong lacks the state-led agenda evident in almost every East Asian nation. Hong Kong has grown prosperous essentially as 'a convenient marketplace-cum-workshop in which systematic social and economic engineering has been conspicuous for its absence' (Ng, 1996a: 297). To label Hong Kong's transition as an exercise in economic restructuring that is reminiscent of First or Third World economic agendas can be an unwittingly simplistic overstatement because:

Hong Kong's activities in the realm of 'economic restructuring' or the 'new international division of labour' have rather been dictated by relatively bizarre market responses and human adjustment, and not in any way by a national strategy or development policy. Moreover, Hong Kong's economic restructuring process to date would not have crystallized in its present form if not for the modernization and economic reforms now going on inside China. Earlier, the inception of Hong Kong as an export-oriented industrial division of labour (for instance, its role as an offshore production base, essentially ancillary to advanced industrial economies like those of the USA and Japan in the 60s and 70s) would not have taken root were it not for the waves of regional upheavals including the Korean War in the 50s, and the Vietnam War in the 60s and 70s.

(Ng, 1996a: 297)

Hong Kong defies the logic of any long-term planned strategy for both the economy and its business management. Its sustained growth, since it became a *de facto* haven for mainland refugees in the 1950s, was actually a sequence of disjointed regional upheavals in Asia, punctuated by incremental and cyclical growth which these crises precipitated. The hybrid nature of business, industrial and work values in Hong Kong has been a product of 'a resilient legacy of Confucian trust and altruistic tendencies, flavored by a classic free market preference of its people for flexibility, adaptability, and contractual individualism and impersonality' (Turner *et al.*, 1980: 157). Indeed, three decades ago, a benchmarking academic enquiry commissioned by the British government into the Hong Kong economy and labour market portrayed the colony as 'a picture of multiple paradox' (Ng, 1996b: 113), leaning upon 'borrowed time, borrowed place' (Hughes, 1976). The research team conducting this work labelled it as 'the world's nearest contemporary equivalent to the nineteenth century ideal of *laissez-faire* industrial capitalism' (Turner *et al.*, 1980: 157). There was compatibility between the fluidity of business and institutions in Hong Kong and the transient nature of this refugee society. In the imagery which they presented, Hong Kong society was predominantly Chinese and yet 'complexly fragmented, stratified, and shifting in ways which have discouraged its crystallization on firm class lines' (Turner *et al.*, 1980: 9). There was a managerial-cum-business elite, allied to the governing colonial echelon, but a managerial class remained fluid rather than deeply ingrained. This 'Hong Kong syndrome' was perceived to be a distinct paradox, long before globalization became a fashionable phenomenon worldwide.

However, it has to be conceded that globalization since the 1990s has affected Hong Kong visibly, especially as its impact is compounded by

Hong Kong's decolonization and its geopolitical reintegration with China. The result is a young Asian society whose people and businesses appear enmeshed perpetually in an insecure, transient and defensive psychological complex, seeking shelter as well as opportunities. Sensitivity, responsiveness, adaptability and an opportunistic strategy for both the individual and the enterprise are essential for survival, hence becoming a normative aspect of Hong Kong culture and crystallizing as a popular managerial ethos. As a former refugee society, an aversion psychology inherited by the post-war generations towards political uncertainty, compounded by the 1997 handover, has derailed Hong Kong and pushed the neurotic bulk of its middle class into emigration. These affluent emigrants, essentially a central class, comprised businessmen, managers, professionals and public sector employees. Their exodus led to a dual process of brain drain and capital attrition, which climaxed in the aftermath of the Beijing episode on 4 June 1989. Such a drain forced many Hong Kong local businesses to internationalize their human and capital resources in order to maintain their competitive competencies, in spite of the 'localization' propensities associated with decolonization.[5]

Ironically, the emigration syndrome of people and capital leaving Hong Kong and resettling abroad because of their political apprehension about China coincided with the attraction of Hong Kong capital back into China. Since the late 1980s, Hong Kong has crept unwittingly into another era of externalization and globalization because of the migrant movement touched off by the 1997 handover. Globalization was later accelerated by escalating business opportunities stimulated by China's economic advances alongside East Asia as well as growth led by Japan. These attractive economic opportunities prompted the emigrants to return, and also attracted foreign capital that actively exploited Hong Kong as a conduit to the potential Chinese market.[6] Therefore, in contrast with the political independence of many East Asian nations, the 'late decolonization' of Hong Kong towards the close of the twentieth century exposed it to the world globalization tide in an accentuated 'paradigm'. Hong Kong's history of 'decolonization' is not likely to be repeated elsewhere, not even in neighbouring Macau, which was also reunified with China in 1999 as a second SAR after almost 400 years of Portuguese rule.

Hong Kong therefore became a modern/post-modern refugee society and a young, vibrant economy. While the First World nations are globalizing their economic and trading relations largely by deregulating the transnational movement of both people and capital and external trade, Hong Kong has apparently benefited also from this globalization process. The embrace of the globalization trend also extended to cover other parts of East Asia, in particular China, during the last two decades of the twentieth century. However, as argued by Christopher Patten and other critics who were sceptical about the logic of East–West convergence, much of this globalization phenomenon, visible in Hong Kong and elsewhere in East Asia, could have distorted the actual picture by presenting modernity/post-modernity simply in a nominal, synthetic and partial form. Their rejoinder is that globalization can be viewed as a myth associated with the fashionable emulation of Western lifestyles and urbanism. Globalization stops at 'global materialism', and beyond that the superstructure and decision-making systems of East Asian management remain conservative, authoritarian and even archaic as sanctioned by Confucian Asian values. Hardly developed, the latter are fragile and lack the resilience of a civil society in the West. Such fragility is attested to by the bursting of East Asia's 'bubble' in the 1997 currency upheavals.

However, globalization still offers a hard-to-refute interpretation of all rapid changes today in the East Asia region. It has been noted that a new horizon is dawning upon these young Asian societies by the freer cross-border migration of labour and capital within the region:

> This Hong Kong feature, suggesting a transient culture which will remain uncrystalized because of (and in spite of) changes, may in future help us understand work values in other new or rejuvenated economies in neighboring societies, which are affected equally, if not more, by the international migration of labour and capital across national boundaries, a migration now clearly on the rise all over the world.
>
> (Ng, 1996b: 113)

## Globalization, business benchmarking, and converging managerial and labour market practices

The globalization syndrome has evidently affected the reshaping of Hong Kong businesses. Globalization, of course, is not as neat a notion as it seems, in spite of its popularization as a fashionable label. As pointed out by Child, even an academic treatment of the concept lacks consensus. The term has been used to describe the geopolitical retreat of 'the national barriers to the operation of economic forces' and, alternatively, it has also been linked metaphysically to 'profound changes in values, attitudes and

personal identity', as a manifestation of modernity/post-modernity
(Child, 1999: 30). It is also imperative to address the globalization
phenomenon largely as a generic transnational process which extends
from the economic arena to institutional emulation and benchmarking
in standards and practices, suggesting a propensity for 'convergence'.[7]
This is a comprehensive perspective on globalization, one which
embraces a market as well as a normative dimension:

> Globalization comprises a host of facts and observations such as the
> accelerated growth of world trade and direct investment since the mid-80s,
> the global distribution of the value added chain of companies . . . or the
> global integration of money and capital markets. Yet globalization is
> not only an economic phenomenon, but rather includes the contracting role
> of the nation-state, and the emergence of other social values and ways of
> life.
>
> (Steger, 1998: 1)

This liberal and generic approach to globalization suggests a world-wide
propensity for ideological integration and harmonization of global
standards across nations and societies – notably in human rights
and employment practices, as well as managerial assumptions and
prescriptions. The process is also conspicuous for bridging the regulatory
regimes of financial and capital market operations world-wide. Hong
Kong's industrial and economic restructuring processes have also
redefined to a certain extent the territory's infrastructure under the
impact of globalization. Yet empirical studies have indicated that these
innovations are limited and suggest the leisurely pace in which Hong
Kong's institutional regime of industrial regulation has advanced towards
First World standards in spite of globalization.

One of these studies investigated the orientation of Hong Kong
business and management towards the agenda of equal pay and
equal opportunities. Hong Kong began to evolve a community-wide
consciousness about human rights in the early 1990s, as its people
came to expect benchmarking the SAR as a civil society against
Euro-American (and global) standards. This was in the currency of
world-wide propagation of civil liberties and human rights, attested and
backed by the Basic Law promulgated by China for the Hong Kong SAR
in 1990 and the 1991 Bill of Rights Ordinance (enacted by the colonial
government as a liberal and comprehensive legal code on civil liberties),
which enshrine the continued practice of the rule of law in Hong Kong in
spite of the transfer of sovereignty.

The rights movement, popularized as a global ideology by the First World, the United Nations, and international agencies like the International Labour Organization (ILO), also prompted Hong Kong to formalize safeguards against discrimination as well as devices sanctioned to equalize opportunities, especially across the gender divide. The pre-1997 government reversed its prolonged indecision and endorsed application of the standard-bearing United Nations Convention on the Elimination of All Forms of Discrimination Against Women (CEDAW) in 1996. Hong Kong started to codify a series of counter-discrimination laws with the introduction of the Sex Discrimination Ordinance and the Disability Discrimination Ordinance in 1995, backed up by the appointment of the Equal Opportunities Commission as the enforcing agency (Ng and Lethbridge, 2000: 218–19). The workplace was evidently affected, and most Hong Kong employers, especially large corporate businesses, and their managements responded with an accommodating and cooperative attitude towards this legislation. Many even acted proactively by presenting themselves as equal opportunity employers. This became a hallmark of fashionable and enlightened people management and human resource policy, and was especially noticeable among the pattern-setting multinational corporations (MNCs). In a study sponsored by the Equal Opportunities Commission in 1997 on the feasibility of introducing to Hong Kong a statutory regime to regulate equal pay by law and enshrine the principle of equal pay for equal worth, indicative findings were yielded on the Hong Kong workplace and labour market as well as managerial practices in this arena. The companies' changing profiles hinted at a propensity both to converge with and diverge from the global patterns of practising equity in the workplace.

Managerial attitudes expressed in this study were dichotomized between those upheld by corporate management in the primary sector and those espoused by smaller employers of petty capital located within the secondary sector of the Hong Kong labour market. The imprints of globalization were noticeable in the large corporate employers as the standard-bearers of the world's enlightened and liberal workplace standards. They were assiduous in pursuing the best practices of the level playing field. At the two corporate businesses investigated (the Hong Kong-based airline Cathay Pacific and the multinational Philips Electronics China Group), equity norms were a 'priority' and governed payment of basic pay, incremental adjustments, bonus payments and promotions. The two companies' personnel policies purported to give maximum latitude for open competition for all employees in pursuing their career advancement and management development free of discrimination and handicaps due to gender, ethnicity, religion and other possibly disabling criteria found in the traditional society of the past (Ng *et al.*, 1997b: 16). Cathay Pacific, in particular, was a leading proponent of the level playing field. The study suggested that Cathay's clear policy to preclude any employment and rewards differentials because of 'gender, marital status, sexual preference, pregnancy, ethnic background or disability' was a sign of its corporate maturity. The adoption of a more sophisticated corporate image was opportune, as Cathay began to globalize from a Hong Kong localized horizon into 'a trans-national airline hiring a cabin fleet which is increasingly multi-racial and multi-cultural in composition' (Ng *et al.*, 1997b: 21).

At Philips Electronics China Group, a subsidiary of the giant Holland-based MNC, the Hong Kong management was on the whole more self-effacing than that of Cathay. It presented a less distinctive image, if not a low profile, in advancing itself as an equal opportunity employer.

However, Philips was a long-established global business, enshrined as a benchmarking employer in human resource policies and practices. Because of this, its austerity drive during the lean period of 1996–97 did not erase its world-wide commitment to continue as an equal pay employer in applying the principle of equal pay for equal worth. The Hong Kong office, Philips' regional head office for its China Group, was laudable in applying the Hay system of job evaluation as a personnel procedure to govern the equitable administration of a fair pay system among its staff members.

It would have been hazardous to construe a picture of convergence of Hong Kong with the First World domain in employment practices on the basis of the above evidence from the aristocratic employing units within the 'primary' sector of the labour market. Actually, interviews with management of both small and medium-sized enterprises and the key labour union centres yielded an observation to the contrary. There was almost a 'consensus' repudiating any proposal to institute for the Hong Kong labour market an equal pay legislation analogous to the UK Equal Pay Act, or comparable provisions in the European Community Law (specifically Article 119, which declares that the principle of equal pay for equal work is legally enforceable against every employer among its member states). The respondents answering the survey, including leaders of the labour movement, articulated a doctrinal faith in Hong Kong's freely self-adjusting labour market as the logic of a performing economy. For them, state intervention in the wage market was likely to bureaucratize production and the labour process. An excessive and obtrusive body of rules was liable to pervert and impede its efficient functioning. This managerial psychology was elaborated as follows:

> An 'equal pay' legislation was hence seen by the bulk of these small and medium-sized employers with cynicism, with little but nominal pay-off to any beneficiaries apart from helping 'package' Hong Kong's regulatory institutions to make the workplace system look more fashionable and analogous to their western counterparts. However, any legalistic intervention in this direction was liable to make these Hong Kong employers of petty capital more susceptible to the perils and burdensome costs of court litigation processes, as well as to compromise again the flexible responsiveness of Hong Kong businesses. These developments were perceived as alien and inhospitable to business of small capital, and hence detrimental to the latter's propensity to invest in Hong Kong. A further argument canvassed pointed to the lukewarm business approval of these institutional advances as they were hardly in stride with the world-wide trend of de-regulating the workplace.
>
> (Ng *et al.*, 1997b: 36)

Even the labour movement was not keen for such an equal pay legislative initiative. The critical perspective espoused by the leading trade union centres was largely a parochial assumption and emphasized Hong Kong's cultural distinctiveness. Deploring the free drift towards civil litigation on rights issues in Euro-American societies, these labour organizations pointed to the cumbersome and even absurd nature of the Western-style legalistic approach towards the equal pay principle. These elements of legalism and bureaucracy were perceived as especially alien to 'the Hong Kong culture of a permissive and individualized labour market free from any legislative or administrative controls and constraints by the government' (Ng *et al.*, 1997b: 44).

The union centres were also reserved over potential costs entailed by an equal pay statutory regime for Hong Kong, in view of the costly nature of the supportive infrastructure. The First World prescription of using job evaluation (JE) and performance appraisal (PA) was seen to have become excessively bureaucratic and expensive, and these procedures' application was not entirely unproblematic. The labour unions specifically opposed any suggestions 'to import . . . specialized areas like job evaluation and performance appraisal' (Ng *et al.*, 1997b: 44). They doubted whether the SMEs in Hong Kong would have the necessary managerial resources, capabilities and interests to institute and develop a sophisticated inventory of these instruments for JE, PA, or both.

The equal pay study took place in the late 1990s during a period when the Hong Kong economy was progressing along its course of restructuring. The large corporate businesses and workplaces had been modernized, catching up in many aspects of people management with fashionable Western practices, partly because of the effects of globalization. And even the SMEs, especially those in the export-oriented manufacturing sector, substantially reshaped their business and production process management by the relocation of their assembly works in a new organizational form of cross-border networking.

Given the changing milieu of Hong Kong's politics, society and economy in the period of study, the equal pay project is an exemplary pointer to the way that continuities are preserved while Hong Kong is modernizing and enhancing its normative and institutional infrastructure. These modernizing and reform activities are popularly perceived as endeavours of benchmarking Hong Kong with global standards. Hong Kong has demonstrated a prudent orientation on this course but still there have been instances of selectivity and stubbornness due to doctrinal adherence to a prized heritage of a free labour market. Although Hong Kong's free labour and employment market has been viewed by critics as a myth, there was, and still is, a society-wide reluctance to waive this label. Both Hong Kong workers and capitalists alike, at least up to the 1990s, were apprehensive about legalistic intervention into the permissive and little-regulated wage market, even in the name of a humanitarian aspiration for equality and equity in employment. Because of globalized values, both organized labour and business management, including SMEs, approve of the principle of equal rights in the workplace. Yet both sides also agree that a regime of legally sponsored normative prescriptions accompanied by a corresponding series of voluntary initiatives in the private sector would work better than mandatory legislation. The present provisions are hence perceived as adequate in advancing Hong Kong and its image in this 'rights' domain.

However, these *status quo* parameters were largely altered by post-1997 recession crises, and it appears that the new paradigm, which Hong Kong enters because of the economic adversity caused by globalized competition, has exposed it even more to the 'dialects' of its institutional immaturity. This immaturity has increasingly polarized society into the rich and poor, the 'haves' and 'have-nots'.[8]

It is useful here to mention another study, conducted by the Workplace Study Group, Chinese Management Centre, University of Hong Kong, on workplace communication and human resource activities among Hong Kong enterprises as they were surveyed in the wake of the 1998–99 recession under the sponsorship of the Labour Department of the SAR government. The study focused on a range of key workplace labour relations features, and found that Hong Kong can converge with Western analogous practices while retaining its distinctiveness.

The study indicated that some enterprises allowed limited negotiation in their dialogues with employees. This is suggestive of employer flexibility, probably Hong Kong style, about the use and application of a workplace device which is supposed to be institutionally distinct from union–management collective bargaining (Workplace Study Group, 2000: 46). The researchers argued that the eclipsing and usurping of unionism and its bargaining functions by using joint consultation as an equivalent can be a purposive personnel strategy, as it 'could have enabled these establishments to hold at arm's length any full-scale collective bargaining with trade unions' (Workplace Study Group, 2000: 47). Second, a workplace legacy of Chinese paternalistic benevolence which is reminiscent of an employment-based 'welfarism' also emerges from the findings, so that 'the firm behaves like an extended family analogous to the notion of "commonwealth"'. However, this nostalgic element appears to be withering away, constituting a third feature documented in this study. This third element pertains to the systematic erosion of the permanent hiring norm 'because of the fashionable move of modern business enterprises and workplaces towards the "competitive" model of a "flexi organization"' (Workplace Study Group, 2000: 48).

A performance-based approach to building an effective, dedicated and committed workforce also engenders its own limits and problems. A notable piece of evidence was the equivocal attitude of the respondents, who were human resource practitioners and managers, as to the work-place protocol on the disclosure of information to the workforce on a collective and representative basis. As an enlightened sign of professionalism, such disclosure has always been endorsed by human resource personnel as instrumental in briefing staff on delicate personnel matters, but there are also situations where managements, especially among the large corporate workplaces, elect to withhold information to the affected staff until the eleventh hour. The researchers lamented that 'even apparently liberal managements at enterprises with an established reputation for their enlightened approach towards staff relations were known to curfew and embargo news about who were to be laid off in downsizing exercises because of their neurosis and suspicion that any advanced notification would invite possible acts of sabotage'. What emerged amid the uncertainties of downsizing and personnel de-establishment was a low-trust workplace syndrome, a label which the researchers used to describe a situation when the firm's human resource calculation and decisions clearly 'put the employing organization's interests before everything' (Workplace Study Group, 2000: 49).

The enterprises studied were also found to be lukewarm about and equivocal in institutionalizing any practice of 'bilateral collectivism' on a formal basis. The workplace culture of trade union recognition by employers has remained as feeble as it was in the 1970s and 1980s: 'The practice of workplace labour relations has stayed as pluralistic, diversified and even loose as it was three or four decades ago, except where the growth of modern managerial practices (like human resource prescriptions) and the enlarged scale of business have led to the denser application of communicative devices' (Workplace Study Group, 2000: 51). However, in an age of globalization and convergence of trade, business and employment standards, a distinctively 'Hong Kong' looseness and diversity can look backward and immature when benchmarked against standards promulgated by the ILO and other international government agencies, such as the World Trade Organization. Hence a profitable strategy might be for the administration to encourage better standardization of labour–management protocols at the workplace level, rather than leaving an evident 'institutional' gap of 'workplace "normlessness" detrimental to Hong Kong's image [as a civil society] in the labour and employment area' (Workplace Study Group, 2000: 51). However, the Hong Kong case, it has to be conceded, has been compounded by historical events, of which the most pervasive are now its reunification with China in 1997 and China's move towards market socialism, alongside the advent of globalization. Therefore, a Hong Kong syndrome of sustained paradoxes and contradictions emerges. Ironically, some of these forces combine well to produce a distinctive synergy which has earned Hong Kong a reputation as a benchmark case of economic success, especially among East Asia's newly industrialized economies (NIEs). However, in other instances, cross-pressures are encountered so that Hong Kong is trapped in an impasse on a number of fronts awaiting further institutional reform and progress. Hong Kong can therefore be viewed as a hybrid melting-pot, 'a borrowed place on borrowed time' that echoes as well as defies the logic of theoretical statements like those of the convergence, culturist and late-development theories.

## Lessons from the East Asian financial crisis

The fragile basis of the apparent strength of the East Asian economies (including Hong Kong's) was unmasked and exposed by the financial crisis of 1997. The collapse also illustrates that there is no short-cut to modernity and economic development. The subsequent East Asian recession revealed an almost endemic weakness in the optimistic statements of the late-development and culturist theories, which assume that all or any evolutionary stages can be side-stepped in the Asian process of development. But are events like the 1997 financial upheavals suggestive that Hong Kong and other young East Asian economies must evolve similar institutional (and normative) arrangements for infrastructure building as those characteristic of Western industrial democracies before they can be expected to perform with the same level of consistency and efficacy?

Yet the core lessons learned from the East Asian financial crisis and the prolonged stagflation that beset Euro-American economies throughout most of the 1980s are the relatively crude prescriptions of cost-cutting as a panacea enabling ailing businesses to recover their competitive power. This 'solution' has been widely labelled as the flexibility strategies of lean businesses, which include fashionable streamlining actions like de-layering, downsizing and de-establishment. Many bureaucratic employers have elected to waive labour force commitment and retention in favour of more transient arrangements of this nature, including measures like outsourcing and atypical employment, because of resulting overhead savings. Part-time work, fixed-term contracts and temporary hiring norms have been popularized as a new form of employment arrangement in the reactivated casual labour market, in a world-wide drift towards flexible arrangements and provisions. However, flexi-hiring norms are hardly more than a disguised form of legitimating the use of cheap labour. Ironically, recourse to a cheap labour strategy such as this becomes a popular prescription at the workplace level, featuring the restructuring and renewal activities of the bulk of businesses and enterprises in both the East and West. The use of part-time employees and other forms of flexi-hiring (atypical employment) epitomize a global feature which has probably grown world-wide at the fastest pace among fashionable human resource prescriptions. Hong Kong management emulates its counterparts in the First World within this domain of applying austerity prescriptions.

In Hong Kong, these cost-cutting measures over labour would not have been adopted and practised on such a near epidemic scale were it not for the East Asian financial upheavals and the ensuing recession. Before the downturn, the buoyancy of the market, especially at greeting the advent of the China domain, sustained in Hong Kong such a mood of business confidence that almost all the business enterprises studied pledged a policy of no retrenchment or downsizing in their development and growth agendas. However, financial upheaval was to follow and the Hong Kong economy became trapped in the doldrums. The drain of business optimism was fast and widespread, causing almost all enterprises to embark upon austerity agendas and begin emulating their Western counterparts in practices like downsizing and flexi-hiring. However, at the core of these so-called deregulatory and restructuring activities to streamline was a crude incentive to revert to cheap labour processing as a way of minimizing labour costs.

Paradoxically, the bulk of these dehumanizing austerity measures were disguised as modern and enlightened practices of human resource management (HRM). However, although HRM has gained global popularity as a prescription for managing people, this approach evidently has an elitist dimension as it differentiates, almost explicitly, between the upper crust of the core personnel and the periphery of the less capable and important. And, in spite of its purported focus on people as assets, HRM has embarked on a world-wide trend of employment dualism, which creates a sharp divide between the core and periphery within the labour force, between those who are the able performers and those who are less able.

The propagation of the human nexus as a key element of value-adding processes in modern enterprises, in both the West and East, has unwittingly led to a drift towards the balkanization of a sub-stratum of less competitive people as hard-core unemployables. They, together with young and new entrants to the full-time labour market, provide businesses with a pool of casual labour available for flexi-hiring as non-core marginal workers. They are almost equivalent to the economically deprived, constituting a sub-class phenomenon of low-paid, transient, contingent workers and hard-core unemployables in industry. Possessing the new labels of atypical, non-regular or non-standard employment, they escape branding as unemployed persons and yet are not entirely immune from the vicissitudes of post-industrial capitalism for their lack of employment and income security, employment benefits and welfare packages.

This creation of a casual labour pool of atypical employees is, at its heart, not much different from, nor superior to, the sweat-shop economies in the Third World. Ironically, such a practice contradicts the people orientation that has been expressly articulated by HRM, which actually endorses and practises it. This irony has been vividly demonstrated, for example, by Cathay Pacific, which has reduced its labour costs and revived its profitability during the recession largely because of a conversion to casual hiring of novice flight attendants on an hourly rate, three-year fixed-contract basis. Similarly, Japanese- and Hong Kong-based retail establishments appear to be best equipped to cope with the recession when they are ready to institute part-time employment as a key lever on labour cost control. The growth in popularity of part-time working and fixed-term hiring in Hong Kong was probably due, in the first place, to an emulation by management of Euro-American and Japanese practices around the mid-1990s, but the economic adversity of the post-1997 recession added to its momentum. However, Hong Kong still lags behind the First World in institutionalizing and managing a secondary tier of part-time and atypical employees within its general labour force.

In the following section, we present two illustrative cases of local firms. (For reasons of confidentiality, the names of the firms and the managers are not revealed.)

## Case studies

### Organization case 9.1 The HKE

#### Company background

The HKE is a monopolistic power plant located on Hong Kong Island. Established over a century ago, it now employs over 1,900 employees. The workforce is composed predominantly of technical and skilled workers who are supervised by an elite group of professional engineers and management staff. Their work conditions to a large extent have been reminiscent of those in the public sector in terms of wages, training and promotion opportunities, and fringe benefits. The employees have enjoyed a high level of job security, reflected by the low company turnover rates and, on average, their long years of service in the company. However, recently, the company faced an impending threat which forced it to initiate a series of policy changes.

## Managerial issues faced

The threat came from the government-imposed Scheme of Control review in the mid-2000s, aimed at market deregulation and enhancing competition in the industry. In response, the company started to convert itself, strategically and structurally, from a conservative engineering technocracy into a versatile, customer-oriented service provider enterprise.

## Strategic response

The HRM function was entrusted with a significant role in the renewal exercise. The key issues involved, first, the cultivation and building of an integrative corporate culture, namely V (Vision), M (Mission) and V (Values); second, implementation of a more 'outcome oriented' performance management system; third, achieving competency enhancement via in-house training; and fourth, improving workforce morale.

Among the key strategic issues, a core concern of management was to steer the enterprise towards evolving a leaner organization and hence a 'flexible' workforce. Key HR initiatives in this respect included natural attrition, pay pause and, above all, hiring of 'contract staff' on a fixed-term, two-year contract. This type of hiring, in contrast to the previous 'permanent' hiring, is conducive to flexibility of the company in dealing with problems related to fluctuation of the market. In 2005, the proportion of this type of staff reached a sizable 6 per cent. Going hand in hand with this was the implementation of a new policy of performance management, linking performance appraisal to employees' pay rise, bonus and promotion opportunities.

Source: fieldwork conducted by the authors.

## Organization case 9.2 Company W

## Company background

Company W is one of the leading property management companies in Hong Kong. It was established in 1997 and has since grown into one of the largest service providers in

continued

the industry. The company now employs over 1,100 people, the majority of whom are security guards providing maintenance and security services for tenants and residents in commercial and residential buildings. Due to the nature of the work, most of the employees are semi-skilled, and these are supervised by a small management nucleus located at the company's headquarters. Some of the front-line staff are senior-aged people who have retired from previous occupations, while a small but growing number are new immigrants from the mainland. In contrast with the previous case, property management is a relatively young industry in Hong Kong. But it has maintained relatively stable growth over the past few decades thanks to the sustained expansion of the private and commercial property sector in the SAR.

## Managerial issues faced

The boom in the industry is paralleled by keen market competition among various service providers who have not yet built strong branding and product differentiation among themselves to rival that found in more established industries. There is also persistent pressure from clients, namely the tenants and their legal representative body (the Occupants' Committee), not to increase management fees, which form the core income of the property management companies. With substantial fee hikes out of the question, the property management companies have usually resorted to cost-cutting measures, leading to an industry-wide downward pressure on employees' wages. This, coupled with the twelve-hour days demanded of front-line staff, has contributed to high turnover rates of security guards. The annual turnover rate is generally between 20 and 30 per cent, resulting in persistent staff shortages and recruitment problems for Company W. In recent years, with the improvement of the labour market in Hong Kong and neighbouring regions, the problem of recruitment has worsened. Many front-line staff have left for better-paid jobs or have returned to their previous jobs and employment fields. Staff with managerial experience have quit because they have been offered much better packages by counterpart companies in Macau, where the property business is booming.

## Strategic response

Company W's response has been multifold. First, over the past few years, it has strived to build a stronger corporate image to differentiate itself from the rest of the service providers. For this purpose, it has set up a comprehensive management system, the Integrated Management System, which is strategically modelled on Western management practices. The new system incorporates clients' needs and offers extended areas of service to clients. In a similar vein, it has succeeded in achieving high publicity and acknowledgement by obtaining ISOs, participating on the committees of public and professional bodies, and winning awards from the Labour Department for its management initiatives.

Second, like the power-generating plant, the company's core values are manifested through articulation and implementation of the company's V (Vision), M (Mission) and

V (Values). Furthermore, a series of policies benchmarked against Western HR policies has been launched in the company. In respect to employment practices, the company has implemented a comprehensive performance appraisal system which is linked to the reward system of the company. Conducted on a biannual basis, the performance appraisal system is dualistic, consisting of both self-evaluation and evaluation by the employee's immediate supervisor. By design, the appraisal process entails reflective dialogue between the supervisor and the employee. Whenever there are unresolved differences between the two sides, the site manager will intervene to mediate. If the matter remains unresolved at this stage, it will be submitted to the corporate head-quarters for adjudication. Three criteria are used in the evaluation: 'quality of service', 'quality of management' and 'general knowledge'. The company has also improved the training opportunities of staff by increasing the hours of on-the-job training and the subsidies for training. In addition, innovative and proactive recruitment methods are employed. It organizes, for instance, on-site recruitment exercises and activities in densely populated residential areas for prospective candidates. It is noteworthy that the company is now offering long-term employment to all staff, except for a small number who are hired on a project basis.

Source: fieldwork conducted by the authors.

Next, we turn to the 'voices' of two managers in the two companies.

## Manager case 9.3 Mr Chan (pseudonym), senior manager, the HKE

Mr Chan is one of the senior managers in the HKE. Trained as an engineer, he has served the company for over twenty years. He has witnessed the course of corporate restructuring of the company over the past decade, and has been involved in the implementation of the new initiatives. He generally agrees that such changes are necessary for ensuring proactive and sustained corporate development.

In describing the company's changing corporate culture and employee commitment, Mr Chan made the following comments:

> The pre-existing management style and employee relationship were characteristic of a 'paternalistic' style of management. To a certain extent the management style was reminiscent of that found in traditional Japanese companies which practise life-long employment. In return, the employees have high identity with and are committed to the company. Indeed, this kind of relationship worked well in the company in the past, when there was trust between management and staff. But now, things have changed: some of the employees are only willing to perform their duties in a minimal manner, while still expecting to enjoy long-term employment and other benefits.

continued

## Hiring of contract staff

Mr Chan considered the Scheme of Control review of the industry by the government to be the primary driving force behind the corporate changes. He concurred with the opinion that the company has resorted to recruitment of fixed-term 'contract' staff as a key to containing the market vicissitudes and uncertainties faced by the company. But he hinted that the company may return to the previous practice of long-term employment in the future if market conditions improve.

## The new performance appraisal system

In describing the shift to a performance-based appraisal system, Mr Chan emphasized the prudent approach adopted by the company during the implementation process:

> Before the setting up of the new performance appraisal system, annual reports on employees' performance were completed by heads of the section in a qualitative manner. To ensure comparability, a new performance appraisal system was implemented. But it was done gradually, and the system was first trial-run in a department before its full-scale implementation in the company. To reduce resentment from staff, at the initial stage of the implementation, the results of the appraisal were not linked to the reward system.
>
> Source: personal interview with Mr Chan (pseudonym), a manager in HKE.

## Manager case 9.4 Ms Lee (pseudonym), human resources manager, Company W

Ms Lee is an HR manager of Company W. She is based at the headquarters of the company, located on Hong Kong Island. She works closely with the corporate general manager of human resources, as well as with the site managers who are deployed at the geographically dispersed commercial and residential buildings. Hence, communicating headquarters' decisions and policies to the various sites is an important part of her daily work schedule.

In recent years, Ms Lee has devoted much effort to tackling staff shortages. Though the company has not participated in the voluntary Wage Protection Movement initiated by the government, it has tried to offer wages that are comparable with those offered in the market. She attributed the upsurge in turnover of staff to a lack of commitment among employees:

> In our industry, wage is our staff's primary concern. This is particularly true of the security guards. These workers will immediately quit the job if another employer

in the market offers them a slightly higher wage than ours. Added to this, many young graduates are unwilling to enter into the industry because of its low prestige. During the period of economic recession, recruitment of staff was not a big problem. At one stage, we were even able to recruit younger security guards who held university degrees. But now, as the economic conditions have improved, it has become more and more difficult to recruit and retain our staff, especially those who are on the front line. For the security guards, we can only hope to recruit those who are middle-aged. The problem of recruitment is particularly serious when hiring night-shift staff.

Source: personal interview with Ms Lee (pseudonym),
an HR manager in Company W.

## Key challenges

What are the challenges faced by management in Hong Kong amid globalization? First and foremost, it should be noted that Hong Kong is both an international city and an SAR of China. The challenges it faces therefore inevitably converge with many of those found in Western market-coordinated economies, but are equally shaped by the indigenous forces of the local market and its (colonial) historical and current institutional forms.

One major challenge is the high turnover rate of employees, reflecting lack of commitment and loyalty towards employers. The downward trend of organizational commitment is echoed by an upsurge in turnover rates in Hong Kong in recent years, once the economy showed signs of substantial recovery. High turnover rates are recorded in the pillar industries: notably, in the banking and finance industry, the insurance industry, and the accounting services industry, as well as in the retail industry, where the labour shortage is particularly acute.

The low organizational commitment of the workforce in Hong Kong is revealed by a recent survey which interviewed 815 employees (Department of Management, 2008). It also indicated that respondents' scores of perceived organizational commitment were significantly lower than their scores of perceived occupational commitment. While this phenomenon may have much to do with the aftermath of the economic recession, it can at least be partially explained by the shifting terrain and profile of the labour market in Hong Kong over the past few decades. As Hong Kong enters an era of late modernity and is becoming a knowledge economy, a larger portion of the workforce possesses higher educational and professional qualifications. This type of workforce is prone to identifying with its occupations and professional associations. When their employing organizations fall short of their expectations, such employees are more willing to leave their organizations. The problem is compounded by the entrance of a young cohort of employees into the workforce, namely Generation Y workers. Born in the later half of the 1970s, its members' work attitudes are distinct from those of their parents. How to recruit, train, retain and motivate these intakes will be new challenges for managers and will necessitate ground-breaking management initiatives.

It is also important to note that organizational commitment is rooted in a context of 'high-trust' relationships which can be hampered by management imperatives during economically adverse situations. The case of the power-generation plant illustrates how organizational commitment, once heralded as an important asset, was discarded when faced with market vicissitudes. During times of uncertainty, the company has chosen to shift from a permanent employment system to a fixed-term contract employment system, thus unwittingly waiving long-cherished employees' trust in the process. In the case of the property management company, a different managerial approach has been taken. As the company wants to establish a stable workforce, a permanent employment system has been instituted. However, it is doubtful that such a policy will engender and enhance organizational commitment in an industry where a 'low-trust' relationship has been the norm.

Another challenge faced by management in Hong Kong is the design of an efficient and efficacious PA system. The two cases above are indicative of the dilemmas faced by management in the implementation of a PA system as the latter is benchmarked increasingly against popular Western management practices. A PA system equipped with comprehensive and explicit assessment criteria has been considered critical to developing and maintaining a highly productive workforce. Such a practice has become fashionable among large and medium-sized companies in Hong Kong. However, it is imperative for management to ascertain the qualifications for successful implementation of PA in the Hong Kong context. First, there must be an open dialogue between the appraiser and appraisee at different levels of the organization. However, in many Chinese SMEs, both managers and employees may treat the task of performance appraisal in a perfunctory manner for fear of jeopardizing their relationships and to avoid open conflict. Second, a 'high-trust' relationship between management and staff is always essential to support the successful implementation of PA. Where 'low-trust' staff relations already exist, the system is likely to breed an air of suspicion and resentment among employees. In the case of the power-generation plant, employees have expressed apprehension about the system for lacking transparency, inadvertently stimulating interpersonal competition among colleagues and contributing to discrimination and favouritism.

Notwithstanding the above, Hong Kong's position as an SAR has led to new opportunities as well as uncertainties, as is evidenced by the inter-regional movement of manpower between Hong Kong and the mainland. While the number of Hong Kong people who shuttle between the two regions for work is increasing, the number of mainlanders entering Hong Kong for work is also on the rise. In an attempt to ease the pressure of a shortage of needed manpower, in 2007 the government relaxed its restriction on mainland youth studying and working in the city, making it possible for mainland talents educated in Hong Kong to obtain work visas (Chief Executive of the HKSAR, 2007). This measure will substantively change the labour market terrain in Hong Kong, and certainly will cause concerns, particularly among local graduates. In the long run, such liberation of immigration policy will also result in a more pluralistic managerial echelon in Hong Kong. Such pluralism suggests, possibly, a growing diversity in the assumptions, ideology, behaviour and style of management in Hong Kong.

# Conclusion

As a modern cosmopolitan city, will Hong Kong continue to advance into post-industrialism along its unique path amid the unpredictable currents of globalization? Or will there be gradual erosion of the institutional (and cultural) differences between Hong Kong and other places, leading to similar configurations of management practices, as predicted by convergence theorists? The authors would argue that while Hong Kong is increasingly entangled in forces of global competition and is steadily converging with other developed, post-industrial societies, its unique historical endowments and Sino-British heritage, as well as its dominant economic ideology, which enshrines the sovereignty of the market, will necessitate and shape the substantial adaptation of these management practices prior to their adoption in Hong Kong.

# Notes

1 Perhaps the most lucid example of Hong Kong's convergence with Western economies in the domain of its financial infrastructure is the linked exchange-rate regime which has pegged the Hong Kong dollar to the American dollar at the official rate of US$1–HK$7.8 since October 1980 (Jao, 2000: 132–33). Hong Kong actually has a high world-wide ranking as an international financial centre (IFC). It is the second-largest IFC (after Tokyo) within the Asia-Pacific region and is seventh in the list of the world's top IFCs (Jao, 2000: 139). For a vivid note on the three-tier financial infrastructure now evolving in Hong Kong and the regulatory role performed by the Hong Kong Monetary Authority in emulation of such comparable agencies as the US Federal Reserve and the Bank of England, see Jao (2000: 136–39).

2 A notable development in the labour market during the growth era of the 1980s indicative of industrial and institutional progress of Hong Kong society was, as observed by Turner and his associates in their landmark labour study between 1976 and 1985, 'a decasualization of the blue-collar labour force' paralleled by 'a lengthening of the work period for which wages are normally paid', which suggested 'a significant stabilization of workers' attachment to particular firms' (Turner et al., 1991: 27).

3 However, the percentage of permanent workers in the general labour force grew to 87 per cent in the 1985 follow-up survey, when wholly casual employees also shrank to a share as low as 5 per cent of the Hong Kong workforce (Turner et al., 1991: 27). See also Levin and Ng (1995: 130).

4 For findings of these APO studies in the late 1980s, see Kao et al. (1989: 142–43).

5 For a lucid exposition of the exodus of Hong Kong's middle-class personnel and families, which reached an almost epidemic scale at the beginning of the 1990s, see Turner et al. (1991: 103–04). See also Emmos (1991), Tang (1995: 117–50) and Ng (1995: 209–10).

6 For a brief review of these socio-political crises and events which hastened the geographical mobility of Hong Kong capital and people, while increasing their cosmopolitan attitude and horizons, see Ng (1998: 212–13, 215). See also Ng and Cheng (1994: 171–204)

7 Hence our observation that 'The globalization of external trade relations has meant a growing need for Hong Kong and its business enterprises to benchmark themselves against their counterparts and competitors, at both the macro and micro levels . . . Hong Kong is steadily converging with other developed industrial or post-industrial societies' (Ng and Lethbridge, 2000: xv, 228–29).

8 On signs of an emerging new 'industrial proletariat' in Hong Kong, see, for example, Ng (1995: 203–05). On the widening gap between rich and poor, see, for example, Wong (2000), *South China Morning Post* (2000) and Slavick (2000). This problem of wealth polarization can be a global phenomenon arising from the ethos of competitive 'individualism' in 'post-modern' societies (Giddens, 1988).

# Bibliography

Cheung, G., Ho, E., Ng, S. H. and Poon, C. (2000) 'Business restructuring in Hong Kong', in S.H. Ng and D. Lethbridge (eds) *The Business Environment in Hong Kong* (4th edition), Hong Kong: Oxford University Press.

Chief Executive of the Hong Kong SAR (2007) 'Policy address', 10 October, http://www.policyaddress.gov.hk/07-08/eng/press.html, accessed on 11 November 2007.

Child, J. (1999) 'Theorizing about organization cross-nationally', Working paper, Hong Kong: Chinese Management Centre, University of Hong Kong.

Department of Management, City University of Hong Kong (2008) 'Employee confidence, industrial relations and work commitment survey', Press release, 15 May.

Emmos, C. F. (1991) *Hong Kong Prepares for 1997: Politics and Emigration in 1987*, Hong Kong: Centre of Asian Studies, University of Hong Kong.

Giddens, A. (1988) *The Third Way: The Renewal of Social Democracy*, Cambridge: Polity Press.

Hughes, R. (1976) *Borrowed Place, Borrowed Time: Hong Kong and its Many Faces*, London: Deutsche.

Jao, Y. C. (2000) 'Monetary system and banking structure', in S. H. Ng and D. Lethbridge (eds) *The Business Environment in Hong Kong* (4th edition), Hong Kong: Oxford University Press.

Kao, H., Ng, S. H. and Taylor, D. (1989) 'Country case studies Hong Kong', in H. S Choi, S. K. Subramanian, C. O. Lee and S. U. Kim (eds) *Hybrid of Man and Technology*, Tokyo: Asian Productivity Organization.

Lethbridge, D., Ng, S. H. and Chan, M. (2000) 'Is Hong Kong entering a new paradigm?', in S. H. Ng and D. Lethbridge (eds) *The Business Environment in Hong Kong* (4th edition), Hong Kong: Oxford University Press.

Levin, D. and Ng, S. H. (1995) 'From an industrial to a post-industrial economy: challenges for human resource management in Hong Kong', in A. Verma, T. Kochan and R. Lansbury (eds) *Employment Relations in the Growing Asian Economies*, London: Routledge.

Ng, S.H. (1995) 'Labour and employment', in J. Cheng and S. Lo (eds) *From Colony to SAR: Hong Kong's Challenges Ahead*, Hong Kong: The Chinese University Press.

—— (1996a) 'The development of labour relations in Hong Kong and some implications for the future', in I. Nish, G. Redding and S. H. Ng (eds) *Work and Society: Labour and Human Resources in East Asia*, Hong Kong: Hong Kong University Press.

—— (1996b), 'Work values and organizations: A glimpse of the Asian syndrome', in I. Nish, G. Redding and S. H. Ng (eds) *Work and Society: Labour and Human Resources in East Asia*, Hong Kong: Hong Kong University Press.

—— (1998) 'Postscript: Hong Kong at the dawn of a new era', in S.H. Ng and D. Lethbridge (eds) *The Business Environment in Hong Kong* (3rd edition with a post-handover postscript), Hong Kong: Oxford University Press.

Ng, S. H. and Cheng, S. M. (1994), 'The affluent migrants as a "class" phenomenon: the Hong Kong case', in S. K. Lau, M. K. Lee, P. S. Wan and S. L. Wong (eds) *Inequalities and Development; Social Stratification in Chinese Societies*, Hong Kong: Hong Kong Institute of Asian-Pacific Studies, the Chinese University of Hong Kong.

Ng, S.H. and Lethbridge, D. (2000) 'Introduction', in S. H. Ng and D. Lethbridge (eds) *The Business Environment in Hong Kong* (4th edition), Hong Kong: Oxford University Press.

Ng, S. H., Stewart, S. and Chan, F. T. (1997a) *Current Issues of Workplace Relations and Management in Hong Kong*, Hong Kong: Centre of Asian Studies, University of Hong Kong.

Ng, S. H., Tse, A., Wright, R. and Cheuk, M. Y. (1997b) *An Interim Report on Equal Pay for Equal Worth: The Case of Hong Kong with a Note on European Practices*, Unpublished monograph, Hong Kong: University of Hong Kong.

Nish, I., Redding, G. and Ng, S. H. (eds) (1996) *Work and Society: Labour and Human Resources in East Asia*, Hong Kong: Hong Kong University Press.

Patten, C. (1998) *East and West*, London: Macmillan.

Slavick, M. M. (2000) 'Hi-tech have-nots', *South China Morning Post*, 11 April, 19.

*South China Morning Post* (2000) 'Haves and have nots', 22 June, 17.

Steger, U. (1998), *Discovering the New Pattern of Globalization*, Ladenburg: Gottlieb Daimler-und-Karl-Benz-Stiftung.

Tang, S. H. (1995) 'The economy', in J. Cheng and S. Lo (eds) *From Colony to SAR: Hong Kong's Challenges Ahead*, Hong Kong: The Chinese University Press.

Turner, H. A., Fosh, P., Gardner, M., Hart, K., Morris, R., Ng, S. H., Quinlan, M. and Yerbury, D. (1980) *The Last Colony: But Whose?*, Cambridge: Cambridge University Press.

Turner, H. A., Fosh, P. and Ng, S. H. (1991) *Between Two Societies: Hong Kong Labour in Transition*, Hong Kong: Centre of Asian Studies, University of Hong Kong.

Wong, M. (2000) 'Rich and poor growing further apart: report', *South China Morning Post*, 22 June, 2.

Workplace Study Group, Chinese Management Centre, University of Hong Kong (2000) *A Report on the Survey Communication and Human Resources: Hong Kong Style, 1998–1999*, Research Report Series CMC-RR 2000-001-01, Hong Kong: Chinese Management Centre, University of Hong Kong.

 **10  Revisiting the changing face of management in China**

Conclusion

*Chris Rowley and Fang Lee Cooke*

- Introduction
- Major findings revisited
- Implications and future trends

## Introduction

In this book we have explored the changing face of management in China through the examination of three key functional areas as well as five issues of business and management. In this chapter, we retrace the main themes, thrust and aspects of these and their main conclusions

## Major findings revisited

We will now revisit the major findings and conclusions of the book's chapters. This is undertaken for both the key functional areas and issues covered.

## Functional areas

We covered the three key functional areas of management: human resource management (HRM), marketing and accounting. First, the critical area of HRM was addressed. This chapter reviewed major changes that had taken place in HRM in China and the reasons for those changes. It outlined changes in the HR environment at a macro level before drawing our attention to some of the changes in HR practices at a micro level. The chapter then provided case studies that illustrated the HR practices that were adopted by two multinational corporations (MNCs) in China and what effect these practices had on employees and organizational performance. It highlighted a number of key challenges in HRM, notably skill shortages and the related talent management problem. And it concluded that HRM in China had undergone significant change, although traditional elements remained influential. In particular, Chinese employees have become more receptive to performance-oriented rewards and career development opportunities. However, tensions clearly remain in the ability, as well as the willingness, of firms to develop good HR policies, including investing in training and development and providing good employment terms and conditions. The chapter also concluded that when firms' HR practices were discussed, we could not simplistically categorize them by ownership forms and assume that Western MNCs are more 'progressive' than domestic Chinese firms. Instead, we are witnessing the emergence of a diverse range of management practices in which ownership forms, regional variations, industrial sectors, product market, and the type of employees firms seek to employ all play important roles. Management outlook and leadership style are also important determinants.

Finally, the chapter argued that HRM was highly context specific, with institutional and cultural factors being enduring influences. However, there is a danger that Chinese practitioners are misguided by the hype of Western HRM and might end up forgetting their own roots. It is important to note that Chinese culture emphasizes relationships. Relationship management plays a vital role in HRM. To a large degree, management is seen as an art rather than a science in China. How to motivate employees and develop their potential is essentially an art in which social value plays an important role. Instead of modelling Western HR theories and practices in an undigested manner, Chinese management needs to develop its own models that are appropriate to the Chinese context (see also Rowley and Poon, 2007).

The second functional area covered was marketing, in particular brand-equity-based marketing strategy. China is a big country with numerous ethnic groups; and the consumption habits are quite different for consumers living in urban and rural areas, as well as in different regions of China. Fast economic development has made the income gap between different areas even larger. So, firms need in-depth research on local customers' income level, consumption habits and the local environment to adjust their marketing strategies to build strong brands and win local customers. Many famous brands, such as Whirlpool, Valentino and NEC, quit the Chinese market after several years' operation because they failed to address this uniqueness of brand building.

Incorporating research conducted in both Western countries and China, this chapter proposed a brand-equity-based marketing strategy to guide practitioners in brand building in China. Brand equity could be divided into four parts: perceived quality, brand awareness, brand associations and brand loyalty. This chapter illustrated and analysed brand-equity-based marketing strategies by focusing on two excellent MNC companies that are famous for their successful brand strategies in China – Haier Group and McDonald's (China).

The chapter introduced the importance of brands in the Chinese market and the uniqueness of the market. The historical development of marketing in China, the unique characteristics of Chinese consumers and unique compositions of customer-based brand equity in China were all outlined. A brand-equity-based marketing strategy framework in China incorporating the four components of the brand equity and marketing mix was presented. And the brand-equity-based marketing strategies two companies implemented to succeed in China's market were presented. Finally, the chapter addressed the challenges confronting brand building in China, such as regional differences, stricter legal and media supervision, crises of customer confidence towards brands and stronger patriotism.

The chapter concluded that as the economy moved from a centrally planned system that was largely closed to international markets to a market-based economy that had a rapidly growing private sector, China was playing a major role in the global economy. Accordingly, local marketing practices developed from a 'manufacturing-capacity-focused' strategy in the 1980s to the 'promotion-and-advertisement-focused' strategy of the 1990s to the recent 'customer-focused' strategy. Local firms gradually began to realize the value of brands and made every effort to enhance their own brand-equity by improving product quality, providing superior service and building good corporate images through public relations efforts. At the same time, the brand-building environment changed quickly. Both MNCs and local firms are now facing more challenges than ever before. As the market changed from a seller's to buyer's market, Chinese consumers became more demanding as more brands and products were available and as their purchasing and consuming habits changed quickly. Besides, Chinese consumers no longer hold the blind faith that famous-brand products are always high quality after so many brand scandals. Therefore, firms need to dig deeper into their customer databases and anticipate consumers' needs in order to create new markets and keep their brands alive.

The third functional area covered was accounting. As companies around the world expand internationally, diverse strategies have been employed to establish global presence. With the internationalization of Chinese enterprises, it has become imperative for executives to understand the differences in the operational environments of home and host countries. While there are several cultural, business, economic and management differences across countries, an important area of examination is accounting practice. This chapter described the current state of accounting in China, identified differences with countries such as the US, cited examples and discussed business implications for internationalizing Chinese enterprises.

Twelve significant accounting issues were identified: revenue recognition, disclosure of related party transactions, disclosure of cash flow statements, intangible assets, borrowing costs, leases capitalization, inventories valuation, fixed assets valuation, research and development (R&D) costs, accounts receivable, effects of currency conversion, and income taxation. In dealing with these issues, the authors recommended a seven-step process for the Management of International Accounting Disparities (MIAD). The MIAD model comprises market environment assessment, accounting system evaluation, identification of key accounting differences, assessment of business impact of accounting differences, implementation of selected measures, evaluation and monitoring, and review and update. The chapter further recommended seven specific measures for internationalizing Chinese firms: consider differences in cross-border accounting practice; provide time for efficient implementation; ensure reliability of information; conduct regular assessments; anticipate organizational disparities and adapt; understand legal and contractual obligations well; and utilize the services of an experienced Hong Kong accounting firm. With a greater level of internationalization, managers will be well served by gaining a good understanding of accounting challenges and planning ahead.

The book also examined five key issues that are important to management and pertinent to business.

## Issues

The first issue comprised changes and restructuring in state-owned enterprises (SOEs). China's economic reform commenced in 1978 with the call for a reduction in the degree of centralization of economic management and reform of the commune structure. The initial reforms focused on agriculture, but in the 1980s they spread to the SOE sector. In the first period of SOE reform, from 1984 to 1993, SOEs were made responsible for profits and losses in the market and contract arrangements were introduced that rewarded managers for meeting specified performance targets. These reforms had some success in reducing government intervention in the management of SOEs, but the rights and responsibilities of SOE managers remained ill-defined. The second period of SOE reform, which commenced in 1993 and is ongoing, has focused on establishing a modern corporate governance structure in China's large and medium-sized SOEs and enterprise groups.

The purpose of this chapter was to examine the outcomes of the latest stage of China's attempts to corporatize its SOE sector and consider some of the major challenges that existed for further economic restructuring of China's large SOEs. A case study of Fushun Petrochemical Company (FPC), an SOE in Liaoning Province under the control of China National Petroleum Corporation, was presented. Drawing on interviews with managers and local government officials, the economic restructuring of FPC that commenced in 1999 was used to illustrate how the reforms were implemented on the ground and some of the major difficulties that further economic restructuring poses. The chapter also examined how a manager in a large SOE used emerging environmental awareness in China in the lead-up to the Beijing Olympics to promote a positive image of FPC.

The chapter's main conclusion was that the SOE sector is an area where the reforms have yielded relatively meagre returns. Attempts to build large SOEs and enterprise groups that can compete in global markets have not been as successful as hoped. The process of gradually improving the accountability and efficiency of SOEs through corporate governance reform and streamlining worker numbers has been slow. Progress has been impeded by a lack of depth of managerial talent and the need to go slow on redundancies because of the underdeveloped nature of the social security system and fear of social unrest. The outcomes of the reforms for FPC were typical of those for many large SOEs. While there was some progress in reducing surplus workers in FPC, the separation of production and service companies was not really successful, with the production company heavily subsidizing the service company until the two were finally remerged. One respect in which FPC was somewhat atypical was that it had an extremely entrepreneurial general manager, who was able to read the signals from Beijing. Without him, the company's performance would have been much worse.

The second issue concerned small and medium-sized enterprises (SMEs). China's development and the importance of its large firms have received an increasing amount of attention in political and popular discourse, the media and academia. Yet, since the 1990s, SMEs have played an increasingly important role in economic growth. They have become important as sources of employment and as contributors to the economy and structural reform. Though SMEs now contribute 60 per cent of the country's gross domestic product and over 75 per cent of urban job opportunities, they face enormous challenges as China integrates more into the world economy. Influences, such as globalization, technological innovation and demographic and social change, as well as the level of technology deployed, innovative ability, financial support and entrepreneurship, can be found in the business environment, impacting as both external and internal factors.

The chapter provided an overview of SMEs in China by looking at their historical development and examining the recent situation in a socio-economic environment. It showed that key political and economic reforms form a backdrop to the development of SMEs in China and demonstrated the significant role of SMEs in the national economy. Case studies of indigenous SMEs and their owner managers were presented. The evidence illustrated that institutions and culture played critical roles not only in SMEs' development, but in shaping SME entrepreneurship in China. Finally, key challenges faced by entrepreneurs in SMEs in China were identified.

Overall, this chapter provided an outline of the changing face of SMEs in China. They are clearly vital to the nation's economy and the development of Chinese entrepreneurship. Yet, increasing competition after WTO entry has brought more difficulties for SMEs. Their importance was confirmed by the shifting role of non-SOEs in the economy and the changing mindset of the government. The chapter suggested that the performance of SMEs and the changing pattern of Chinese entrepreneurship were not determined solely by environmental factors in the market economy, but by other factors, such as institutional determinants. It is evident that the development of Chinese SMEs, and entrepreneurship within them, is strongly associated with key economic reforms. And it is clear that Chinese entrepreneurship has been actively encouraged, as there has been a rapid shift in formal institutions related to entrepreneurship in China. While the government has played an important role in SME development, an assemblage of factors linked to China's integration into the world economy has pushed through fundamental changes in institutions related to Chinese entrepreneurship. As one of the world's most entrepreneur-friendly countries, overcoming those challenges while promoting and facilitating entrepreneurial thinking and practice has been critical in SME future development.

The third issue concerned performance management (PM) (see also Rowley and Poon, 2009). This chapter identified recent developments in PM in China, particularly in knowledge-intensive industries. Economic reforms, new labour legislation, accession to the WTO, as well as the focus on 'informatization' strategy, have brought significant changes to the practice of management in China. An important consequence of the change has been the introduction of greater market mechanisms in HRM practices (see Chapter 2) with commensurate changes in PM. The literature shows that HRM practices, including PM, can be shaped by many factors, such as the Chinese institutional environment, cultural values and type of firm ownership. The chapter compared and contrasted the PM used by different types of firm ownership to indicate which elements and functions of PM have changed (*change content*). It also discussed which factors facilitated or hindered the implementation of new PM in knowledge-intensive industries (*change context*). Cases were provided to highlight the characteristics of PM and explored issues during the change process. The first two cases examined the context of change from an organizational perspective and the later two investigated the implementation of PM from a managerial perspective. These cases provided detail and 'real-life' examples and gave 'voice' to issues, developments and experiences in the area.

The chapter concluded that many changes in PM have swept through the knowledge-intensive industries in China. It showed that change in the content of PM has been observed in all types of firm ownership in key elements, such as criteria of judgement, evaluation methods, the appraisal process, and so on. However, the content of change has varied. Organizational inertia, employees' resistance and the role of HR have all affected the implementation of PM change. The process of PM change in China has therefore not been easy and companies have faced delays and challenges. The chapter also argued that the shift in the content of PM practices requires support from many other areas, such as having a strategic HRM role in PM as well as involving line managers in the process. Nevertheless, the complexity of the economy could involve the field of change forces operating in different system areas. Some idiosyncratic cultural and institutional heritages have been crucial constraints on HRM change. As long as the facilitators and barriers of

HRM change continue to be present, future changes could occur and new practices could be expected in China. The chapter suggested that future research on change in PM needs to be conducted using a comparative approach across different types of firm, at different time periods and for different PM elements. In summary, this chapter showed the changing face of PM in China to be complex and ongoing.

The fourth issue was mergers and acquisitions (M&As), a major strategy deployed by firms to grow, strengthen their market positions and exploit new market opportunities in the Western economies. M&A activities started to emerge in China only from the mid-1980s and gained popularity from the mid-1990s. However, much M&A activity has taken place between Chinese firms. But cross-border M&A deals remain a relatively small proportion and are insufficiently understood. This is in spite of the fact that China is one of the largest foreign direct investment (FDI) recipient countries in the world. Cross-border M&As in China have mainly taken place in the form of acquisitions, and acquisition activities in the twenty-first century have shifted away from traditional industries towards new, high-tech and high-value-added industries. With the explosive growth of mobile phone and Internet subscribers in the last decade, the Chinese information communication technology (ICT) market has been a lucrative, as well as a competitive, arena for many Chinese and foreign firms.

This chapter first provided an overview of the brief history of M&A in China, with a focus on foreign investors' acquisition activities in China. It then provided case studies of acquisitions of private Chinese firms by US-owned MNCs in the IT and telecom industry. These case studies revealed the motives and processes of the M&A, the bargaining power held by the parties and the new business dynamics that emerged during the post-acquisition integration. The chapter then outlined some of the key challenges facing cross-border M&A in China. These included: regulative confusion, limited availability of professional services to facilitate M&As, competence deficiency of Chinese management in handling cross-border M&As, and intervention from the local government.

The chapter concluded that post-acquisition integration and development was often an emerging process rather than an execution of a predefined plan and that a value-added business strategy and high-commitment model of HRM were crucial factors for successful M&A. At least this is the case in the fast-growing and highly competitive IT and telecom industry, in which human resources and innovations play a vital role in business success. Although M&A has been a major business strategy for firms to grow and survive in the dynamic ICT market world-wide and in China, so far this area has received little attention from academic studies in the Chinese context. This chapter therefore contributes to an understanding of the dynamic development of the IT and telecom industry, the role foreign and Chinese businesses have played, and the way competition has evolved and new products have been developed. However, foreign investors face a number of regulatory and management challenges in acquiring Chinese firms, in addition to barriers to accessing certain types of industry and business due to national protectionism.

The fifth issue was management in Hong Kong, which owes its features and patterns largely to the cultural and normative heritages of both Chinese and British custom and practice. In this chapter the evolution of management and management practices in Hong Kong in the context of globalization and Hong Kong's reversion to China in 1997 were traced. In the first part of the chapter a number of key issues which provided the historical and theoretical backdrop to the development of management practices in Hong Kong were discussed. It was acknowledged that there was a propensity for Hong Kong businesses to benchmark themselves against industrially advanced economies and societies, while evolving practices to emulate them. However, it was argued that Hong Kong has attained its current position not only through convergence, but due to experiences that are unique to its history. In this respect, two issues relevant to developing economies were discussed: the role of the state in fashioning the development process; and the alleged excellence of Asian values, as popularized by the thesis of the spirit of Chinese capitalism, which has purportedly contributed to the 'Asian economic miracle'. The next part of the chapter drew on several studies conducted during the 1980s and 1990s to illustrate how the contextual variable of culture affected managerial characteristics and performance in the territory. These indicated that, although globalization has affected Hong Kong visibly since the 1990s, Hong Kong has remained a hybrid melting-pot that echoes, as well as defies, the logic advanced by convergence, culturalist and late-development theories. The last part of the chapter took a closer look at the managerial issues raised by the Asian financial crisis and their impact on HRM practices in Hong Kong firms. Two illustrative cases, one from the power-generating industry and the other from the property management industry, were presented with the objective of illustrating the resultant readjustment processes in the firms.

The chapter concluded with a set of thought-provoking questions. As a modern cosmopolitan city, will Hong Kong continue to advance into post-industrialism along its unique path amid the unpredictable currents of globalization? Or will there be a gradual erosion of the institutional (and cultural) differences between Hong Kong and other places, leading to similar configurations of management practices as predicted by convergence theorists? The chapter argued that while Hong Kong is increasingly entangled in the forces of global competition and is steadily converging with other developed post-industrial societies, its unique historical endowments and Sino-British heritage, as well as a dominant economic ideology that enshrines sovereignty of the market, will necessitate and shape the substantial adaptation of these management practices before their adoption in Hong Kong.

## Implications and future trends

The implications from the key findings of this book and predictions of future trends are myriad, as summarized in Table 10.1. They are listed in terms of present situation and future focus and are general as well as specific to sectors and issues.

There are still many functional areas and issues which we have not been able to cover in this book. Many of these are of growing pertinence to China as a nation, with wider repercussions for the world: for example, managing the global supply chain, corporate social responsibility and environmental protection, sustainable business and social development. In addition, the impact of the global financial crisis triggered by the banking sector in 2008 was still unfolding when this book was published. Future studies can look into how Chinese businesses have been affected by the global economic downturn and the subsequent action plans launched by many national governments, including China's. They can also examine how these actions may have induced new changes in business management in China in order for firms to survive and thrive. Just as Chinese firms have benefited from learning from Western MNCs in the last thirty years of economic reform of the country, so too may the Chinese experience provide important lessons for other economies.

**Table 10.1** Implications and future trends

| General | Present situation | Future focus |
|---|---|---|
| Objective | Growth | Sustainability |
| Nature of growth | Export-driven | Domestic as well as export |
| Measurement | Economic | Economic, environment and social |
| **Issues** | | |
| HRM | • Performance management<br>• Performance-related reward<br>• Hire and fire<br>• Low HR competence<br>• Law avoidance | • Human capital development<br>• Total reward strategy (e.g. financial reward, benefits, training and career development)<br>• Organizational culture<br>• Employee engagement<br>• Improved HR competence<br>• Compliance to laws |
| Marketing | • Price-driven competition<br>• Low brand recognition<br>• Poor marketing techniques | • Brand management<br>• Customer relationship management<br>• Value chain<br>• Professionalization of the marketing function |
| SOEs | • Managing downsizing and organizational restructuring<br>• Under-employment<br>• Clashes of traditional cultural values (e.g. paternalism, egalitarianism, seniority, nepotism) and new cultural values (merits-based employment and reward) and new management techniques | • Improved competitiveness<br>• Realignment of employer–employee expectations<br>• More strategic management of business and people convergent to MNCs and leading private firms' practices |
| Firm growth and strategy | • M&As<br>• Business diversification<br>• Emerging internationalization | • Organic growth as well as M&As, JVs and strategic alliances<br>• Strategic management<br>• Internationalization that is market-seeking and resource-seeking<br>• Leadership development<br>• CSR and sustainability |

# Bibliography

Rowley, C. and Poon, I. (2007) 'Contemporary research on management and HR in China', *Asia Pacific Business Review*, 13, 1: 133–53.

—— (2009) 'Performance management for a global workforce in turbulent times', *Effective Executive Magazine*, 12, 8: 69–73.

# Index

Note: Page numbers followed by 'f' refer to figures. Page numbers followed by 'n' refer to notes. Page numbers followed by 't' refer to tables.